HOOSIER SCHOOLS

MIDWESTERN HISTORY AND CULTURE

GENERAL EDITORS

JAMES H. MADISON AND THOMAS J. SCHLERETH

HOOSIER SCHOOLS

Past and Present

Edited by William J. Reese

INDIANA UNIVERSITY PRESS   BLOOMINGTON & INDIANAPOLIS

The paper used in this publication meets the minimum requirements of American
National Standard for Information Sciences—Permanence of Paper for Printed Library
Materials, ANSI Z39.48-1984.

Manufactured in the United States of America

Library of Congress Cataloging-in-Publication Data

Hoosier schools : past and present / edited by William J. Reese.
p.   cm. — (Midwestern history and culture)
Includes bibliographical references and index.
ISBN 0-253-33362-8 (cl : alk. paper). — ISBN 0-253-21154-9 (pa : alk. paper)
1. Public schools—Indiana—History. 2. Educational change—Indiana—History.
3. School management and organization—Indiana—History.
I. Reese, William J., date   II. Series.
LA283.H67   1998
370'.9772—dc21   97-21565

1 2 3 4 5   03 02 01 00 99 98

To the Memory of

Ray "Ike" Blemker

and

Ray "Buddy" Blemker

CONTENTS

ILLUSTRATIONS

Acknowledgments

WILLIAM J. REESE

This volume had its origins in a lively graduate program in the history of education at Indiana University at Bloomington. For a number of years I had the pleasure of working with many talented doctoral students there, in the School of Education as well as in the history department, whose contributions made this volume possible. I am very grateful to my friend and colleague, Barry Bull, a philosopher and policy analyst, for joining our effort to offer readers a wide-ranging look at the history of school reform in Indiana.

James Madison of the I.U. history department as well as Joan Catapano of Indiana University Press showed kindness, patience, and encouragement as this project moved through its various phases. Terry L. Cagle, managing editor, and Ruth Albright, our copyeditor, were unfailingly helpful. Three other people deserve especially high praise. My long-time friend and coconspirator in the history of education, Ed McClellan, characteristically read the entire manuscript and offered helpful suggestions for improvement. Such a friend and colleague appears once in a lifetime. Amy Schutt, my former colleague-in-arms at the *History of Education Quarterly*, also served as a friendly but critical reader. Ron Cohen of the history department at I.U. Northwest deserves my thanks for different reasons: for his exemplary studies on the history of the Gary schools and for sharing materials on the history of the Steel City's schools after World War II. For their camaraderie and irreverence, I tip my cap to the regulars of the Thursday Night Seminar, especially its cofounder, Frank Lester, and Bob Orsi, Lanny Beyer, Dan Mueller, and Pete Kloosterman.

This book is dedicated with affection to the memory of Ray "Ike" Blemker and his son, Ray "Buddy" Blemker. Both were graduates of Huntingburg High School, whose mascot was the Happy Hunters. I will always remember the happiness that Ike and Buddy helped bring to me, their family, and friends.

William J. Reese
Madison, Wisconsin

Introduction

Writing in the inaugural issue of the *Indiana School Journal* in 1856, the editor urged readers to take pride in the Hoosier state. "We trust we shall not be obnoxious to the charge of boasting," he wrote, "if we say to our professional brethren that we believe no State offers superior inducements to the Teacher than our own." Forty years before, the editor continued, Indiana was "almost unbroken forest and prairie. To-day a million and a quarter of human beings find their home within her borders." Moreover, "civilization" was advancing across the state. "Behold the growth of her cities. Mark the mighty tide of emigration which is ever setting towards the golden West, sweeping away the forests, covering the prairies, and filling the vallies [*sic*], and remember that our earliest settlers are as yet but middle aged men; our pioneers are those whose heads are scarcely silvered."[1]

Now that railroads increasingly crisscrossed the state, the editor saw further signs of progress: easier travel, enhanced communication, and better access to eastern markets for Indiana's surplus agriculture. As commerce expanded, farsighted citizens increasingly turned their attention to improving their children's education, as a veritable educational "awakening" commenced. Schools would rescue children from the darkness of ignorance and advance the cause of "civilization." Contrary to a popular view, claimed the editor, "our people are not conservative; they are generous and impulsive." Indeed, Indianans were "looking forward, not backward, and we feel the fresh life and bounding pulse of youth."[2]

School reformers and educators who labored to build a comprehensive system of public education in Indiana in the nineteenth century were hopeful individuals. They were a proud part of a larger common school movement in the northern states, led by famous individuals such as Horace Mann of Massachusetts and Henry Barnard of Connecticut, champions all of tax-supported schools for the children of the republic. When ignorance and public apathy were defeated, they believed, victory would be theirs. As the editor of the *Journal* concluded, "We have no past. No crumbling monuments rear their frowning heads and bid us pause." All things seemed possible.[3]

Scholars have long remarked that Americans, lacking a feudal, never mind an ancient past, were born without the historical shackles of the Old World. Every generation of school reformers, however, from the mid-nineteenth century to the present, has understood that all men, women, and children have a past, decisively shaping the present and future. No matter how worthy their goals or prescient their observations, advocates of school improvement have never had the luxury of working with a historical *tabula rasa*. This was the hard truth when public schools were first organized and would frustrate many advocates of school improvement in successive generations. In all times and places, the twin impediments to rapid change—the power of tradition and slowness of institutional response—usually guaranteed that school reformers always remained just that, reformers, not revolutionaries.

Historian James Madison has remarked that Indiana has historically been populated and thus led by cautious individuals, searching for a middle ground between standpat politics and rapid innovation. Even the editor of the *Indiana School Journal* hoped to dispel the image of Hoosiers as foot-dragging citizens, as early as the 1850s! Yet Madison's generalization aptly describes as well the fate of most school reform movements, in Indiana as elsewhere. Dire social ills in other nations sometimes provoke a revolution. In America, men and women aroused by injustice or social distress instead often turn to the schools, believing that a new course, a new program, or some educational solution will ease the pain or cure the disease.[4]

Since the earliest days of the republic, Americans have often believed that social, economic, and political crises can be resolved to a large degree through educational reform. Fears of economic changes, of the widening gap between rich and poor, of foreign immigration and competition, of political apathy or instability, of a declining family structure: these and other perceived ills arose across the nation in the antebellum period, at the turn of the century, and in the 1980s and 1990s. And, like citizens elsewhere, Indianans have assumed that the schools should play an important role in addressing these problems, which do not primarily have an educational cause.[5]

Before the Civil War, Indiana's leading educational evangelist, Caleb Mills, and many fellow activists bemoaned the pedagogical sins of their day, highlighted the failings of current educational arrangements, and demanded immediate change. They pressed for legislation to fund schools well and to strengthen the educational profession; they also lectured the public on their civic responsibilities and warned about the pressing need to educate youth to become more upright, productive, and responsible citizens. Such jeremiads resonate even today, in a so-called postindustrial world. And the slowness with which contemporary schools change and improve, despite the proliferation of sophisticated computers and a highly credentialed citizenry, reminds us that to secure a popular consensus around educational improvements and then transform these ideas into concrete reality has never been easy.

Since Hoosiers, like other Americans, have long believed that schools are a fundamental means by which to improve society, the recurrent discovery of our personal and social imperfections has often placed them in the center of debates about the very nature and future of the nation. The chapters in this volume demonstrate that from their earliest years important cultural battles have been waged in Indiana's schools, over the meaning of democracy, opportunity, morality, social trends, and other important issues.

Reforms designed to improve the public schools became so commonplace in Indiana and throughout the nation by the 1980s and early 1990s that one needed a veritable scorecard to keep track of them, as the chapter by Barry Bull makes clear. What interested citizens lack, however, is a clearer understanding of the broad historical development of Indiana's schools. Only history can provide a long view of change over time, illuminating what gave the past its distinctive cast and what elements survived to shape the modern world. A few books exist on the history of public schools in the Hoosier state, but they are outdated and fairly uncritical of their subject. This volume presents the work of a new generation of scholars, whose contributions explore critical moments in Indiana's educational past while hopefully stimulating further inquiries.[6]

To be dissatisfied with schools is a perennial American condition, yet again and again citizens have turned to them to improve society. This reflects both a laudable hopefulness about the future and some naivete about how to reach the promised land. In different decades, citizens have variously expected schools to teach the three R's, an ever-expanding curriculum, the worthy uses of leisure time, personal hygiene, driver training, Cold War civics, AIDS prevention, and strategies to beat Japanese car makers at their own game through tech prep, vocational training dressed in a new suit. Still other citizens have occasionally cared more about keeping taxes low, or about building larger basketball gyms and winning the sectional and state championship. To suggest to anyone over the past century and a half that schools should do less, not more, to concentrate on academics, not everything else, or to leave the problems of the economy to someone other than principals, teachers, and students would have left a blank look on the faces of many reformers, whatever their particular ideological orientation.

Knowing more about the history of public schools might give today's reformers and taxpayers pause. Expecting schools to address every imaginable problem is a fruitless task. But, as John Dewey wrote nearly a century ago, the fundamental way Americans envision reforming society is by improving their schools, and the actions of liberals as well as conservatives continue to confirm the wisdom of his observation. Whether the demand is for better discipline, or better links between school and work, superior language training, higher math and science test scores, or solutions to drug abuse, violence, or immorality, many citizens seem to regard schools as something of a panacea, however disappointing they often find them. It is the American way, and it fits well the Hoosier predisposition to move slowly and cautiously.[7]

NOTES

1. "Our State," *Indiana School Journal* 1 (January 1856): 1.

2. "Our State," 2–3.

3. "Our State," 3.

4. James Madison, *The Indiana Way: A State History* (Bloomington, 1986).

5. David Tyack and Larry Cuban, *Tinkering toward Utopia: A Century of Public School Reform* (Cambridge, Mass., 1995), chap. 1.

6. William J. Reese, "Indiana's Public School Traditions: Dominant Themes and Research Opportunities," *Indiana Magazine of History* 89 (December 1992): 293–98.

7. Reese, "Indiana's Public School Traditions," 290.

HOOSIER SCHOOLS

SCOTT WALTER

"Awakening the Public Mind": The Dissemination of the Common School Idea in Indiana, 1787–1852

Who built the common schools of Indiana? Their names are legion, of course, because the common school movement in Indiana was primarily a grassroots affair. Beginning as early as the first settlement of the Indiana territory, the call went out for the public support of education. Teachers, preachers, and politicians, all in their own time, added their voices to the rising chorus of support for the common school movement in the Hoosier state. Historians often overlook the chorus, however, and turn their attention to the soloists. Jacob P. Dunn, for example, offers the standard answer to the above question, noting that "It is a singular fact that Caleb Mills has been commonly regarded as 'the father of the Indiana [common] school system.'" The common school movement in Indiana was far from a "singular" affair, though, and Mills's was not the only voice to rise above the roar of the crowd.[1]

Historian Michael B. Katz has written that history is best understood as "a choice among alternative possibilities." This is certainly the case when one considers the course of the common school movement in Indiana. Publicly supported, socially inclusive "common" schools existed in early Indiana alongside private academies, sectarian religious institutions, and even radical educational experiments such as those undertaken at New Harmony under the auspices of Robert Owen and William Maclure. Rather

Caleb Mills: Indiana's
Famous School Reformer,
ca. late 1840s. Courtesy
Indiana State Library

than as a staging ground for alternative possibilities, however, the common school movement in Indiana has typically been portrayed in the same narrow fashion as it was by Indiana University Professor Richard G. Boone in his *History of Education in Indiana* (1892). Praising this work as "the best general history of education in the United States" available at the time, a contemporary of Boone described how his study narrated "the rise and progress of the public school idea in Indiana; its slow and sure growth from decade to decade; its final victory over all effective opponents in 1851, and its complete triumph as the logical close of the splendid war record of the State in the final school system of 1865." For over a century, historians of education in the Hoosier state have painted the Indiana common school movement in monochrome and have identified the movement almost exclusively with the name "Caleb Mills." Mills, however, was not the only "leader" of this broad-based effort, nor was his vision of common schooling the only one promoted during its most critical years.[2]

Mills's chief biographer, Charles W. Moores, referred to his subject as an "apostle of enlightenment." With no apparent sense of hyperbole, another biographer claimed that Mills single-handedly brought common schools to the Hoosier state "by the sheer power of his sharp pen . . . [which was] the greatest and most effective weapon against ignorance ever known in Indiana." Most historical accounts concur in this evaluation of Mills's place on the rolls of Hoosier common school reformers, but such accounts are misleading. Standard works by Boone, James H. Smart (1875), and Fassett A. Cotton (1904), among others, discuss the common school movement in Indiana as if it were somehow isolated from the larger experience of the common school movement nationwide. By these accounts, a vision of common schooling seems to have appeared anew in the mind of Mills and to have been translated into reality by his work alone. Mills's contribution to the movement was unquestionably significant, but he was only one prominent local representative of that select group of reformers who, like their preeminent member, Horace Mann, worked to ensure the victory of a particular vision of common schooling between 1830 and 1860.[3]

Other leading reformers, including Indianapolis's Calvin Fletcher and the peripatetic H. F. West, were equally responsible for the triumph of this vision of common schooling in Indiana. As important were the hundreds of local reformers who organized grassroots support for the common schools. Still others promoted visions of common schooling that were at odds with the one outlined by Mills. In Indiana, as elsewhere, the common school movement was a loosely organized effort at social reform that drew inspiration and support from myriad sources. Mills's was not the only vision of common schooling contributing to that victory. His triumph, therefore, was not only over the opponents of common schooling, but also over those among his fellow reformers who did not wholly subscribe to his particular vision of educational reform.

The common school movement in Indiana was characterized both by broad consensus and by significant conflict. Common school promoters disagreed over salient aspects of educational reform, and they generated opposition from those who doubted the wisdom of establishing free, tax-supported schools. Like other young states, Indiana gave birth to her earliest public schools in a highly charged atmosphere.

Conflict, both internal and external to the movement, dogged the efforts of common school reformers to disseminate their ideas to the Indiana public in the decades prior to the passage of the "Free School law" in 1852. Even this famous law proved only that a majority of state legislators had become converts to the common school cause. The state Supreme Court declared vital sections of the law unconstitutional within two years of passage, and many citizens remained likewise indifferent to the educational crusade. A truly free system of common, or "public," schooling was not firmly established in the Hoosier state until after the Civil War. What tensions underlay this mixed record of success? How did local activists, alone and in groups, articulate and disseminate their visions of common school reform? To what degree did these local visions conflict with the more familiar reform package associated with Mills? Why, in the end, did the people of Indiana choose to support the "public school" over the various alternative models of formal education available in the antebellum period?

By the dawn of the Civil War, the generally accepted vision of common schooling in Indiana was unquestionably the one promoted by Mills and his colleagues. The question of how this was accomplished, however, still requires clarification. As many historians have asked: "Why should a *common* school for people in all walks of life have become the dominant form of education? How did the school promoters persuade Americans to support *public* education?" The lion's share of credit in Indiana has long gone to Mills and to the famous set of missives that he directed to the state legislature under the pseudonym, "One of the People." In a recent study, however, William J. Reese claimed that the "history of how reformers successfully mobilized action throughout the state through speeches, newspapers, and other forms of political lobbying . . . remains somewhat of a mystery." Not solely reliant upon the legendary commitment of Mills to educational reform, common school supporters in Indiana brought all available weapons to bear in their struggle to convince the public of the righteousness of their cause and to popularize a particular vision of common schooling. Mills referred to this effort as the struggle to "awaken the public mind."[4]

If the "public mind" to which Mills hoped to appeal was a product of the Hoosier schools, general opinion likely suggested an uphill battle. Popular education in early Indiana was not the envy of the nation. In 1790, the governor of the Northwest Territory labeled the inhabitants of the Wabash Valley "the most ignorant people in the world." Half a century later, according to Moores, "the name Hoosier [remained] the synonym for ignorance." The cherished belief of all early nineteenth-century schoolmen that any boy educated in the common schools might one day become president seemed out of reach in Indiana. Abraham Lincoln, the very embodiment of the dream, had few kind words for the schools of his Hoosier youth: "There was absolutely nothing to excite ambition for education, somehow, I could read, write, and cipher to the rule of three; but that was all." Lincoln passed a harsh judgment on the common schools of Indiana, one in which many concurred.[5]

Lincoln's sour evaluation of his early educational experience echoed the criticisms hurled at those same schools by contemporary reformers. To one group in particular, the American Home Missionary Society (AHMS), Indiana's early schools seemed in desperate need of improvement. Articles appearing in the Society's journal, *The Home Missionary*, decried the state of common schooling in Indiana. Among these articles was one written in 1833 by the Rev. James Thompson of Crawfordsville. Evaluating the support that local schools might give to the Society's evangelical mission, Thompson concluded: "The state of the common schools in [the

Wabash Valley] is perhaps less flattering than anything else regarding our prospects, and calls for decisive and vigorous efforts." Mills, long considered the most important leader of the Indiana common school campaign, was one of the would-be missionaries whose attention was captured by Thompson's plea for help.[6]

Motivated by this bleak picture of the Hoosier schoolhouse, Mills and innumerable lesser-known reformers dedicated themselves to the common school cause. In a letter written to Rev. Thompson, Mills captured the sentiments that drew these men (and women) to the West. "My thoughts," he wrote, "have been directed of late to the subject of common-schools, and the best means of awakening a more lively interest in their establishment in the Western country. Public sentiment must be changed in regard to free schools; prejudice must be overcome, and the public mind awakened to the importance of carrying the means of education to every door. Though it be the work of years, yet it must and can be done."[7]

Nearly twenty years separate Mills's letter to Thompson from the Indiana state legislature's passage of the landmark Free School law of 1852. The record of those two decades reflects the insight that lies at the heart of James H. Madison's recent history of the Hoosier state, *The Indiana Way* (1986). "There have been no revolutions in the history of Indiana," Madison wrote. Change, when it has come, "has been evolutionary rather than revolutionary." Nowhere was this facet of the "Indiana way" more evident than in the campaign for publicly supported, "common" schooling. From a loose network of formal educational institutions made up of locally controlled and financed schools (many of reportedly dubious quality), both "public" and "private," sectarian and nonsectarian, there slowly evolved a broad consensus in support of a vision of common schooling similar to the one championed by prominent reformers. Schools, in this view, should be nonsectarian and socially inclusive (although racial inclusion remained largely taboo); controlled, if only nominally, by a centralized state authority, and supported by a combination of state funding and local taxation.[8]

Prior to the rise of the common school movement in the 1830s, one found throughout America "a patchwork quilt of public, quasi-public, religious, and pauper schools." Despite its early reputation, Indiana supported an impressive variety of such institutions. District schools, county seminaries, and private academies were among the many "alternative" educational institutions that drew fire from Mills and his fellow common school supporters.[9]

The district school, which later histories celebrated as the foundation of American public education (marred, if at all, only by its submission to local control), was neither the first, nor the most prevalent form of institutionalized education in early Indiana. The earliest Hoosier schools were Sunday schools. Mills, himself, first came to Indiana as an agent of the

American Sunday School Union. Although the Sunday school was often the pioneer, it was quickly joined on the Hoosier frontier by the county seminary, the private academy, the college, and, of course, by the one- and two-room district schoolhouses of lore. Already by the first years of statehood, Indiana boasted numerous county seminaries and private academies: the former provided publicly supported, "secondary" schooling; the latter, instruction in both the higher and the lower branches for a fee. "Practically every case was an experiment," noted an early historian of the county seminaries, "different schemes being tried in every new school." This was true at every level of formal education in Indiana; local control and initiative typified most early efforts at schooling.[10]

An educational landscape characterized by locally controlled institutions such as these was typical of early nineteenth-century America, and it is consistent with what Madison identifies as an enduring Hoosier commitment to "a local, decentralized, democratically oriented strategy" in matters of public policy. So deeply committed to democratic localism, Indiana's public mind would, indeed, need to be "awakened" to the virtues of a bureaucratically centralized and uniform system of common schooling. During an 1837 debate over a proposed school tax, one state legislator reportedly announced: "When I die I want my epitaph written, 'Here lies an enemy of the free schools.'" Given such confirmed opposition, one must again question the manner in which educational reformers successfully disseminated, and garnered support for, their visions of common schooling.[11]

The effort to awaken the public mind of Indiana to the virtues of common schooling did not begin with Mills, nor with the particular vision of common schooling that he shared with fellow reformers. Revolutionary-era leaders such as Thomas Jefferson, Benjamin Rush, and Noah Webster proposed systems of publicly supported formal education decades prior to the rise of the common school movement. More relevant to Indiana were the Ordinance of 1785 and the Northwest Ordinance of 1787. These statutes governed the Indiana territory in the years prior to statehood and were clear in their support of popular education. In its most famous passage, the Northwest Ordinance proclaimed: "Religion, morality, and knowledge, being necessary to good government and the happiness of mankind, schools and the means of education shall forever be encouraged." The Ordinances truly were "the founding documents of public education in the Old Northwest."[12]

Whatever ideological support the Ordinances lent to educational reformers in the Indiana territory during those early years, the financial support was insufficient to ensure the permanent establishment of common schools. The Ordinances were better at popularizing the importance of public responsibility for education than at establishing any firm financial foundation. It would take decades of labor by a diverse group of reformers to rally support for binding legislation such as the Free School law of 1852.

Reflecting the influential precedent set by the Ordinances of 1785 and 1787 in matters of schooling, the Indiana state constitution of 1816 included an educational clause unprecedented in scope. Article IX, Section 2 of the 1816 constitution was generally lauded by educational reformers nationwide. It reads: "It shall be the duty of the General Assembly, as soon as circumstances will permit, to provide by law for a general system of education, ascending in regular gradation from township schools to a State University, wherein tuition shall be gratis, and equally open to all."[13]

This provision has been aptly described as "the Ordinance of 1787 translated into Western Institutions." The promise of the 1816 constitution was understood to exclude Indiana's black population, of course, but even this racially limited constitutional promise was never realized. Hoosier taxpayers were freed from any immediate demands by the constitutional caveat that educational provisions should be made "as soon as circumstances shall permit." The creation of the free system of education promised in Article IX, therefore, was left to the discretion of individual communities. Although an impressive variety of educational institutions flourished in pioneer Indiana, the citizenry demonstrated no broad commitment to public support of the common schools. Indianans believed in the value of education, but not necessarily in publicly supported, socially inclusive school systems. Over the next thirty-five years, common school advocates rallied followers by pledging to fulfill the lost promise of the state constitution.[14]

Despite its failure to ensure the development of a publicly supported system of common schooling, the constitutional commitment to popular education remained a potent symbol. Common school supporters were able to secure the passage of a series of school laws in the first decades of statehood by drawing upon this symbolism. The most significant of these early laws were the statutes of 1824 and 1833.

The law of 1824 was "[the] first systematic effort to establish a plan for state schools." This law mandated the division of congressional townships into local districts and empowered township trustees to appoint district trustees. Trustees were also granted the right to examine prospective teachers and to grant teaching certificates for local schools. Revising the 1824 statute, the law of 1833 made the district trustee a locally elected position and increased the number of district trustees from one to three. It empowered the district trustees (subject to township approval) to enumerate district children, to examine and employ teachers, and to direct the erection of district schoolhouses. This latter power was the most significant because it affirmed the right of officials to levy a local tax that might be used, in addition to the funds available through the state Common School Fund, to support the erection and maintenance of schoolhouses.

Again, however, the decision to levy such a tax was left in the hands of individual communities. Rarely did any Hoosier community vote to tax itself in support of the district school. Many believed that state funds were sufficient, while others simply could not afford an additional tax (no matter how small). Significant revisions of the 1833 law included the formal recognition of women as eligible for the teacher's position (1834), and the provision that, in the absence of an elected district trustee, an individual householder might legally employ the district teacher (1836). These early statutes were so loose that one historian has concluded that "there were but few people left that were not [school] officials of some kind."[15]

Thus, even before the arrival of Mills to the Wabash Valley, Indiana common school advocates successfully supported the passage of a series of educational laws by the state legislature. Unfortunately, the nonbinding character of these laws rendered them ineffectual. "Weak" school laws allowed Indiana to sidestep its constitutional commitment to the support of a system of free schooling for all citizens. As late as 1850, Indiana school officials chafed at the weakness of their school laws. As superintendent of common schools J. P. Drake wryly concluded: "Indiana is far behind some of her sister States on the subject of common schools. Not that we lack legislation; we have entirely too much of it." Said one historian: "For twenty years statute had been added to statute, and the resulting school system was little more than a jumble of wheels within wheels."[16]

Early advocates of common schooling in Indiana drew successfully upon the symbolic power of the Northwest Ordinance and the state constitution to support the passage of school laws. Unfortunately, they were unable to ensure that these laws had sufficient strength to mandate public support for universal common schooling. By 1833, local advocates had reached the limits of their persuasive powers. Thanks in part, however, to the rise over the next two decades of a series of prominent spokesmen in the figures of Mann (Massachusetts), Henry Barnard (Connecticut), and Calvin Stowe (Ohio), the common school movement rose to national prominence. The revitalization of the movement at the national level gave new support to the Hoosier common school promoters. The passage of toothless laws might have failed to awaken the public mind of the Hoosier state to the virtues of common schooling, but the next two decades brought a number of reformers to Indiana who were well versed in the persuasive methods pioneered by common school reformers to the east. Together (albeit sometimes in name only), these men and women brought the common school movement to Indiana.

Based upon the influence of his now-famous "Educational Messages" to the state legislature and his service as the second state superintendent of public instruction (1854–57), Mills has been celebrated in history and popular memory as the "father" of the common school movement in

Indiana. Presented to both houses of the legislature and to the 1851 Constitutional Convention in the form of six annual reports (1846–52), Mills's proposals regarding the establishment and support of a system of common schooling have been referred to as "the most important documents ever prepared on the subject of education in Indiana." They have likewise been called "the basis of the Indiana system of common schools." Whatever their broader significance, Mills's messages to the legislature remain the clearest statement extant of the educational reforms promoted by prominent common school activists in Indiana.[17]

Written under the pseudonym "One of the People," Mills's letters reflect both the local progress of the Indiana common school movement and the influence of the national movement on his thinking. Mills's messages addressed issues of local interest, including the literacy rate in Indiana, the 1848 referendum on free schools, and the educational provisions to be included in the revised state constitution of 1851. Each promotes a particular vision of the proper shape, scope, and goal of common school reform. In general, Mills outlined an educational reform program remarkably similar to that of prominent common school reformers nationwide.[18]

The basic outline of Mills's plan for a publicly supported system of common schooling in Indiana was presented in his first message to the legislature. In this message, Mills emphasized the importance of establishing sound financial support for the proposed common school system, partly through local taxation. The teaching profession, too, needed firmer support. Normal school training, expert supervision, and a provision for higher salaries would combine, in Mills's opinion, to improve both the individual teacher and the profession of which he or she was a part. Textbooks needed improvement and standardization. Public interest in the common school needed vitalization and support. Finally, according to Mills, a state superintendent was needed to coordinate the work of the entire system. Accountability to a central authority was to replace the earlier emphasis on local control. Each of these reform proposals echoed the views of common school leaders across the northern states.[19]

Mills's messages to the legislature are the most easily accessible and the most eloquent examples of support for the common school idea in antebellum Indiana. The eloquence of Mills's voice, however, should not be allowed to drown out others found among the larger chorus of reformers abroad in the state during this same period. Common school reformers were a diverse lot, and reformist voices were heard from across Indiana. Each voice was crucial to the projects of spreading the idea of common schooling throughout the state and converting each local community to the cause. Local organizations such as the Association for the Improvement of Common Schools in Indiana, educational periodicals such as the *Common School Advocate*, and individual local activists all promoted ideas central to school reform. Thus, the public mind of the Hoosier state was awakened to the virtues of a common school system both through missives to the mighty and through the work of grassroots reformers.

Formal associations devoted to educational reform were one of the most popular means of gathering support for the common school movement. Organized at both the state and local levels, such associations drew their membership not only from the ranks of eminent, "public-minded" men, but also from the missionary reformers and the ordinary men and women concerned with the conduct of formal education. Public figures such as Indianapolis's Fletcher and New Harmony's Robert Dale Owen were common school reformers. So were teachers such as Richmond's James Poe and Ebeneezer Bishop. James Shields of Greencastle quietly seconded the work of Mills, his more prominent colleague in the AHMS; Keziah Fletcher, a teacher, the work of her husband, Calvin. The credit for persuading the traditionally recalcitrant Hoosier taxpayer to endow a system of free schools has gone to prominent individuals, but local associations of anonymous reformers were equally important to the larger movement.[20]

The Association for the Improvement of Common Schools in Indiana (AICSI) is a case in point. Unlike many other local associations of reformers, the AICSI was comprised of individuals of sufficient means (and ambition) to publish a record of their first meeting. Published in 1833, literally weeks before Mills's arrival in the Wabash Valley, this report reflects the status of the common school movement in Indiana prior to the arrival of its most acclaimed advocate. The AICSI began in strong fashion: "Few subjects of vital importance to society in all its relations have received as little attention, or been as little understood as primary education." The report catalogued both the weaknesses of existing educational institutions and the virtues of a common school system. Even at this early stage of the common school movement, the criticisms and suggestions for reform found in the AICSI report were very similar to those being made by their counterparts across the northern states.[21]

For example, Hoosier common school reformers claimed that the lack of qualified teachers crippled the existing network of educational institutions. According to the AICSI, "[no] station in society is more important or responsible than that occupied by him to whom a crowd of little ones look up for instruction, by precept and example; and no where is correctness of principle, integrity of heart, an uprightness of life so indispensable." Unfortunately, the report continued, the locally supervised teaching profession was largely "in the hands of unprincipled men." If Indiana's common schools were to play their part in the larger reform program, the teaching profession needed a drastic overhaul. Improvement could come only with a more rigorous examination of prospective (and current) teachers and a more widely standardized means of certifying their command of academic material. Teachers also required greater knowledge of pedagogical innovations and an elevated moral character.[22]

The AICSI also echoed popular ideas about the role of the common schools in providing citizenship education. As the boundaries of the United States expanded across the former wilderness of the Old Northwest, and the twin processes of urbanization and industrialization began to transform social life in the settled areas of the northeast, the common school was heralded as a powerful weapon in the struggle to protect and maintain America's "republican experiment." In this view, an evolving democracy needed the common school as a neutral social institution open to the children of all, regardless of socioeconomic status, political affiliation, or religious background. The AICSI report emphasized the common school's role in providing a basic education to the future voter: "True, it is not necessary for the preservation of our government that a liberal education should be extended to all—and were it necessary, it would not be possible; but to maintain our Republic, the people must be able to watch their servants . . . where all can read and write, *there* the public officers must and will be amenable to the control of their rightful sovereigns."[23]

Another representative local experience with formal association among common school advocates emerged in Greencastle, where Mills's fellow missionary, Shields, attempted to foster support for educational reform. His efforts were largely unsuccessful, but his failure in central Indiana's Putnam County may be as informative to historians as are any of the AICSI's successes on the Ohio River. "[Meetings] were called," Shields reported to the AHMS, "addresses delivered, and considerable interest in the subject generated; but little seems to have changed." By Shields's account, one might assume that the general populace of Putnam County remained lukewarm to the idea of a publicly supported common school system. Indeed, such pessimism was warranted. Putnam was one of nine Indiana counties, mostly in the southern half of the state, to vote most decisively *against* common schooling during the 1848 referendum on "free schools" that has long been considered a bellwether of the movement's success at the state level.[24]

Why was Shields's work in Putnam County such a failure in regard to generating public support for the common school idea, and why were his counterparts in other Indiana counties so much more successful? Neither Putnam County, nor southern Indiana, in general, were opposed to popular education. Both, however, reflected a broader southern consensus about the private nature of educational responsibility. Popular adherence to the traditional southern commitment to private funding for one's formal education necessarily conflicted with the goals of common school reformers such as Shields.

Markedly more successful than its counterpart in Putnam County was the local association of common school reformers in eastern Indiana's Wayne County. Founded in 1838 by Richmond teachers Poe and Bishop, the Wayne County association of common school reformers was able to elicit considerable support from the general public. As late as 1846, this group was still drawing praise from state school officials for its profound effect on Wayne County schools. superintendent of common schools Royal Mayhew (1844–46) emphasized in one report his belief that Wayne County "will be at once recognized as a county where literature has not been neglected; but whose common schools, public and private, are probably not secondary to those of any other county in our State."[25]

Unlike their counterparts in Putnam County, the Wayne County reformers were not forced to contend with a regional sentiment opposed to the public financial support of common schools. Set on the Ohio border, Wayne County was instead influenced by the blossoming common school movement in her neighbor to the east. Such influence could be specific, as it was in Benton County, where a wealthy reformer from Cincinnati influenced local school politics throughout the 1840s and 1850s, but more significant was the generally positive sentiment toward the public support of formal education. Settled largely by migrants from the east and by Quakers, Wayne County accepted a commitment to the public support of popular education that was to a large degree absent in counties settled predominantly by southerners.[26]

The relative success achieved by the associations of common school reformers in Putnam and Wayne counties are extreme examples of the fortunes of antebellum school reform in Indiana at the local level. Educational societies of all sorts existed in many Indiana counties during this period, and they undoubtedly encountered a broad variety of both successes and failures. Given the changing character of antebellum school reform at the local level, it is impossible to come to any final conclusions regarding the success or failure of local groups as an instrument of reform.[27]

Historians have characterized these groups as models of democratic organization for school reform at the local level. Boone, for example, claimed that much of what is "valuable" in the history of the common school movement could be found in a study of local groups. Working independently of central authority, but with the blessing of state officials, in this view, local groups of reformers paved the way for the passage of the Free School law of 1852. Local associations were undoubtedly instrumental in collecting grassroots support for school reform, but their motives bear closer scrutiny than they have received to date.[28]

Common school activists at any level were rarely altruists. What other motives might underlie one's role in a local group of reformers? Shields, for example, like Mills, was an agent of the American Home Missionary Society. The society defined one important role for the common school as the promotion of its evangelical mission. Shields's concern for the success of his Putnam County association of reformers undoubtedly rested on his concern for the success of his mission. Likewise motivated by ulterior concerns was Richmond's Poe. Poe cofounded the Wayne County group in 1838; by the following year, he had opened a private academy for the instruction of paying youths in the "higher branches." Might not Poe's passion for common school reform have been fueled to some degree by his desire to see potential academy students provided with a publicly supported elementary education?[29]

The history of these local associations of reformers is as complex as that of the larger common school movement of which they were a part. Historians of education in Indiana have repeatedly paid homage to the importance of local groups, but information on specific groups remains sketchy, buried in local and county histories. A survey of surviving records of such local associations would aid immeasurably in the task of understanding the way in which the common school idea was disseminated and promoted in local communities during this period.

Whatever the motivations of its cofounder, Wayne County's association of common school reformers drew repeated notice from prominent school reformers. Superintendent Mayhew's praise was echoed by West, the editor of Indiana's educational reform periodical, the *Common School Advocate*. As West exclaimed in his inaugural issue: "Wayne County—we believe to be the only county in the State that has an Educational Society. It has undoubtedly done more, and is now doing more in the cause of education, than any other county in the State. We hail it as the banner county of Indiana." West was incorrect to assume that Wayne was the only Indiana county with a local association of common school supporters, but the bridge built between the work of local reformers and periodicals such as the *Advocate* was important. Like local associations of reformers, educational periodicals enabled common school supporters to disseminate their proposals to a larger audience than would have otherwise been possible.[30]

Published under the banner, "Devoted to Common Schools—the only guaranty of our Republic," the *Advocate* was reportedly "the first educational publication known in the State." Whatever the truth of that claim, the *Advocate* represented a local adaptation of one of the common school movement's most potent weapons nationwide. Periodicals like the *Common School Advocate* (1846), the *Indiana School Journal* (1848), and the *Educationalist* (1852), provided vital support to Hoosier common school reformers in their efforts to lobby for educational change.[31]

The educational periodical was a familiar approach to shaping public opinion in favor of school reform. More than sixty periodicals devoted to the common school movement in various states were founded between 1825 and 1850. These periodicals were extremely risky ventures, rarely surviving beyond their second year. Publishing only one volume (1846–47), Indiana's *Common School Advocate* was characteristically short-lived. Like the local associations of reformers, periodicals such as the *Advocate* worked to awaken the public mind to the virtues of common schooling.

"[There] were all types of opposition to the concept of a common school," as one scholar notes, ". . . the journals had to create an interest in this concept in order to garner support for the ideas they espoused."[32]

Advocate editor West was new neither to the common school movement, nor to Indiana, when he began publication of his biweekly periodical in 1846. Often described simply as "an educator from Ohio," West traveled across the Hoosier state in 1844–45, visiting the local common schools. He was recognized in 1845 as a man with a broad understanding of the common school movement in Indiana. "[He] traveled over Indiana," one representative state history reports, "trying to arouse sentiment for better schools, and started a paper, the *Common School Advocate,* in Indianapolis. For several years this journal made a campaign for state schools, and is credited with being an important influence in making possible the free school system." Forgiving the factual error concerning the periodical's longevity, this account is typical of the historical image of West. An itinerant preacher spreading the gospel of reform from township to township, West has been pictured by contemporary and later reports as an altruist, concerned only with the promotion of a publicly supported system of common schooling in Indiana.[33]

Like the founders of local reform associations, however, periodical editors and publishers were often motivated by personal interests. Some periodicals, for example, served as promotional organs for the publishers of new school textbooks, and this was clearly the case with West and his *Common School Advocate.* West was not simply an itinerant educator traveling through Indiana in order to observe and promote public support for her common schools. He was a salesman peddling a new line of school books, the Sanders Series. This fact was noted by common school Superintendent Mayhew, who described West as a man who had "been traveling in part for the purpose of introducing a new and improved series of books for children and youth in the primary departments." Mayhew expressed confidence in the quality of West's product, but, regardless, West's motivation for helping advance the common school movement seems clear.[34]

The "Prospectus" of the *Common School Advocate* assured its reader that "no advertisements [would] be permitted" on its pages, but West continued to promote the textbook series throughout his tenure as editor. He wrote editorials on the evils of the "endless variety of school books" then in use and solicited further support of the Sanders Series from prominent individuals. The call for improved, uniform textbooks was a commonplace of educational reform, but with West, self-interest and the public interest were clearly intertwined.[35]

Whatever their motivation, editors like West were genuinely committed to the improvement of local schools. In an 1845 letter to Superintendent Mayhew, West criticized the incompetence of common schoolteachers who had "obtained certificates of qualification on the ground of expediency, and not of merit." He also criticized the apathy of parents and community members, who ignored the lack of discipline in the schools, the lack of communication between schools, and, of course, the "want of a regular progressive series of school books." Each of these criticisms, along with proposed remedy, reappeared in the pages of the *Advocate*. Chief among West's concerns in 1845 was Indiana's "isolation" from the pedagogical innovations associated with the common school movement in the eastern states.[36]

According to West, the local reform effort had stalled because its supporters were unaware of the pedagogical reforms and political stratagems successfully pioneered by eastern common school leaders such as Mann and Barnard. "Within the last five years," West wrote, "there has been a great improvement in the manner of communicating instruction, as well as in the system of government in common schools; and why should not the schools of Indiana be benefited by these improvements? There is no copy right for them—they are free. If they have revolutionized New York, and done so much good in Ohio; why may not Indiana reap the benefit of their experience?" West promised to bridge the gap between the ideas of eastern reformers and the work of Hoosier activists; the *Common School Advocate* would be his vehicle. Like other professional reformers, West may have exaggerated both the good that such intellectual contact would bring to the local common schools of the Hoosier state, and the harm that would come from continued isolation. In an age of local boosterism and institution building, however, West saw in the *Common School Advocate* a means both of standardizing formal education in Indiana and of professionalizing Hoosier teachers.[37]

The role of educational periodicals in the success of the Indiana common school movement, like that of local associations of reformers, is complex. West was clearly not the altruist that earlier histories have lauded, but he did provide a forum for the exchange of important reform proposals during a critical period in the history of the movement. At the very moment that Mills penned his first message to the state legislature in 1846, he had ready access to the distilled wisdom of eastern reformers in the pages of the *Common School Advocate*.

The *Advocate* was characteristic of the regular periodical literature of antebellum educational reform. The common school idea, however, was also spread across the country at the state and local levels by an irregular literature of "reports, lectures, pamphlets, brochures, memorials, and petitions." West engaged in the most common form of this type of educational propagandizing, the local lecture, as he rode the Indiana circuit in 1844–45. Typically and unfortunately, he left no written record of his local efforts. A representative sample of such addresses and lectures survives, though. One example of this promotional literature has already been examined (the AICSI report of 1833), but a veritable flood of such reports deluged the Hoosier state throughout the 1830s and 1840s. Promotional speeches of this type, joined in 1846 by the first of Mills's annual messages, represent the most common means of spreading the common school idea to local communities. Much of this literature promoted a vision of common school reform consonant with the one outlined by Mills, but a handful of these reports promoted discordant ideas. Slight variations on the common school theme emerged in this literature to reveal the subtle complexities and conflicts internal to the Indiana common school movement.[38]

What was likely the first statewide meeting of common school supporters in Indiana convened in Indianapolis in 1837. Andrew Wylie, the first president of "Indiana College," gave the keynote address on the subject of "common school education." One Mills biographer has claimed that the famous educational reformer became "publicly interested in the cause of public education" only after attending this meeting and hearing Wylie's address. This seems unlikely, however, given Mills's expression of interest in common school reform in his earlier letter to Thompson. Moreover, the model of popular education promoted by Wylie in his address differed considerably from the one steadfastly promoted by Mills.[39]

Rather than directing his comments to the Hoosier schoolhouse, and eschewing even the term "common school," Wylie began his address by proclaiming that "the best part of a common education, that is, such an education as all children may, and ought to, obtain, must be gained, if gained at all, not in schools, but at home in the family circle." Wylie identified moral training and religious instruction as "the most essential branch of a common education," and concluded that this crucial moral education was best left to the home.[40]

Most of Wylie's contemporaries concurred with his conclusion that moral education must comprise the greatest part of "common education." The definition of the common school classroom as a "crucible of character," as historian B. Edward McClellan has called it, was a distinctive feature of educational reform rhetoric throughout the nineteenth century. Common school wisdom, however, held that moral education must be sharply distinguished from religious instruction; the former was nondenominational, the latter sectarian. Even Mills, an ordained Presbyterian minister who gave much of his life to the service of sectarian Wabash College, believed nonsectarianism to be essential to any common school system. Wylie's acceptance of religious instruction as part of "common education" and his focus on the home as the proper site for such education put him at odds with many of his fellow reformers.[41]

Education, formal and informal, must begin in the home. No common school reformer would have argued against this point. Wylie's insistence, however, that the heart of "common education," the moral aspect, be left solely to the private sphere contradicted a crucial feature of the reform rhetoric of people like Mann, Barnard, and Mills. One of the larger social concerns that helped give rise to the common school movement was precisely the belief among elite segments of society that certain homes (especially those of the poor) were proving increasingly incapable of providing appropriate moral education. In such cases, moral education left to the home would be worse than insufficient; it would be positively harmful. Moreover, one of the fundamental tenets of the common school movement was that, to be socially effective, "common education" must take place within a common school building. It was precisely the mixing of social classes within the public institution of the common school that was to allay the threat of social class conflict in the rising generation. These twin concerns, that the children of morally suspect homes receive an appropriate moral education in the public sphere and that the children of different socioeconomic and religious backgrounds learn mutual civility in a common social institution, could not be met by Wylie's definition of an appropriate "common education." In short, Wylie's vision of common *education* did not provide for a common *school*. Wylie's address could have had only limited influence on a reformer like Mills, who argued throughout this period for publicly supported, nonsectarian, socially inclusive common schooling.

Reviewing Wylie's work as president of the state college, Madison concludes that "[he] had little understanding of or interest in the state's common people and only a narrow vision of a public university." Wylie's vision of higher education lies beyond the scope of this study, but his comments to the 1837 common school convention certainly suggest that he had a narrow vision of "public" education at the elementary level. Overall, Wylie apparently had little faith in the social role to be played by public education. These views may have distinguished Wylie from the most prominent of common school reformers, but he was not alone in holding them.[42]

Wylie's unusual vision of "common education" may have been influenced by a lecture delivered on the Indiana College campus only a few months prior to his Indianapolis address. In 1836, Charles Caldwell spoke on "popular education" to the college's Philomathean Society. "As respects the *moral* education of the community," he said, "which offers the surest guaranty of all that is most estimable in social, safe and valuable in political, and desirable in individual life, we must look to other sources than popular schools." Caldwell, like Wylie, concluded that moral education, the central goal of "common" education, was best left to the home.[43]

Wylie and Caldwell offered an alternative vision of common education to the school-based one successfully promoted by reformers like Mills. Another alternative appeared in an *Indiana State Journal* editorial prepared by George Kent in 1845. Regarding school reform, Kent wrote: "Education must be free—free, we had almost said, as the air we breathe. There must be no royal road to learning—to be rattled over only by the gilded coaches of the great, or trod only by the dainty foot of the purse-proud aristocrat. It must not be the king's highway but *the people's*—trodden over, and macadamized even, by their hard hands and flinty feet." Egalitarian to its core, Kent's argument for the necessity of common school reform was clearly distinct from those made by Mills or Wylie.[44]

Unlike the usual plea for social harmony, Kent's rationale for common schooling directly addresses social class conflict. The "purse-proud aristocrat" is compared unfavorably to the hardy American worker; the common school as a social institution must serve the interests of the latter. The egalitarian overtones of Kent's editorial are strongly reminiscent of the argument for common school reform given nearly two decades earlier by the Workingmen's parties of the East. One of the strongest arguments given by common school promoters in support of their proposed reforms concerned the problem of maintaining social order in a rapidly changing society. Kent's argument for common schooling, like that of the Workingmen's parties, identified a different concern: the empowerment of the increasingly distinct American working class. Elite concern for social order and popular concern for empowerment rarely gibed, and arguments for common schooling like Kent's were only superficially in accord with those promoted by men like Mills.[45]

Although more conservative rationales for common schooling tended to dominate the literature of the movement in Indiana, Kent's vaguely radical rationale was not without its Hoosier roots. An egalitarian ethic informed the innovative educational practices of the utopian community at New Harmony earlier in the century. Following the collapse of the New Harmony experiment, Owen became a prominent speaker for the Workingmen's Party of New York on educational and social reform. Owen abandoned public support for his radical positions upon his return to Indiana, but the belief in the egalitarian potential of common schooling continued to resonate in the state movement. Occasionally, as in the Kent editorial, the egalitarian rationale resurfaced; when it did, it provided a glimpse into a reform program fundamentally different from the one outlined by Mills and his colleagues.[46]

Reform leaders, according to historian Carl F. Kaestle, "came to the common school cause with different values and different purposes in mind." Historians have highlighted the work of Mills and have suggested that his proposals represent a standard around which all other Indiana common school reformers flocked. The truth, however, is not so simple. Alternative visions of the proper nature and direction of educational reform surfaced throughout the critical decades of the Indiana common school movement leading up to the passage of the Free School law of 1852 (occasionally supported by individuals as prominent on the state level as

Mills was himself). Again, only further research into local histories can tell us how heated such conflict became at the grassroots level.[47]

Wylie, Caldwell, and Kent presented visions of common schooling at odds with the "mainstream" vision associated with reformers such as Mills, West, and the members of the Association for the Improvement of Common Schools in Indiana. In 1847, Hoosier common school reformers prepared for another convention in Indianapolis. A similar convention, one decade before, had produced Wylie's address on the virtues of "common education" outside the schoolhouse. Kent had published his farewell editorial in the Indianapolis-based *Indiana State Journal* only two years before. Convened in the shadow of Mills's first message to the legislature, however, the 1847 meeting was devoid of any conflicting visions of common school reform (or, at least, any such discord was excised from the convention's official report). The reform program outlined by Mills captured the day.

These "friends of education," like virtually every common school supporter before them, placed moral education at the heart of the proposed common school program. Also like their predecessors, this group of reformers saw the common schoolteacher as a role model for the student body and lamented the moral and intellectual weaknesses exhibited by current members of the profession. "Very much," they claimed, "is said of the influence of the press, of our legislators and of the clergy. But none of them exert such an influence as the schoolteacher. The mind of his pupils is cast into the mould of his own, and the impress is made with astonishing exactness." In other words, "as the twig is bent, so the tree inclineth"; there was no more popular sentiment among common school reformers.[48]

In the eyes of these reformers, improving the morals of each child would prove a wise social investment. The common man trained in a common school, they argued, was a more productive citizen, both politically and economically. To the charge that a statewide system of publicly supported common schooling might prove an unbearable expense to the young state, they replied:

> It is believed that nine-tenths of the whole have had little or no early moral training, which has cultivated the affections and inspired good moral principles in the child. Even our hospitals and poor houses are extensively filled by the indirect influence of ignorance and vice. So far then from increasing our annual State expenses, by establishing upon a broad and generous basis, a system of Free Common Schools, it will doubtless in the end, greatly diminish our expenses by diminishing crime, and pauperism, and poverty.

Perhaps the extension of American civilization onto the frontier had stretched thin the bonds of social cohesion, and perhaps an increasing amount of immigration from foreign ports had introduced a frightening ethnic and religious diversity into the American population. Perhaps the related forces of urbanization and industrialization, nascent though they were, had redefined social relations between the classes, and, perhaps, higher rates of "crime, pauperism, and poverty" were the result. According to this view, however, all might be set aright by the proper education of the rising generation in America's common schools.[49]

The claim that popular education, properly conducted, would alleviate social problems such as crime and public vice is virtually a universal feature of common school rhetoric. It appears in the proposals of Mills, in the editorials of West, and in the addresses of Wylie. The common school's potential as a "preventative" to crime and social discord was central to the rise of broad public interest in the movement. Wylie's 1837 address contained a representative approach: "To prevent evil, fellow-citizens, is proverbially easier than to cure. This, then, we must do to prevent the ruin of our country, we must effect a great and permanent improvement in the system of common education." In an age of systemic reforms aimed at renovating social institutions that served to rehabilitate the deviant (e.g., asylums and prisons), the common school was called upon to eliminate such problems before they required individual remediation. Given the successful execution of educational reform, it was argued, no other social reform should be necessary.[50]

The reform proposals found in the report of the 1847 common school convention are representative of the rhetoric associated with the preeminent figures of the common school movement in America. They strongly echo Mills's own proposals, first published in the previous year. Even if certain facets of the 1847 proposals were sympathetic to the unorthodox vision of Wylie, it was only because there were some features of common school reform upon which virtually every notable reformer could agree. Since the 1847 report is much closer to the "mainstream" position on common school reform than are some other extant documents, it is not surprising to find that on the few occasions when previous historians of education in Indiana have expanded the focus of their inquiry beyond the figure of Mills, they have turned most frequently to the work of the common school convention of 1847.

In one sense, the work of Indiana's "friends of education" culminated in the Constitutional Convention of 1851 and the Free School law of the following year. Calling themselves and their predecessors to task for leaving unfulfilled the educational promise of the 1816 constitution, the authors of the revised constitution reiterated the Hoosier state's support for the common school idea. In 1852, this support was finally translated into binding legislation, the landmark "Free School law." Historian A. D. Mayo called this statute "the most advanced and comprehensive of all the new States," and concluded (with characteristic exaggeration) that "the Indiana constitutional convention of 1851 and the legislature of 1852 gave to the whole country assurance of a brilliant educational career for the Hoosier state."[51]

Like its predecessor, the Indiana state constitution of 1851 made provision for a publicly supported system of "free schooling." Article VIII of the 1851 constitution, like 1816's Article IX, reconstituted the educational rhetoric of the Northwest Ordinance. An important distinction, however, was made in the later document. Instead of calling for the establishment of a system of free, public education continuing through the university level, the 1851 constitution made provision only for "a general and uniform system of common schools, wherein tuition shall be without charge, and equally open to all." Public support for formal education no longer encompassed secondary or higher education, even in theory.[52]

Following this constitutional change, there was a narrowing of possibility for the "public" sector of education in Indiana. The mainstream vision of common schooling had always been limited to "elementary" education. In states like Michigan, where the common school vision had expanded to include every level of formal education, reform plans had been curtailed for lack of funds and lack of agreement over the appropriateness of public support for "higher learning." The county seminary, a familiar landmark on the Hoosier educational landscape since its public funding in 1818, lost its source of support as a result of the constitutional changes of 1851. County seminaries, like private academies, provided a means of pursuing one's formal education beyond the limits of the common school curriculum. Unlike the academies, however, county seminaries had long been subsidized by public funds, thus bringing the cost of "secondary" education within reach for a greater number of Indiana families than might have otherwise been the case. After 1851, secondary education of this sort could no longer be part of the "public" sector. Public support was denied secondary education even in cases where such education could be proven to directly benefit the common schools, for example, through the provision of teacher training in a state-supported normal school. Private academies and preparatory departments of colleges and universities would have to fill this gap on Indiana's educational ladder until the permanent establishment of the public high school as a social institution later in the century.[53]

Pursuant to the educational provisions made by the 1851 constitution, the state legislature passed the Free School law of 1852, widely regarded as the ultimate accomplishment of the common school movement in Indiana. While the 1852 law did include some new mandates, including the identification of civil townships as school townships, the elaboration of the duties of the superintendent of public instruction, and the provision of support to township school libraries and to a state board of education, its most important function was to reaffirm, and make mandatory, many of the earlier statutes regarding common schooling. As late as 1849, the legislature was still passing nonbinding school laws. The purpose of the 1852 law was to make local compliance to state statutes compulsory. No longer would the provision of universally accessible common schooling come "as soon as circumstances shall permit." Public support for a free system of common schools in Indiana was at hand, or so its promoters believed.[54]

Unfortunately, the "friends of education" were premature in their celebration, and the final establishment of a system of publicly supported common schooling in Indiana did not come until after the close of the Civil War. One important battle in the war for the common school *had* been won by 1852, though: the public mind had finally been awakened. While not every Hoosier was yet convinced of the virtues of common schooling, activists on both sides of the issue now shared a common vocabulary. Few would question the public responsibility to provide for a universally accessible common school education; conflict now centered on the proper source and scope of that support. In the end, the day belonged to Mills.

As this chapter has suggested, though, the triumph of the common school idea in Indiana did not belong solely to Mills. Several prominent voices seconded Mills's call for common school reform, as did innumerable less prominent ones. Moreover, the vision of common schooling associated with Mills was only one among a number of competing alternatives. We may never fully understand how the program of reform advocated by Mills and his colleagues overcame competition from alternative programs, such as those suggested by Wylie and Kent, but there can be no doubt that each, in its own way, contributed to popularizing support for the idea of common schooling. If anything, this chapter suggests that we have only just begun to understand the complicated nature of the common school movement in Indiana, and that considerable further research is required at the local level.

One such study, an examination of local newspaper coverage of Mills's death in 1879, suggests that his contemporaries associated Mills more closely with his work in higher education than with his support for the common school movement. Given the diversity of Indiana's common school reformers, and Mills's identification by contemporaries with his long service to Wabash College, one must ask: How did "Caleb Mills" become the one name most commonly associated with the Hoosier common school movement?[55]

As an eloquent common school activist and former superintendent of public instruction, Mills entered the historical record as a "schoolman" (a generic term often applied to nineteenth-century educational reformers and administrators). As Reese has noted, early historians of education in Indiana, as elsewhere, were also schoolmen. Boone, for example, was a professor of pedagogy at Indiana University, while both Smart and Cotton were former superintendents of public instruction. Searching the past for historical predecessors, men such as these looked for the familiar. In short, they searched the past for men who reminded them of themselves. Not for them the unorthodox views of an Andrew Wylie, a George Kent, or even a Robert Dale Owen. Professional schoolmen-as-historians sought out noble and uncomplicated ancestors; Mills fit the mold perfectly.[56]

In background and temperament, Mills was the most "like" the nationally recognized leaders of the common school movement. A New Englander by birth and a clergyman by training, Mills fit easily into the pattern cut for men such as Samuel Lewis (Ohio), John Pierce (Michigan), and John Swett (California). Each of these men was promoted, in his turn, as a "Horace Mann" for his state; Mills was little different. Mills's contemporaries may have regarded him primarily as a college professor, but to a later generation of schoolmen-historians, he was an archetype. This, as much as the continued accessibility of his "educational messages," explains why the Wabash professor was plucked from his rightful place among a chorus of reformers and placed at center stage.

Whatever his actual role in the larger common school movement, Mills was correct on one count: the struggle to awaken the public mind was essential to the movement's success. To the degree that this struggle was completed by 1852, Mills played an important part. He did not play a "singular" part, however, or even a decisive one. Local associations of reformers, educational periodicals, and speakers on the stump all contributed their visions of common schooling to the struggle. Mills's position at the vanguard of reform was made possible only by the work of an anonymous mass. The struggle to awaken the public mind to the virtues of common schooling was won at the grassroots, not at the state capital. Missionaries in Greencastle, businessmen in Madison, and teachers in Richmond all played their part in disseminating the common school idea to the Hoosier public. To discount the complicated and sometimes conflicted nature of the common school movement in Indiana is to do an injustice both to those who argued against educational reform, and to those who supported educational reform but disagreed with Mills and his colleagues on the particulars.

NOTES

1. Jacob P. Dunn, *Indiana and Indianans: A History of Aboriginal and Territorial Indiana and the Century of Statehood* (Chicago, 1919), 474.

2. Michael B. Katz, *Reconstructing American Education* (Cambridge, 1987), 1; Richard G. Boone, *A History of Education in Indiana* (New York, 1892); A. D. Mayo, "Education in the Northwest during the First Half Century of the Republic, 1790–

1840," in *Report of the Commissioner of Education for the Year 1894–95,* vol. 2 (Washington, D.C., 1896), 1537.

3. Charles W. Moores, *Caleb Mills and the Indiana School System* (Indianapolis, 1905), 364; Andrew A. Sherockman, "Caleb Mills, Pioneer Educator in Indiana" (Ph.D. diss., University of Pittsburgh, 1955), 3; Boone, *A History of Education in Indiana;* James H. Smart, ed., *The Indiana Schools and the Men Who Have Worked in Them* (Cincinnati, 1875); Fassett A. Cotton, *Education in Indiana: An Outline of the Growth of the Common School System* (Indianapolis, 1904).

4. David Tyack and Elizabeth Hansot, *Managers of Virtue: Public School Leadership in America, 1820–1980* (New York, 1982), 23; William J. Reese, "Indiana's Public School Traditions: Dominant Themes and Research Opportunities," *Indiana Magazine of History* 89 (December 1993): 301; Caleb Mills to the Rev. James Thompson of Crawfordsville, Ind., 18 March 1833, in Joseph F. Tuttle, "Caleb Mills and the Indiana Common Schools," a paper read to the Indiana Teachers Association, 31 December 1879 (reprinted in Moores, *Caleb Mills,* 382–83). The entire text of Mills's six letters to the state government in support of his vision of common schooling are reprinted, in full, in Moores, *Caleb Mills,* 397–638.

5. Moores, *Caleb Mills,* 363; Governor St. Clair quoted in Mayo, "Education in the Northwest during the First Half Century of the Republic," 1535; Stephen B. Oates, *With Malice toward None: The Life of Abraham Lincoln* (New York, 1977), 11. On Lincoln, see also Louis A. Warren, *Lincoln's Youth: Indiana Years, Seven to Twenty-One, 1816–1830* (Indianapolis, 1959).

6. Rev. James Thompson, "Common Schools," *The Home Missionary* (January 1833), quoted in Everett E. Jarboe, "The Development of the Public School System in Indiana from 1840 through 1870" (Ed.D. diss., Indiana University, 1949), 23–24. For a study of the relationship between the work of the American Home Missionary Society and the common school movement in Indiana, see also W. William Wimberly II, "Missionary Reforms in Indiana, 1826–1860: Education, Temperance, Antislavery" (Ph.D. diss., Indiana University, 1977).

7. Mills to Thompson, 18 March 1833, in Moores, *Caleb Mills,* 382–83.

8. James H. Madison, *The Indiana Way: A State History* (Bloomington, 1986), xiii. "Public" and "private" are modern terms, ill-suited to the description of the educational landscape of early nineteenth-century America. On the nature of this difficulty, see, for example, Carl F. Kaestle, *The Evolution of an Urban School System: New York City, 1750–1850* (Cambridge, Mass., 1973); and *Pillars of the Republic: Common Schools and American Society, 1780–1860* (New York, 1983).

9. Lawrence A. Cremin, *American Education: The National Experience, 1783–1876* (New York, 1980), 149.

10. Donald F. Carmony, ed., "Public Schools in Congressional Township 13, Range 7 East, Shelby County, Indiana, 1829–1852," *Indiana Magazine of History* 58 (December 1962): 280; Walter Johnson Wakefield, "County Seminaries in Indiana," *Indiana Magazine of History* 11 (June 1915): 151. On the Sunday school as the predecessor of the common school on the early nineteenth-century frontier, see Lloyd P. Jorgenson, *The State and the Non-Public School, 1825–1925* (Columbia, 1987), 13, 53. On the American Sunday School Union, see Anne M. Boylan, *Sunday School: The Formation of an American Institution, 1790–1880* (New Haven, 1988). On private academies, see, for example, John Hardin Thomas, "The Academies of

Indiana," *Indiana Magazine of History* 10 (December 1914): 331–58; 11 (March 1915): 8–39; and Wimberly, "Missionary Reforms in Indiana," 140–53.

11. Madison, *The Indiana Way,* 81; Boone, *A History of Education in Indiana,* 87.

12. Gordon Lee, ed., *Crusade against Ignorance: Thomas Jefferson on Education* (New York, 1961); Frederick Rudolph, ed., *Essays on Education in the Early Republic* (Cambridge, 1965); The Northwest Ordinance of 1787, in Francis N. Thorpe, ed., *The Federal and State Constitutions, Colonial Charters, and Other Organic Laws of the States, Territories, and Colonies Now and Heretofore Forming the United States of America,* vol. 2 (Washington, D.C., 1909), 961; Carl F. Kaestle, "Public Education in the Old Northwest: 'Necessary to Good Government and the Happiness of Mankind,'" *Indiana Magazine of History* 84 (March 1988): 60. See also Carl F. Kaestle, "The Development of the Common School Systems in the States of the Old Northwest," in Paul H. Mattingly and Edward W. Stevens, Jr., eds., *". . . Schools and the Means of Education Shall Forever Be Encouraged": A History of Education in the Old Northwest, 1787–1880* (Athens, 1987), 31–43.

13. Indiana Constitution of 1816, Article IX, in Thorpe, ed., *Federal and State Constitutions,* vol. 2, 1069.

14. Boone, *A History of Education in Indiana,* 13. On the influence of the rhetoric of the Northwest Ordinance on state constitutions, see, for example, Paul H. Mattingly and Edward W. Stevens, Jr., "Introduction," in Mattingly and Stevens, eds., *". . . Schools and the Means of Education Shall Forever Be Encouraged,"* 3. See also David B. Tyack, Thomas James, and Aaron Benavot, *Law and the Shaping of Public Schools, 1785–1954* (Madison, Wis., 1987). On the status of African Americans in early Indiana, see Emma Lou Thornbrough, *The Negro in Indiana: A Study of a Minority* (Indianapolis, 1957).

15. Boone, *A History of Education in Indiana,* 24; Otho Lionel Newman, "Development or [*sic*] the Common Schools of Indiana to 1851," *Indiana Magazine of History* 22 (September 1926): 250. It is precisely this state of affairs that is satirized in Edward Eggleston's classic, *The Hoosier School-Master* (Bloomington, 1984 / reprint of 1871 edition). A concise description of early educational legislation in Indiana can be found in Jarboe, "The Development of the Public School System in Indiana," 1–26.

16. J. P. Drake, *Report of the Superintendent of Common Schools* (Indianapolis, 1850), 227; Boone, *A History of Education in Indiana,* 39.

17. Madison, *The Indiana Way,* 113; Moores, *Caleb Mills,* 376; Val Nolan, Jr., "Caleb Mills and the Indiana Free School Law," *Indiana Magazine of History* 49 (March 1953): 81.

18. The general outline of this plan for common school reform may be found in Kaestle, *Pillars of the Republic.* For a summary of the key points of the highly influential plan formulated by Horace Mann, see Lawrence A. Cremin, ed., *The Republic and the School: Horace Mann on the Education of Free Men* (New York, 1957).

19. Concise summaries of Mills's messages to the legislature may be found in Moores, *Caleb Mills,* 367–70; and, Nolan, "Caleb Mills and the Indiana Free School Law."

20. Lawrence A. Cremin, *The American Common School: An Historic Conception* (New York, 1951), 49.

21. Association for the Improvement of Common Schools in Indiana (hereafter

AICSI), *First Annual Meeting of the Association for the Improvement of Common Schools in Indiana, read September 3, 1833* (Madison, Ind., 1833), 3.

22. Ibid., 7–8. On the significance placed upon the moral reform of the teaching profession by prominent reformers during these years, see Paul H. Mattingly, *The Classless Profession: American Schoolmen in the Nineteenth Century* (New York, 1975).

23. AICSI, *Report of the First Annual Meeting of the AICSI*, 14.

24. James H. Shields of Greencastle, Ind., to the Corresponding Secretary of the American Home Missionary Society, 15 March 1842, quoted in Wimberly, "Missionary Reforms in Indiana," 170; Ellwood P. Cubberley, *Public Education in the United States* (Boston, 1934), 136.

25. Smart, *The Indiana Schools and the Men Who Have Worked in Them*, 117; Royal Mayhew, *Report of the Superintendent of Common Schools* (Indianapolis, 1845), 104.

26. L. A. McKnight, *Progress of Education in Benton County, Indiana* (Benton County Board of Education, 1906); Ethel Hittle McDaniel, *Contributions of the Society of Friends to Education in Indiana* (Indianapolis, 1939). The notion that Indiana's progress in common school reform was based on the work of transplanted "Yankees" has long been a staple of educational history. Cubberley, in particular, gave credence to this "New England interpretation" of the common school movement in his *Public Education in the United States*. More recently, this interpretation has been reevaluated by Kaestle in his "The Development of the Common School Systems in the States of the Old Northwest." Despite its simplicity, Kaestle concludes, there remains an important degree of truth in the New England interpretation. It should be reiterated, however, that southern migrants were not opposed to education, in general, but to the model of publicly supported, socially inclusive formal education that was brought to the Old Northwest by transplanted northerners.

27. See, for example, Boone, *A History of Education in Indiana*, 63.

28. Ibid.

29. Thomas, "The Academies of Indiana," 336.

30. *Common School Advocate*, 1 October 1846, 6.

31. Smart, *The Indiana Schools and the Men Who Have Worked in Them*, 127. Smart was incorrect in his statement about the periodical, the *Common School Advocate*. It was not the first educational journal published in Indiana, but it *was* the first to focus on the Indiana common school movement. An earlier periodical, also called the *Common School Advocate*, was published in Madison, Ind., in 1837, but it was concerned with the Ohio common school movement. Publication of this periodical later moved to Cincinnati. A useful study of these educational periodicals is Sally Harris Wertheim's "Educational Periodicals: Propaganda Sheets for the Ohio Common Schools" (Ph.D. diss., Case Western Reserve University, 1970). Wertheim's study, although focused on the Ohio movement, is relevant to a study of Indiana's *Common School Advocate* (1846), not only because of its general conclusions about early educational publishing, but also because West, editor of the Indiana periodical, had been trained in a similar position in Ohio. A comprehensive study of educational periodicals during this period may be found in Sheldon Emmor Davis, *Educational Periodicals during the Nineteenth Century* (Washington, D.C., 1919). None of the journals listed in this chapter have any relationship to the *Indiana School Journal* that began publishing in 1852 and became the official organ of the Indiana State Teachers Association.

32. Davis, *Educational Periodicals during the Nineteenth Century*, 11, 92–95; Wertheim, "Educational Periodicals," 14.

33. George S. Cottman, *Indiana: Its History, Constitution, and Present Government*, revised edition (New York, 1936), 97. See also Mayhew, *Report of the Superintendent of Common Schools* (1845), 107.

34. Wertheim, "Educational Periodicals," 25, 29; Mayhew, *Report of the Superintendent of Common Schools* (1845), 107.

35. "Prospectus," *Common School Advocate*, 1 October 1846, 16; "School Books," *Common School Advocate*, 1 October 1846, 16; Royal Mayhew to H. F. West, 6 November 1845, reprinted in the *Common School Advocate*, 13 October 1846, 23.

36. Wertheim, "Educational Periodicals," 23; H. F. West to Royal Mayhew, quoted in Mayhew, *Report of the Superintendent of Common Schools* (1845), 108–109.

37. West to Mayhew, quoted in Mayhew, *Report of the Superintendent of Common Schools* (1845), 109.

38. Cremin, *The American Common School*, 51.

39. Andrew Wylie, *Address on the Subject of Common School Education, delivered before the convention of the Friends of Education, in Indianapolis, January 3, 1837* (Indianapolis, 1837); Sherockman, "Caleb Mills," 88. This was the first of a series of similar common school conventions held in Indianapolis over the next several years. Smart, it should be noted, has incorrectly identified this address as having been given in 1836 (*The Indiana Schools and the Men Who Have Worked in Them*, 118).

40. Wylie, *Address on the Subject of Common School Education*, 3, 9.

41. B. Edward McClellan, *Schools and the Shaping of Character: Moral Education in America, 1607-Present* (Bloomington, 1992), 24. See also David Nasaw, *Schooled to Order: A Social History of Public Schooling in the United States* (New York, 1979), esp. 29–43. As Jorgenson notes, it was typical of evangelical Protestants such as Mills to advocate a nonsectarian Christianity in the common schools. Jorgenson links the work of interdenominational groups such as the American Sunday School Union and the American Home Missionary Society (both of which claimed Mills as a member) to the development of a commitment to interdenominational (i.e., nonsectarian) social reform movements among the evangelical Protestant clergy (Jorgenson, *The State and the Non-Public School*, passim).

42. Madison, *The Indiana Way*, 111.

43. Charles Caldwell, *Thoughts on Popular and Liberal Education with Some Defence of the English and Saxon Languages, in the form of an address to the Philomathean Society of Indiana College, delivered September 28, 1836* (Lexington, 1836), 23.

44. George Kent, *Indiana State Journal*, 12 March 1845, quoted in Jarboe, "The Development of the Common School System in Indiana," 48.

45. On the Workingmen's parties' support for common school reform, see, for example, Rush Welter, *Popular Education and Democratic Thought in America* (New York, 1962), 45–59; and Jay Marvin Pawa, "The Attitude of Labor Organizations in New York State toward Public Education, 1829–1890" (Ph.D. diss., Teachers College, Columbia University, 1964).

46. On the educational practices of Owenite New Harmony, see, for example, John F. C. Harrison, ed., *Utopianism and Education: Robert Owen and the Owenites* (New York, 1968). For Owen's early writings in support of the common school movement, see R. D. Owen and Frances Wright, *Tracts on Republican Government and National Education* (London, 1847). On Owen's later, more conservative in-

volvement in the Indiana common school movement, see, for example, Harlow Lindley, "Robert Dale Owen and Indiana's Common School Fund," *Indiana Magazine of History* 25 (March 1929): 52–60; and Richard Leopold, *Robert Dale Owen: A Biography* (New York, 1969/reprint of 1940 edition), 142–62.

47. Kaestle, *Pillars of the Republic*, 75.

48. E. R. Ames, et al., *An Address in Relation to Free Common Schools by a Committee of the State Education Convention, Held May 26, 1847* (Indianapolis, 1847), 10.

49. Ibid., 19.

50. Wylie, *Address on the Subject of Common School Education*, 8; On the common school as the "ultimate" social reform, see Nasaw, *Schooled to Order*, 33. The idea that the public school may serve as a panacea for contemporary social ills has, of course, remained with us; see, for example, Henry J. Perkinson, *The Imperfect Panacea: American Faith in Education*, fourth edition (New York, 1995).

51. A. D. Mayo, "The Development of the Common School in the Western States from 1830 to 1865," in *Report of the Commissioner of Education for the Year 1898–99*, vol. 1 (Washington, D.C., 1900), 375.

52. Article VIII of the Indiana State Constitution of 1851, quoted in Boone, *A History of Education in Indiana*, 139.

53. Jarboe, "The Development of the Public School System in Indiana," 104; Boone, *A History of Education in Indiana*, 137. On the Constitutional Convention of 1850–51, see also Charles Kettleborough, *Constitution Making in Indiana* (Indianapolis, 1916); and John I. Morrison, "A Fragment of the Inside History of the Constitutional Convention," *Indiana School Journal* 23 (October 1878): 435–37 (Morrison was the chairman of the Educational Committee of the Constitutional Convention). On the early history of the public high school, see William J. Reese, *The Origins of the American High School* (New Haven, 1995).

54. On the particulars of the Free School law of 1852, see, for example, Boone, *A History of Education in Indiana*, 143–64; and Jarboe, "The Development of the Public School System in Indiana," 113–18.

55. Stephen D. Short, "Mulling Over the Mills Myth" (unpublished mss., Department of Educational Leadership & Policy Studies, School of Education, Indiana University, 1993). Among the newspapers sampled by Short were the *Kokomo Saturday Tribune*, the *Goshen Democrat*, the *Brownstown Banner*, the *Richmond Palladium*, the *Indianapolis News*, and the (Indianapolis) *Saturday Herald*.

56. Reese, "Indiana's Public School Traditions," 293. On the influence of schoolmen such as these on the larger field of educational history, see Bernard Bailyn, *Education in the Forming of American Society* (Chapel Hill, 1960), and Lawrence A. Cremin, *The Wonderful World of Ellwood Patterson Cubberley* (New York, 1965). For a radical critique of this so-called "celebrationist" school of thought in the field, see, for example, Michael B. Katz, *The Irony of Early School Reform: Educational Innovation in Mid-Nineteenth Century Massachusetts* (Boston, 1968), esp. 1–5. On the broader nature of historical scholarship of this type, see, for example, Herbert Butterfield, *The Whig Interpretation of History* (London, 1950); and Daniel Walker Howe, *The Political Culture of the American Whigs* (Chicago, 1979), esp. chap. 4.

WILLIAM J. REESE

Urban School Reform in the Victorian Era

The creation of tax-supported public school systems was one of the major social and political developments in the American north in the nineteenth century. Like fellow reformers in other states, Caleb Mills and his contemporaries at mid-century dreamed of the day when Indiana's schools might receive adequate funding, teachers might be honored and well paid, and white youth would be given educational opportunities unknown in a previous generation. Reformers everywhere despaired at the slow pace of change, despite continual efforts at better support for free common schools in many communities. Most distressing was the realization that most children who received an education did so in the Spartan confines of little country schools, the bane of the professional educator's existence for the next hundred years.[1]

The rise of public schools in the era before the Civil War has often dominated the historiography of education. Scholars have debated the causes leading to the formation of public schools and have quarreled over who supported and opposed their creation and their ultimate purposes once established. Most agree that, in Indiana as elsewhere in the north, schools were part of a larger evangelical Protestant movement, which emphasized the importance of state responsibility for promoting basic literacy, an ethos of personal accountability and self-discipline, and social uplift among the citizenry. As market relations expanded in the antebellum period, giving rise to the formation of more distinct social classes, businessmen, professionals, and other members of the middle classes joined together to press for the establishment of tax-supported public schools.[2]

Despite legal setbacks in the 1850s and 1860s that temporarily invalidated tax support for free schools, Indiana's educational leaders on both the state and local levels had reason for cautious optimism about the future. Throughout the nation, educators who dreamed that schools might become more sophisticated knew that towns and cities, not the countryside, would serve as their best hope. Earlier condemned by Thomas Jefferson and others as the cancer on the body politic, urban areas became lively centers of educational reform throughout the north. By mid-century, Yankee schoolmen agitated for more graded classrooms, a more sequenced curriculum, the hiring of women as teachers, more professional supervision, and safer and more commodious school buildings. In the next century, these innovations had become familiar enough that citizens could easily forget that they were once reforms, pathways to an educational millennium.[3]

In 1852 Indiana's General Assembly empowered towns and cities to establish their own school systems, separate from local townships. Most urban children in previous years did not attend schools regularly or for free. Existing schools were diverse, some church affiliated, some run for profit, others dependent upon private tuition or upon some local tax support. After the 1850s, the idea of locally controlled, tax-supported, publicly maintained schools grew more popular in Indiana. The 1852 law provided for the creation in towns and cities of a board of school trustees, usually three men appointed by city council, sometimes later elected directly by the voters. To the relief of many educational reformers, urban areas had gained enough autonomy to attempt to build more modern systems of instruction.[4]

While most historians of education who focus on the nineteenth century have written about the origins of the schools, the period from the late 1860s through the 1890s has received far less attention. Yet it was then that villages, towns, and cities experimented with new ways to educate children and organize and supervise schools. Urban schools, which came under more professional direction, enlarged their curriculums and provided models for change that many educators hoped the country schools would emulate. Indiana remained largely rural, yet little villages and towns as well as booming cities became noteworthy centers of educational innovation.[5]

The reformist zeal that stimulated the formation of schools in America in the antebellum period did not disappear in the late nineteenth century. Educators still spoke in hopeful terms about the promise of schooling, its ameliorative effects upon poverty, racism, social class injustice, and so forth. But the language of reform was increasingly transformed into a culture of professionalism, into concrete plans for curricular and organizational reform, and into careers for an increasingly self-conscious and better-organized class of educators, particularly male administrators. Some critics by the end of the century believed that reformers had succeeded too well, as reformist zeal was converted into rigid bureaucracies. They ominously warned that while country schools fit the school to the child, the most sophisticated urban systems approached the other extreme, serving as straitjackets for the young. "Thirty-five years ago there was little of system or method in the educational efforts of this state," wrote one observer in the *Public School Journal* in 1893. Now, however, "a prescribed system and order prevails everywhere. The authority of this order dominates everything. Its spirit permeates every department of the school system."[6]

Whether such alarm was warranted, change had come fairly quickly to a range of places. After the Civil War, villages and towns as well as bona fide cities such as Indianapolis started to build rudimentary school bureaucracies, which emphasized routine, order, and compliance. This was especially true in the largest places, but in remarkably rapid fashion even little hamlets pressed for a more modern school system. While the vast majority of Indiana's children late in the century attended modest ungraded country schools, even the smallest towns wanted something different and better for their children.

School trustees hired superintendents to oversee the expanding urban systems, adding to the growing division of labor becoming more common in the larger economy. From that day forward, those who supervised were paid more and gained more public influence than those who taught. School trustees also approved elaborate rules and regulations that tried to monitor and discipline the behavior of superintendents, principals, teachers, and pupils. More sophisticated courses of study were proposed and gradually implemented. Graded classrooms became more common, school subjects increased in number, and high schools emerged as the pinnacle of local systems. A new educational order was emerging.[7]

In the larger towns and cities, school trustees gave local superintendents increased power to hire teachers, supervise their labors, and direct the system—much like the men who directed the work of subordinates in new commercial establishments or factories. As paved roads and railroads increasingly connected small places with major urban centers, quickening the pace of commerce and communication, schools were caught up in a whirlwind of change. The whole society was being transformed, said W. H. Sanders, superintendent of the Rensselaer schools, late in the century. Like others before him, Sanders emphasized that "a very serious question for educators of today to consider, is how to adjust the work of the School to the demands made by the changed conditions of society on the one hand and to the limitations of teachers and pupils, and the board's finances, on the other." Superintendents saw themselves as boldly charting the future, often appearing in retrospect overly optimistic that their solutions would work for country folk, too. But these captains of learning were the envy of many educators, especially men, who aspired to their lofty status, high-salaried positions, and a life away from the dullness of farms and rural routine.[8]

Superintendents in all communities served at the pleasure of the lay-men on the local board of trustees, often moving from job to job in search of more secure employment. But they nevertheless enhanced their author-ity as the decades progressed. For example, after the Civil War, superinten-dents Abram Shortridge of Indianapolis and James Smart of Fort Wayne led the local efforts at grading their schools, hired more women as primary teachers, strengthened their high schools, helped separate administration from teaching, and became commanding figures in state educational circles. Their counterparts in little villages a fraction of the size of the capital city pursued similar reforms on a smaller scale in the ensuing decades. Smart, more ambitious and successful than most urban adminis-trators, used his position as a stepping stone to the office of state school superintendent.[9]

Urban administrators showed their growing influence in many ways. They sometimes edited journals, became influential within the state teach-ers' association, conducted popular teachers' institutes in the county seats, and otherwise served as counselors to the educational community at large. In the early 1870s Shortridge and a fellow administrator from Indianapo-lis, George P. Brown, edited a short-lived journal, *The Educationist,* to help spread their professional ideas. Urban areas were crossroads of commerce and growing industrial development as well as of intellectual ferment, home to publishing houses, bookstores, and often impressive public li-braries. In every way possible leading schoolmen publicized the idea that educators should universally embrace city models of administration and organization.[10]

"One of the most serious evils connected with our Public School System is the frequent changes that occur in the administration of the schools," claimed *The Educationist* in 1873. "This is especially true of cities and towns," even though these places offered the best models for school im-provement. "It is to these that we look for the organization and develop-ment of a system of schools that shall have a definite object in view, and each department of which shall do a specific work necessary to the accom-plishment of that object. Here we need Superintendence, and heads of departments who shall oversee and direct the work of the subordinate teachers." And lay trustees needed to learn that "No superintendent . . . will be content to work in the harness of someone else." Superintendents never gained such independence, yet they continually criticized the situ-ation in the countryside. Country schools were too self-contained, offering a meager curriculum to children and youth, forced to sit in drafty buildings in ungraded classes taught by an often poorly prepared teacher. So said the city-oriented educators.[11]

Like other professional journals, *The Educational Weekly* (1883–86) similarly held country schools up to the candle of the city systems. An editorial in this Indianapolis-based journal confidently illuminated the way for the folks in the countryside: "The organization of the country schools into a system resembling that which obtains in a well-managed body of city schools is a movement in the right direction. The proper gradation of a country school is a matter as necessary for its greatest good as gradation needed in a city school." And, the editors gravely warned, "we can in no sense afford to return to the schools of our fathers." There was no retreat from progress.[12]

The greater administrative sophistication of villages, towns, and cities was already evident by the late 1880s, as the superintendent of public instruction proudly published more and more information on their emerging "systems." Throughout these decades, state superintendents extolled the benefits of expert supervision and denounced one- and two-room schools, so common throughout the state. They also regularly published beautiful pencil sketches of the latest expensive graded school or high school in Hoosier towns and cities. Country folk who might have read these reports, which were printed by the thousands to spread the ideology of professionalism, knew that few urban educators had complimentary things to say about their work.[13]

Of the 331 towns and cities listed in the state superintendent's report in 1888, 42 percent had hired a superintendent, 80 percent had hired a high school principal, and 24 percent an assistant high school principal, with the larger communities leading the way. While women quickly became the vast majority of primary and grammar schoolteachers in these systems, men overwhelmingly dominated the top administrative positions. Only 2 (1 percent) of the 139 superintendents, 35 (13 percent) of the 266 high school principals, and 36 (46 percent) of the assistant high school principals were women. In Indianapolis in 1879, the local superintendent earned $2,500, compared with the $420 to $570 for women elementary teachers. As the local enrollments burgeoned and more and more money was spent on the system, the president of the board of school commissioners boasted that the local schools "are running smoothly and are believed to be doing as good work as is done in the best schools in the land."[14]

In the state's largest urban districts—such as Indianapolis, Fort Wayne, Terre Haute, and Evansville—growth was the order of the day after the 1860s. Growth seemed synonymous with goodness and progress. These school systems had much longer school terms than country schools, sometimes up to 180 days after the Civil War. Between 1869 and 1879 the number of schools in Indianapolis increased from 13 to 25, the teaching staff grew from 78 to 212, and daily pupil attendance jumped from 5,160 to

13,336. The boom continued in the following decades. Terre Haute employed 18 teachers in 1860, 66 in 1875; the number of pupils increased from 1,122 to 3,647. Between 1853 and 1892, Evansville's schools increased from an enrollment of 750 pupils taught by 8 teachers to 6,893 pupils taught by 171.[15]

Little towns and villages obviously had smaller numbers to report, but expansion was common, leading to more administrators and more emphasis on expert supervision, rules and regulations, and efforts at standardization. While the bigger places got excessive attention in the teachers' periodicals and praise from state officers in the capital, smaller places were hardly educational backwaters, as some examples demonstrate.

Bedford, a community south of Bloomington and the county seat of Lawrence County, had about 2,000 residents in 1870. Its leaders consciously abandoned district school organization, which in outlying areas meant more parental control, shorter school terms, and an ungraded curriculum. The town hired a superintendent and in 1871 built an expensive, graded, central school, which burned to the ground a few months after it opened. It was uninsured, but the city fathers rallied public support and erected an equally expensive school within three years. As in other small towns, Bedford's superintendent doubled as the high school principal, where he was assisted by one female teacher. The ten other teachers employed in the "system," which enrolled fewer than 500 pupils, taught in the lower grades and were all women, except for a male teacher of German.[16]

Even at this early date, the school trustees codified a long list of rules and regulations for the superintendent, teachers, pupils, and janitor. Since all the "grades"—primary, grammar, and high school—were in the same building, it was relatively easy for the superintendent to ensure that teachers kept certain kinds of records, were at their desks at the appointed hour, and marked students tardy or truant in a reasonably consistent manner. As in other little towns as well as large cities, Bedford had a formal course of study, graduated from the lowest grades up through the high school department, and a specified list of textbooks from which teachers could not deviate. No doubt the "system" failed to function as smoothly as the rules and regulations specified, but the attempts at disciplining and shaping the behavior of everyone in the central school were insistent.[17]

Many other little places worked diligently in the 1860s and 1870s to standardize the behavior of those who worked in the local schools. When Salem built its impressive two-story "graded school" in the early 1870s, the local trustees evinced the booster spirit of the times. Wrote the trustees, "Our people are enterprising, intelligent, and cultured, and can boast of a good, substantial School Building, being well constructed in reference to light and ventilation. It will seat at present near 500 pupils." When William Russell was hired as principal in 1870—he soon became the superintendent—the trustees instructed him to keep Salem abreast of the latest educational developments. "I commenced organizing the schools in accordance with the graded school system adopted by most of the towns and cities throughout our State." Here, as elsewhere, local educators emphasized that while new buildings and improved salaries were costly, schools were cheaper than prisons and the enemy of vice.[18]

The pressure of little towns to conform to their urban counterparts stemmed from the broadened circulation of ideas as markets broke down the isolation of Indiana communities after the Civil War. Contemporary reports from the grassroots reveal a powerful sense of pride in an emerging educational professionalism, and the booster spirit remained characteristic as the century progressed. By 1875, Spencer had built a central schoolhouse and established graded classrooms. The school trustees applauded the benefits of living in their "pleasantly situated" and "rapidly improving" town, certain that "if we increase the advantages for education, families of wealth and influence" would be attracted there. The city fathers of Knightstown, whose school enrollments exceeded 500 by the turn of the century, proudly emphasized that it "was a city of about 2,000 inhabitants . . . located in a rich and picturesque farming district, 34 miles from Indianapolis, at the junction of the P.C.C., and St. L. and the Big Four railroads." There were abundant gas wells, a fine water works, and many "new sidewalks." And the schools were as progressive as those of other advanced towns and cities. Rails carried produce to market and ideas and goods back and forth from the capital, ensuring that Knightstown did not become mired in the past.[19]

After the 1860s, therefore, even towns with a few hundred students slowly began to try to imitate their urban counterparts. As the size of systems expanded, the need to order, monitor, evaluate, and control the work of education expanded. Little Edinburgh was not going to be left behind, noted the Board of Education in 1895, as it justified its adoption of elaborate rules and regulations to ensure a smoothly working system. "A little reflection will show that an institution owes its very existence to the surrender of individual preferment in a measure, to the interests of many; and the individual cannot reasonably claim the privileges of the institution without cheerful compliance with the rules adopted for its government." Schools never became perfectly well-oiled machines, but efforts to discipline and order lives at school, to anticipate problems and prevent them, remained common in hamlets throughout the state.[20]

Villages, towns, and cities all desired a more advanced curriculum to match what was perceived as the more complex needs of the time. Whether in Peru or Lebanon, the pressure everywhere was to expand the curriculum and to make it more uniform across the state. In the 1880s and 1890s, a professional group within the Indiana State Teachers Association, the Town and City Superintendents, gathered annually; members exchanged letters and reports, laboring to popularize their ideas. The "graded" course of study was the great panacea, an alternative to the mixed age groupings so common in the majority of small rural schools throughout the state. No idea so captivated schoolmen at the time. It allowed the hiring of relatively inexpensive women teachers, deemed superior in the instruction of young children in the lower grades and less expensive. And it furthered the goal of building a graduated curriculum that grew more difficult as children were promoted from grade to grade.[21]

If only all children of the same age were in the same grade, claimed countless reformers during the Victorian period, most pedagogical problems would disappear. In the ubiquitous country schools, however, teachers taught pupils of all ages, at all levels of preparation. Pupils memorized their lessons, learned from whatever books parents had at their disposal, and recited them to their teacher, each in their turn. Critics doubted that rural pupils actually studied a "curriculum" or "course of study." Since there were no common tests, comparing one's academic achievement with others was impossible, too. After reciting a lesson to the satisfaction of one's teacher in a country school serving a mixed age group, a pupil simply moved on to a more difficult text, thus promoting a highly subjective and nonscientific pedagogy. Graded classrooms promised relief from this educational anarchy and lack of system.[22]

Exactly how villages, towns, and cities went about the task of grading their schools must be pieced together from disparate sources and based on educated guesses. Few superintendents left much documentation on exactly how they proceeded. With the earliest formation of a single, "central" school in towns like Bedford, or countless other little places, the newly appointed superintendents first separated all the children and youth into broad grades or levels: primary, grammar, intermediate, and for the older and more accomplished students, high school. Within these rough designations superintendents then organized classes into what later generations called grades, from first to second upward through eleventh and twelfth. Ideally, these graded classes were organized on the basis of one's age, but differing levels of achievement led to a broad age range within many classes. A combination of factors determined placement, especially recommendations by teachers and performance on recitations from specific textbooks designated for particular grades. Within a decade or so in the establishment of a village school system, the primary level was usually subdivided into grades one to four, grammar from five through eight, and high school from nine to twelve. Little Monticello reported this familiar pattern in 1889, when it had three high school graduates.[23]

By no stretch of the imagination were little villages or even city schools perfectly age graded in the late nineteenth century. But the tendency was in that direction, with pupils increasingly though imperfectly clustered around similar ages in particular grades. Even Indianapolis, the most

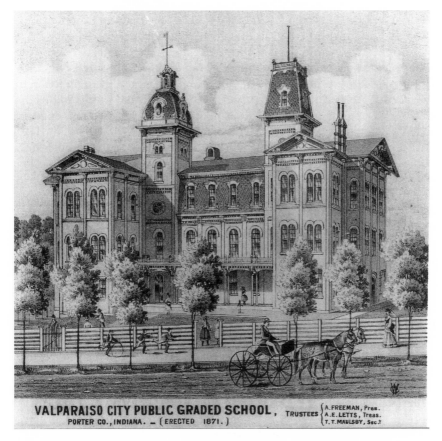

Booster Pride in the Valparaiso Schools. Courtesy Indiana State Library

advanced city system, did not have perfectly age-graded classrooms. But the average age in each grade gave credence to the claim that it had graded schools. In 1879, H. S. Tarbell, the superintendent, was able to report that the average age of children was 7.8 in first grade, 8.4 in second grade, 9.7 in third grade, then 11.1 in fourth grade, 12.1 in fifth grade, and so on. A range of ages appeared in every grade, but age clustering was evident. Graded classes were not to be confused with the typical schools of the countryside.[24]

Schoolmen liked to speak with pride about the efficiency of their schools. But villages, towns, and cities in Indiana were constantly absorbing pupils from the country into their budding systems, which meant that children with varying levels of achievement were continually in their midst. "The High School is growing each year," wrote Lebanon's superin-

tendent in 1896, "and the fact that so many of the country school graduates" sought entry to it led to overcrowding and his appeal for a new
building. Again, while classification remained an imperfect science, the
urban schools were clearly not simply larger versions of rural schools. A
system of classification was being put into place, and it gave direction to
the labors of superintendents, principals, teachers, and pupils in dozens
of communities and ultimately had an enormous influence on country
schools when they consolidated in the next century.[25]

Professional journals and the state superintendent's office consistently praised the virtues of graded classrooms. Grading allowed for a more
sequenced and uniform course of study, made teachers more specialized
and in theory expert in their work, and thus contributed to that greater
division of labor so extolled by society's leaders as sound political economy. The *Indiana School Journal* continually criticized rural schools for
moving so slowly toward consolidation, which was essential for grading and the formation of high schools. Belle Fleming, who taught at the
Vincennes High School, wrote in 1880 that without a division of labor,
teaching would never become a profession. The following year the *Journal*
typically editorialized that grading would cut costs, allow a teacher or
pupil to transfer to other schools more easily, "and find classes corresponding to the ones he left." It seemed "essential" that the country
schools abandon their ungraded plans and promote a more uniform state
system.[26]

Little places by the early 1870s embraced the idea that graded schools,
with the high school at the head of the system, were the wave of the future.
In 1870, with a grand total of twenty-two high school students, a Cambridge City official heartily endorsed graded schools, anticipating the day
when it would establish "a Scientific and Classical High School. One that
will not only give our sons and daughters a scientific and business education, but also prepare young men for the Junior Class in college. Opportunities will also be afforded for instruction in the Modern Languages; also
in Music, Painting, etc." In 1872 Shelbyville's boosters also waxed eloquent on the benefits of its new graded plan and more formalized high
school curriculums. So did other communities. By the turn of the century,
critics said that Indiana, like other states, had high schools more in name
than in fact, with a handful of teachers trying to cover too many subjects,
with predictably poor results. Still, dozens of villages and towns praised
their high schools as "people's colleges," a grassroots expression of popular democracy.[27]

The high schools in little villages were often really a room on the top of
a central school building, with the superintendent sometimes serving as
principal and part-time teacher, aided by a few women assistant teachers.
Petersburg had a graded school in the 1870s, and M. D. McShane served as
the superintendent and high school teacher; the "high school" claimed to

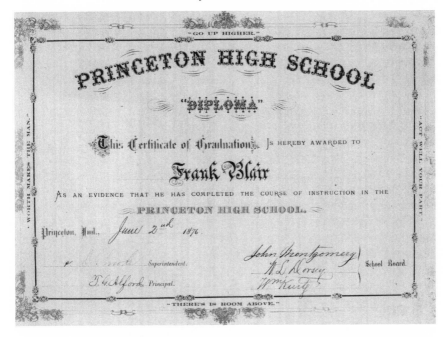

"GO UP HIGHER."

PRINCETON HIGH SCHOOL

"DIPLOMA"

This Certificate of Graduation Is HEREBY AWARDED TO

Frank Blair

AS AN EVIDENCE THAT HE HAS COMPLETED THE COURSE OF INSTRUCTION IN THE

PRINCETON HIGH SCHOOL.

Princeton, Ind., June 2nd 1876.

Superintendent.

T. G. Alford Principal.

John Montgomery
N. L. Dorsey
Wm Kurtz

School Board.

"THERE'S IS ROOM ABOVE."

The Pinnacle of Academic Success in the Public Schools.
Courtesy Indiana Historical Society

offer a three-year advanced course, with four different courses per term, three terms per year. In 1872 Princeton had two high school teachers, one male, one female, with twenty pupils in the first-year class, ten in the second year, and four in the senior class. Village and town high schools, nonetheless, served as a source of tremendous pride. Rockville High was the only commissioned high school in Parke County late in the century, which meant that its graduates could attend a state university without further examination; this seemed an envious achievement to children in the outlying township schools. High schools were usually modest institutions but were the apex of the graded plan and offered the sort of specialized, some said esoteric, knowledge that brought status to local systems.[28]

The higher learning held particular importance to some of Indiana's African American citizens. Indiana was a horribly racist state, its negligible commitments to public education for the freedmen and native black Hoosiers an embarrassment to radical Republicans and civil rights' activists after the Civil War. Rural schools, following state law and local prejudice, often excluded blacks from their schools in the 1860s; towns and cities, which did somewhat more for black children, still practiced widespread segregation. Despite the segregationist character of most of

The "People's College": Knightstown High School, ca. 1900.
Courtesy Indiana State Library

Indiana's town and city schools, blacks took advantage of even scanty opportunities in their search for literacy, knowledge, and claims to equal citizenship.[29]

Throughout the southern part of the state, with its strong identification with the slave south, African American children usually attended segregated elementary schools as well as high schools. Facilities were often rudimentary and poorly equipped, with many "colored high schools" in the larger towns resembling the modest white high schools found in villages. But high school departments in Evansville, Princeton, New Albany, and elsewhere offered important job opportunities for black teachers and a place of learning for some talented pupils, who often later became elementary teachers and community leaders. While segregated elementary schools were also common in towns and cities in central and northern Indiana, people such as Shortridge of Indianapolis somewhat heroically integrated their local high schools in the 1870s and afterward. Indeed, some Indianapolis educators who espoused the doctrine of racial

Urban School Reform in the Victorian Era

High School Consolidation in the Townships: Yorktown, 1901.
Source: *Twentieth Biennial Report of the State Superintendent of
Public Instruction* (Indianapolis, 1901)

equality were outspoken in their defense of the rights of black people to
secure better educational rights for their children.[30]

Both Indianapolis and Evansville operated night schools for white and
black working-class adults, and white officials in both cities applauded
the efforts of older African Americans to improve their lot. In the 1870s
"gray-headed" blacks flocked to Indianapolis's night schools, leading the
superintendent to report that, unlike most of the poorly behaved whites
who attended, they were hard-working students who asked only for the
chance to learn. Evansville's superintendent said the same thing about
blacks attending evening schools in the early 1890s. "These schools have
been largely attended by colored people who, not having had the opportunities to secure an education earlier in life, now eagerly strive to acquire,
at least, the ability to read, write, and spell. For this class of people, the
evening schools are accomplishing a noble work." In contrast, he said, the
working-class whites in attendance at segregated evening schools were
lazy, tardy, and mostly a burden to their teachers.[31]

While evening schools were part of the specialized course offerings feasible in larger places, with their larger concentration of population and tax base, they were another example of the specialized forms of learning more difficult to fund in the countryside. Evening schools helped expand the mission of urban schools, adding to their complexity. Indeed, villages, towns, and cities often marveled at how the enrollments of both black and white pupils mushroomed in the late nineteenth century.

That, however, did not make these school systems faceless bureaucracies. In the earliest reports of graded schools in the 1870s and after, especially in villages and towns, one senses that their "systems" were caught between two worlds: clearly working to imitate places like Fort Wayne, Terre Haute, or Indianapolis but also having some characteristics reminiscent of country schools. Again, villages and towns were moving toward more graded plans, but schools of even 400 or 500 pupils had highly personal qualities. Annual school reports, even for towns with 700 pupils, often included the names of every student in the system, not just the usual small list of high school students found in the published reports in the larger urban areas.[32]

This information stood alongside the growing number of charts and graphs generated by the central office, by which the superintendent and high school principal showed their flair for scientific pedagogy and modern organization. Towns with populations of a few thousand residents remained suspended to some degree between a face-to-face world and one in which ideas and goods drawn from distant markets were subtly and sometimes dramatically altering the texture of community life. In the larger cities, with bigger schools, thousands of pupils, and a more complex division of labor, impersonality and red tape were already in evidence by the 1880s. No one imagined that Indianapolis—with many thousands of students by the end of the century—was going to reprint the names of each student in a published report.

The movement toward making the curriculum more uniform, better sequenced by grades, and taught by female teachers nevertheless occurred with increased rapidity in the decades following the Civil War, making village and town schools qualitatively different from the ungraded, much less supervised schools of the countryside. By the 1860s and 1870s, pupils in villages, towns, and cities studied a more rigidly defined and expanded curriculum, teachers had more specialized teaching responsibilities, and rules and regulations were more formalized and specified. Behavior never perfectly reflected the best-laid plans of urban school trustees or superintendents, but there was also no mistaking the tendency of bringing more system, order, and rationality to the inner workings of local schools.

In the largest places, the system began to work so well that critics feared the loss of attention to teachers' rights and pupils' individual needs. A former Indianapolis official told the state teachers' association in 1883 that complaints were growing about the "machinery" of education and the "Procrustean" system, especially in the city systems. He agreed with the critics, saying that schools, like growing businesses, too easily became rule bound, forgetting that the schools should help individual children, all of them. Other critics accused the big cities of "cast-iron formalism" in terms of the curriculum and treatment of pupils and teachers. In the country schools, said one writer in 1885, the individual was taught; in the city schools, a class was taught. The individual was frequently lost in the process.[33]

What disappeared in terms of personal attention was gained, said some educators, in the slow but steady transformation of the curriculum in the graded schools following the Civil War. Long before John Dewey became identified with a cluster of ideas known as progressive education, movements were under way that laid the basis for a new curriculum and approach to teaching. Basic subjects—reading, writing, arithmetic, plus some grammar, history, geography, and moral instruction—had long been the core of common school education in Indiana and other northern states; these subjects also remained the basis for the primary and grammar level curriculum in urban schools. Towns and cities nevertheless moved into new directions after the 1870s, experimenting with new subjects that subtly and later demonstrably altered prevailing conceptions of schools. They did not eliminate the older subjects but competed with them by taking more hours away from the familiar course of study.[34]

Town and city superintendents after the Civil War pressed for more uniform courses of study while also experimenting with new pedagogies and subject matter. While it seemed paradoxical, they called for more experimentation in terms of curriculum and pedagogy as they simultaneously demanded more uniformity in terms of common written tests and control over classroom practices. Superintendent Shortridge of Indianapolis sent Nebraska Cropsey to study the Oswego plan of object teaching in the 1860s; she also studied other urban systems that emphasized teaching through the use of objects, not just mastery of knowledge from books; and she brought these progressive ideas to bear at home as a renowned primary school supervisor. Many village, town, and city schools adopted the teaching of drawing, music, and other subjects in the 1880s and 1890s, reflecting the belief that the training of the mind was insufficient in one's education; educating the heart and hand and senses generally were equally vital. In larger towns and cities, manual training courses, first drawing and then woodworking, grew popular, with Indianapolis opening Manual Training High School in 1895. That pupils legitimately learned through the manipulation, creation, and handling of objects was later reduced to the famous cliché, learning by doing. Initially, however, it promised to enliven the curriculum, tap student interests, and connect schooling better to life.[35]

In the 1880s and 1890s, the Town and City Superintendents of the state teachers' association pressed for the systematic adoption of these new experimental approaches to the curriculum. One prominent superintendent, LaPorte's William N. Hailmann, remained proud of his role in reorienting the curriculum there, despite local opposition and resistance. As he later recalled, when first hired in the early 1880s, he was asked to shift the curriculum away from its orientation around the Three R's and a little history and geography. In 1892, however, he admitted that many parents remained skeptical despite the obvious benefits of the change. "To this day, however, there are indications of well-meaning doubt among patrons concerning the value of drawing, color-work, and other manual training in the schools, the practical abandonment of oral spelling and the shrinkage of technical grammar, the diminished importance of the school-reader and the use of much reading-matter incidental to other instruction, the substitution of experiment and investigation of matters formerly given over to the text-book, and other matters of similar import." Sensitive to the criticisms, he hoped that the critics, if really "well meaning," would ultimately support his reforms. Superintendents in Peru, Rensselaer, and other communities similarly boasted that they had also altered the curriculum in response to the reforms appearing in the leading towns and cities in the 1880s and 1890s.[36]

Providing local superintendents with the power to change the curriculum, build graded classes, hire women teachers, and overall expand their authority would have not made much sense to school trustees without specifying in great detail the new division of labor in emerging systems. And so villages and little towns rapidly formalized rules for disciplining and molding the behavior of everyone within their purview. To claim to discipline and mold is not synonymous with effecting the deed. At the same time, however, school trustees contributed to the building of more stable systems by working with superintendents and their subordinates to secure as much order and predictability as possible. Elaborate statistical charts appeared in local reports to document the attendance, deportment, and promotion rates of different graded classes, the number of high school graduates, and other information to prove to taxpayers and other professionals that the schools were moving forward.

School trustees routinely published formal rules and regulations for school employees, indicating that in their growing systems that rule-of-thumb methods, excessive individualism, and ideas rooted in a less time-oriented world increasingly were unwelcome. The rules governing the behavior of teachers were remarkably similar from place to place, revealing the conforming effects of market behavior, as ideas circulated with remarkable speed and tended toward similar results. School trustees told superintendents to secure everyone's "cheerful" acceptance of every rule.

Getting teachers to work toward the goals set from above was the first step. For example, once high schools were formed, they provided the majority of teachers for the lower schools, often young women who were among the most academically successful pupils, whose success as teachers continued to depend upon compliance and obedience to authority. Some of the largest systems established teacher training classes or schools as part of the high school curriculum, but most trustees appointed their primary and grammar level teachers directly from their own village or town high schools, without special pedagogical training. J. W. Layne, superintendent of schools in Evansville, called for the creation of a local teacher training school in 1892, noting that "it has been the general policy of the Board for many years to recruit the corps of teachers principally from the graduates of the High School." This was a widespread phenomenon.[37]

Elementary and grammar schoolteachers—nearly all women in many urban areas after the Civil War—faced demanding superiors, large class sizes, and restrictions on their behavior in and out of school. Class sizes could range up to 50 or 60 in the lower grades. It is impossible to tell with certainty how much the rules governing teachers' work were followed in every community, year in and year out. But between the 1860s and 1890s little communities as well as large cities made it clear, reflected by the status and pay, that teachers were subordinates, as superintendent Shortridge of Indianapolis had early claimed.

Lafayette's trustees, like their counterparts elsewhere, early approved a few dozen rules for teachers to follow. Teachers in 1872 were admonished to show "a faithful compliance with all the rules" or face termination. They were to arrive at school at a specified time, principals being responsible for setting the clocks in their respective schools to promote time discipline. All classes had to begin with the Lord's prayer or "appropriate singing"; teachers were told to avoid partisan topics with the children, to discipline youth with love and kindness only, to report miscreants who deserved suspension to the principal, to attend meetings and institutes when requested, to keep school records in a uniform way, and to use only texts formally approved by the trustees. The list of dos and don'ts was extensive.[38]

In addition, while scholars have long noted the authoritarian behavior of big city superintendents by the late nineteenth century, teachers' independence was also fairly circumscribed in little villages and towns as well once graded classes became more common. It is remarkable how much the job of the teacher was seemingly directed by those who did not teach. Even though there was surely never full compliance with any rule, those in power increasingly forced teachers to teach a more uniform curriculum, one in which certain amounts of material had to be covered in a specified period of time, or again face dismissal. Superintendents in communities throughout the state, and not just in the big cities, pressed teachers to comply. Whether they did so consistently and productively remains unclear.

An example drawn from Sullivan, located south of Terre Haute, is representative of developments across the state. Like their peers elsewhere, Sullivan's trustees placed the superintendent in charge of the actual running of the system, specifying what would be taught, drawn from which books, limited to what pages during any given term. Rules about what material to cover, for each grade, in each subject, must have been stifling to some teachers. Teachers received pages of instructions about every aspect of their job. For example, in the teaching of grammar in the fifth grade, one of five subjects taught, they were in part expected to do the following:

> Composition, oral and written. Letter-writing and other work of the Fourth Year continued. Write simple business letters, with care as to form, punctuation, and expression. Reproduce with accuracy and rapidity, stories to be read in class. Use as a text book, "Parts of Speech and How to Use Them, Part II," by Mrs. Knox-Heath. Master work to page 137. Give much attention to the meaning of all words used. Require many different statements about the same word. Illustrate principles by numerous simple examples. In all of this year's work there should be given the greatest variety of expression for a given idea or thought.[39]

Each subject was supposed to be taught as directed from above, to such and such a page in a specified text, whether in history, geography, arithmetic, or other subjects.

Clever teachers, then as now, undoubtedly found ways to subvert the system, or to seem to comply while engaging in imaginative pedagogy. But dissent was probably minimal since principals and superintendents increasingly used common written tests, not just individual oral recitations, to ensure that the curriculum was being followed and to check if pupils were mastering the specified material. Since women teachers lacked many good job opportunities outside of teaching, and since so many had already successfully come through the system, the rules and regulations may not have been especially oppressive to those who saw the benefits of the graded plan and overhead guidance.

Some vocal critics, however, believed that teachers had lost much independence due to the graded plan, that they, like the pupils, were part of a system that stressed order over other important values. The leading pedagogical journals in the state continually emphasized the importance of expert male supervision of schools at all levels, and this grated on the nerves of those who defended teachers' prerogatives. Every time officials in Wabash or Crawfordsville or Michigan City said that teachers were supposed to "cheerfully comply" with the rules and regulations, a minority of educators stood their ground to complain. Uniformity meant the destruction of respect for the individual pupil and teacher, said one observer in the *Educational Weekly* in 1884. "The teacher's energies are bent towards making the child fit into the system, rather than towards adapting the system to the child. The same routine of study is marked out for all; the same code of laws and penalties regulates the conduct of both the weak and the strong. The boy of genius and promise receives the same treatment and the same intellectual nourishment as the dullard or the fool."[40]

A writer in the *Indiana School Journal* in 1890 was particularly incensed at the arrogance of superintendents in their professional relationships with teachers. At a time when the "new education" claimed to prize experimentation, the very people who thought themselves progressive in terms of curriculum—adding new subjects despite public skepticism—simultaneously worked to ensure that teachers did not show too much independence. The author was especially angry to hear some superintendents say that they planned to let teachers keep some of their freedoms. Said the critic, "It is much to boast of when a teacher can use his own free choice as to whether he will stand or sit in the recitation; use a thumb bell or a pencil in calling a class; or in those more weighty matters, such as using diagrams and outlines in teaching grammar and history! Yes, very much; for he is no longer under a despot. But the amusing thing," he sarcastically concluded, "is that, in this age of liberty and personal rights . . . we should call attention so exultantly to this mere matter of the civil liberty of the teacher, in relation to the superintendent."[41]

In the emerging public school hierarchy, there was a clear set of distinctions about the authority and responsibilities of the trustees, superintendents, principals, teachers, and finally the students. Unlike teachers, who at least usually wanted to teach and were paid for their labors, pupils were even less likely to be ready conformists, toeing every line and following every request for dutiful behavior. At a time when schools suspended and expelled pupils when it seemed justified, when the age of student rights was a century in the future, the rules and regulations were effective ways to buttress the authority of those running the system as well as uphold the classroom teacher. In the larger cities, where schools were not built quickly enough to meet the demand, the rules hastened the departure of those who behaved inappropriately, who left through a revolving door that quickly delivered a replacement.[42]

Graded school systems across Indiana had elaborate rules for the student body. By the early 1870s, dozens of communities specified a wide range of behaviors that were expected, permissible, or to be avoided. Pupils had to arrive at school at a certain time, not loiter to and from school, be in one's seat at the appointed minute, be clean in appearance and wear suitable clothes, be respectful of teachers and all adults, complete homework as expected, provide proof of vaccination before seeking admission, and so forth. Much of what pupils were told referred to what they should not do. Like officials elsewhere, those in Lafayette in 1872 issued ominous warnings: "The pupils are strictly enjoined to avoid idleness and profanity, falsehood and deceit, obscene and indecent language, and every wicked and disgraceful practice, and to conduct themselves in an orderly and decent manner, both in school and out." That was just one of many rules to be followed.[43]

Teachers were products of the system and as adults were more likely to conform, but pupils were not always predisposed to order and civility. Teachers likely approved of the elaborate rules for pupils as a way to curb youthful indiscretions. Undoubtedly most adults in Rochester and other places were happy that the schools forbade the use of tobacco by the students and that teachers tried to eradicate profanity, fighting, and other annoyances from the school grounds or the carving of one's initials in a school desk. School officials in Wabash warned youth in 1887 not to "throw stones, snowballs, or missiles of any kind upon or about the school premises," and to "refrain from screaming, shouting, pushing, or rough play." One can assume that the rules may have helped maintain order, but they hardly turned pupils into automatons. When Connersville banned "concealed weapons" from the schools, few adults likely dissented, though it did not mean that children never brought a slingshot to their classroom or otherwise wrecked the quiet of an otherwise peaceful school day.[44]

The villages, towns, and city school systems that emerged in Indiana during the Victorian period were thus the sites of numerous educational reforms. Many of the changes that professional educators advocated—the grading of classrooms, the expansion of the curriculum, the creation of high schools, the hiring of women as teachers, and the separation of administration and teaching—were increasingly implemented in many corners of the state. Change occurred in dozens of communities, not just in the big cities, as markets spread new ideas about educational reform to county seats, overgrown farming towns, and countless hamlets that expanded after the end of the Civil War. Indiana was still mostly a rural state at the turn of the century, but dozens of villages, towns, and cities offered new examples of how to organize schools and educate the young.

The era separating the conclusion of the Civil War and the turn of the century was therefore a fertile time in the history of Indiana school reform. In the new century, schools would expand enormously, both in size and in their social functions. High school departments would give way to well-graded four-year high schools. Smaller schools would be consolidated, teacher credentials would increase, and the gap between professional administrators and the teaching staff would widen. Early in the new century, the curriculum would expand, and vocational education would become the rage in many urban schools. The millennial expectations of schools would remain powerful, even as they grew more secular, as citizens continued to turn to schools to solve a host of economic, social, and political problems, problems that were not necessarily educational in character. The Victorians had bequeathed to the state new ideas about school organization, curriculum, and education that would be tested by the challenges of the new century.

NOTES

1. For an overview of the history of school reform movements in Indiana, see William J. Reese, "Indiana's Public School Traditions: Dominant Themes and Research Opportunities," *Indiana Magazine of History* 79 (December 1993): 289–334.

2. The most important interpretations of the rise of common schools are by Lawrence A. Cremin, *The American Common School: A Historic Conception* (New York, 1950); Michael Katz, *The Irony of Early School Reform: Educational Innovation in Mid-Nineteenth Century Massachusetts* (Cambridge, 1968); and Carl F. Kaestle, *Pillars of the Republic: Common Schools and American Society, 1780–1860* (New York, 1982).

3. Harold Littell, "Development of the City School System of Indiana—1851–1880," *Indiana Magazine of History* 12 (September 1916): 193–213, 299–325.

4. James H. Madison, *The Indiana Way: A State History* (Bloomington, 1986), 109–11, 179–80.

5. On the urban dimensions of school reform, see especially Kaestle, *Pillars*, chaps. 3, 6; Stanley K. Schultz, *The Culture Factory: Boston Public Schools, 1789–1860* (New York, 1973); and Selwyn K. Troen, *The Public and the Schools: Shaping the St. Louis System, 1838–1920* (Columbia, Mo., 1975).

6. The article was reprinted as "Educational Indiana," *Indiana School Journal* 38 (October 1893): 604. On the shifting nature of ideology and reform, see John L. Thomas, "Romantic Reform in America, 1815–1865," *American Quarterly* 17 (Winter 1965): 656–81.

7. For a self-congratulatory examination of male administrative leadership, see the contemporary portrait by James H. Smart, *The Indiana Schools and the Men Who Have Worked in Them* (Cincinnati, 1875).

8. *Nineteenth Annual Report of the Rensselaer City Schools, 1897–1898* (Rensselaer, 1898), 7.

9. William J. Reese, "Education," in *The Encyclopedia of Indianapolis*, ed. David J. Bodenhamer and Robert G. Barrows (Bloomington, 1994), 73–76; Emma Lou Thornbrough, *Indiana in the Civil War Era 1850–1880* (Indianapolis, 1965), 478–81; and Amy C. Schutt, "Abram Crum Shortridge," in *Encyclopedia*, 1259.

10. On the history of urban school administrators and administration, see David B. Tyack, *The One Best System: A History of American Urban Education* (Cambridge,

1974); and David B. Tyack and Elisabeth Hansot, *Managers of Virtue: Public School Leadership in America, 1820–1980* (New York, 1982).

11. Untitled editorial, *The Educationist* 1 (June 1873): 3.

12. "It Is a Good Thing," *Educational Weekly* 2 (May 24, 1884): 328. Articles in various educational periodicals, such as the *Indiana School Journal*, frequently praised the movement toward more graded schools.

13. On town and city school buildings, see *Twenty-Eighth Report of the Superintendent of Public Instruction of the State of Indiana* (Indianapolis, 1880), 257–318; and *Forty-Second Report of the Superintendent of Public Instruction* (Indianapolis, 1896), 498–511.

14. State of Indiana, *Thirty-Sixth Report of the Superintendent of Public Instruction* (Indianapolis, 1888), 376–81; *Eighteenth Annual Report of the Public Schools of the City of Indianapolis, for the School Year Ending June 30, 1879* (Indianapolis, 1879), 56; *Twentieth Annual Report of the Public Schools of the City of Indianapolis, for the School Year Ending June 30, 1881* (Indianapolis, 1881), 11.

15. Reese, "Education," 73; *Twelfth Annual Report of the Terre Haute Public Schools* (Terre Haute, 1875), 11; and *Annual Report of the Public Schools of Evansville, Indiana, for the School Year Ending August 31, 1892* (Evansville, 1892), 136.

16. *Bedford Public Schools, Bedford, Indiana, Officers and Teachers for 1875 and 1876* (n.p., n.d.), 9–13. Superintendent J. H. Madden gave a speech at the Indiana State Teachers Association in 1879 that noted that the hiring of women as teachers accelerated in Indiana after the Civil War; see "Minutes of the Indiana State Teachers Association," *Indiana School Journal* 20 (February 1880): 71.

17. *Bedford Graded Schools*, 14–19.

18. *First Annual Report of the Salem Public Schools, for the School Year Ending May 24, 1872* (Salem, 1872), 11, 18. The belief that schools could combat crime by eliminating ignorance was widespread among educators in the nineteenth century. School trustees, superintendents, principals, and teachers often gave speeches or wrote essays that affirmed that spending more on schools would mean spending less on jails.

19. Spencer Public Schools, *Course of Study, with Rules and Regulations of the Board of Education* (Spencer, 1875), 16; and *Report of the Knightstown Public Schools for the School Year 1897–1898 and Announcements for 1898–1899* (Knightstown, 1899), 32–33.

20. *Annual Report and Catalogue of the Public Schools of Edinburgh, Indiana* (Edinburgh, 1895), 5.

21. To understand the educational reforms in the wider context for change, read Clifton J. Phillips, *Indiana in Transition: The Emergence of an Industrial Commonwealth 1880–1920* (Indianapolis, 1969), 386–408; William A. Rawles, *Centralizing Tendencies in the Administration of Indiana* (New York, 1903), chap. 2; and Madison, *The Indiana Way.*

22. Professional educational journals were usually merciless when it came to evaluating rural schools. Their unprofessional, ungraded, simple character offended the rising class of educational leaders in the state after the Civil War. On the need for the country schools to adapt to urban models, and their resistance, see "'That Will Do Very Well in the City, but It Is Impracticable in the Country,'" *Indiana School Journal* 27 (July 1882): 325–26; W.A.B., "Country vs. City Methods," *Indiana School Journal* 35 (October 1890): 544–45.

23. *Manual of the Public Schools of Monticello, Indiana, 1889–1890* (Monticello, 1889), 3.

24. *Eighteenth Annual Report of the Public Schools of the City of Indianapolis*, 66.

25. *Report of the Lebanon Public Schools, for the Year 1894–1895* (Lebanon, 1896), 7.

26. "Minutes of the Indiana State Teachers Association," 63; and "Grading the Public Schools," *Indiana School Journal* 26 (September 1881): 437.

27. *First Annual Catalogue of [the] Cambridge City Graded School* (Indianapolis, 1870), 17; *Annual Report of the Public Schools of the City of Shelbyville, for the School Year 1871–72* (Shelbyville, 1872), 13; and State of Indiana, *Twentieth Biennial Report of the State Superintendent of Public Instruction* (Indianapolis, 1901), 877. In response to critics, who thought the local high school was a needless response, the superintendent of Franklin typically responded: "It should be a matter of pride to the citizen[s] of Franklin that their High School has taken rank among the best of the state. . . . Let no man that 'has the fear of God before him,' or that desires the best interests of society, lift his hand against the High School. It is the poor man's college." See *Eighth Annual Report and Catalogue of [the] Franklin Public Schools, for the School Year 1880–81* (Franklin, 1881), 14.

28. *Fourth Annual Announcement of the Petersburg Graded School, for the Year 1876–77* (Evansville, 1876), 8; *Annual Report of the Graded School of Princeton, Gibson County, Indiana, for the Year Ending June 20, 1872* (Princeton, 1872), 7; and Rockville Public Schools, *High School Catalogue with a List of Alumni* (Rockville, 1899), 5.

29. Historians remain heavily in debt to Emma Lou Thornbrough's masterful study, *The Negro in Indiana before 1900: A Study of a Minority* (Indianapolis, 1957), chap. 12.

30. Herman Murray Riley, "A History of Negro Elementary Education in Indianapolis," *Indiana Magazine of History* 26 (December 1920): 288–305; Darrel E. Bigham, "The Black Family in Evansville and Vanderburgh County, Indiana, in 1880," *Indiana Magazine of History* 65 (June 1979): 121; Darrel E. Bigham, *We Ask only a Fair Trial: A History of the Black Community of Evansville, Indiana* (Bloomington, 1987), 43–48; and Thornbrough, *The Negro in Indiana*, 340–43.

31. *Eighteenth Annual Report of the Public Schools of the City of Indianapolis*, 80–81; and *Annual Report of the Public Schools of Evansville* (Evansville, 1892), 32–34.

32. Listing the names of all the pupils obviously helped popularize the public schools in local communities. See *Fifteenth Annual Report of the Brookville Public Schools, for the Year 1893–1894* (Brookville, 1894), 22–26; *The First Annual Catalogue of [the] Cambridge City Graded School*, 5–13; *Twelfth Annual Report of the City School of Huntington, Indiana* (Huntington, 1885), 8–15; and *Fourth Annual Report of the Tipton Public Schools, with Course of Study and Rules* (Tipton, 1880), 5–10.

33. W. A. Bell, "Recent Criticisms on [*sic*] the Public Schools," *Indiana School Journal* 28 (August 1883): 399; and "The Pendulum in Education," *Educational Weekly* 3 (July 26, 1884): 25. For contrary evidence, which reported on Joseph Mayer Rice's very positive appraisal of the Indianapolis schools, see "The System vs. the Child," *Indiana School Journal* 38 (January 1893): 35–37.

34. The standard interpretation of "pedagogical" progressivism remains Lawrence A. Cremin, *The Transformation of the School: Progressivism and American Education* (New York, 1961). His interpretation has been challenged by Tyack, *The One Best System,* and a host of other authors. Also read Timothy L. Smith, "Progressivism in American Education, 1880–1900," *Harvard Educational Review* 31 (Spring

1961): 168–93. For further information on the rise of progressive movements on the local level, see William J. Reese, *Power and the Promise of School Reform: Grass-Roots Movements in the Progressive Era* (Boston, 1986).

35. Laura Gaus, "Nebraska Cropsey," in *The Encyclopedia of Indianapolis*, 483; Ted Stahly, "High Schools," in *The Encyclopedia of Indianapolis*, 674–75; and *Catalogue of the Industrial Training School* (Indianapolis, 1898).

36. *Report of the Public Schools of LaPorte, Indiana, for the School Year 1891–1892* (LaPorte, 1892), 11; Barbara Beatty, *Preschool Education in America: The Culture of Young Children from the Colonial Era to the Present* (New Haven, 1995), 56; *A Manual and Course of Study for the Public Schools of the City of Peru, Indiana, 1899–1900* (Peru, 1900); and *Nineteenth Annual Report of the Rensselaer Schools, 1897–1898*, 8.

37. *Annual Report of the Public Schools of Evansville, Indiana, for the School Year Ending August 31, 1892*, 22.

38. *Annual Report of the Board of Trustees of the Public Schools to the Common Council of the City of Lafayette, Indiana, for the Year Ending June, 1872*, 67–71.

39. *A Manual of the Public Schools of Sullivan, Indiana, 1895–1896* (Sullivan, 1896), 13.

40. B. "Individuality vs. Uniformity," *Educational Weekly* 3 (August 9, 1884): 57.

41. Arnold Tompkins, "Liberty!" *Indiana School Journal* 35 (September 1890): 492.

42. These generalizations about the rules and regulations governing villages and towns are based on my reading of annual school reports for a few dozen places between the 1860s and the turn of the century.

43. *Annual Report of the Board of Trustees of the Public Schools to the Common Council of the City of Lafayette, Indiana*, 73. Similar rules and regulations were approved to govern student behavior in every graded school system. See, for example, *First Annual Report of the Wabash Public Schools, for the School Year Ending June 3rd, 1887* (Wabash, 1887), 52–55; *Eighth Annual Report of the Public Schools of Warsaw, Indiana, Including Course of Study, Rules and Regulations, and a Report of the Public Library for the Year 1888–1889* (Warsaw, 1889), 56–59; *Rules and Regulations of the Board of Education of the City of South Bend* (South Bend, 1871), 10–11; and *Twelfth Annual Report of the Terre Haute Public Schools for the School Year Ending August 31, 1875, with the Course of Study and the General Rules and Regulations* (Terre Haute, 1875), Appendix.

44. *Seventeenth Annual Report of the Public Schools, Rochester, Indiana, 1897–98, together with Course of Study, Rules and Regulations* (Rochester, 1898), 31–33; *First Annual Report of the Wabash Public Schools*, 53; and *Rules and Regulations for the Government of the Connersville Public Schools* (Connersville, 1872), 13.

.3.

Ted Stahly

Curricular Reform in an Industrial Age

The flurry of attention devoted to school reform and restructuring since the 1980s echoes many of the concerns expressed a century ago as Hoosier schools underwent what historian Lawrence Cremin has dubbed "The Transformation of the School." Then, as now, there was much talk of international competition, lowered standards, the need for efficiency, skill, and thus a "new" kind of education. Then, too, Germany and other industrial nations were seen as competitors advantaged by better-skilled workforces whereas America's traditional curriculum hindered progress and social salvation. School reformers, professional and lay alike, spoke of the need to create schools and curricula that would meet the needs of a new school population, one that would benefit from courses more accurately reflecting the "realities" of modern life. The critics had their day and helped reshape American education as historians of education have accurately noted. The results, however, were not always what the reformers intended, nor do they suggest a simple strategy that will guide us safely through our renewed insistence that schools again save us from social and economic ruin while educating and socializing a more "diverse" population of students.

In 1923 the General Education Board of the Rockefeller Foundation published a survey of Indiana's schools. Commissioned by the Indiana General Assembly in 1921 in response to charges that the state system of schools lagged behind the rest of the nation, the survey set out to assess scientifically Indiana's educational status and to offer suggestions for improvement. A five-person commission composed of a lawyer, school

board president, dean of women at Purdue University, county superintendent, and professor of literature, all Hoosiers, found many positive features in the existing school system, but they found even more to condemn.
Noting that Indiana schools enjoyed a generally positive reputation nationally, they added: "As a matter of fact the state has in this matter a better
reputation than it deserves," owing more to past progressive efforts than
to current ones. They concluded by stating: "Socially, politically, agricul-
turally, industrially, Indiana is hurting itself through its failure to give
thousands of its children, especially its rural children, a more effective
preparation for life."[1]

They conceded that Hoosier schools had taken a lead in introducing
vocational subjects into schools, as well as in organizing their teaching on
the township, if not yet the county, level, thus allowing for a more diver-
sified and efficient curriculum; but the committee was clearly dissatisfied
with the overall pace of change. Their language came straight from the
rhetoric of educational reform at the time and repeated earlier calls for a
new kind of education. For the past thirty years, Indiana had kept pace
with a national trend to enlarge the curriculum and extend average
attendance and years of schooling. Still, the commissioners found the
system wanting. Although in 1922 Indiana had more than 800 high schools,
they found them to have low standards, generally poor instruction, and
excessive costs. Worst of all, those graduating from these burgeoning
high schools were "not well equipped to take up the duties of life, or
well qualified to enter the higher institutions of the state." In general, they
found the organization of the high schools too rigid, inefficient, and clearly inferior, unable to meet the needs of "children of varying types."[2]

Unmindful perhaps that the schools were victims of their own self-
promotion, the commissioners complained of the myriad small town high
schools whose academic reach exceeded their grasp. Trying to keep up
with their urban cousins, "Schools able to provide a satisfactory two-year
program aspire to a three-year program; schools able to provide a three-
year program attempt a four-year course; noncommissioned high schools
strain to become commissioned high schools; and the competition
progresses almost indefinitely under the stimulus of popular and professional ambition." Having noted these unhealthy effects of recent school
growth, the committee then recommended changes reminiscent of policy
debated thirty years earlier. The school term was too short, a situation no
longer necessitated by the demands of the farm. The work in the second
and fourth years was too academic. Algebra was required in the first year
in 93 percent of the high schools, whereas home economics was required
by only 23 percent and manual training by just 14 percent. Latin was still
the required language in 95 percent of small high schools. Civics was
generally a mere appendage to U.S. history, thus typifying superficial
efforts at coordinating subjects. Articulation between the grade school,

high school, and college was equally faulty. Too much of the high school curriculum centered on formal education and college entrance requirements. Too many of these schools were inefficient and badly organized. Just as the use of a commission of "high-minded and competent men" to resolve thorny social issues in a businesslike way was a product of the late nineteenth century, so too were these educational complaints.[3]

This period was also characterized by rapid social and economic changes and their attendant problems. Depression, labor unrest, economic boom, burgeoning immigration, and technological development came in rapid succession and in increasingly complex combinations. The last three decades of the nineteenth century were thus marked by great contrasts and societal turbulence for Hoosiers and the nation at large. Wealth and opportunity stood side by side with destitution and uncertainty, technological wonders with rural hardships and simple lives, the gospel of wealth with ingrained republican egalitarianism, materialism with parsimony and spirituality and, most significantly for education, a rising acceptance of corporate values with an almost religious attachment to individualism.

The nation celebrated the centennial year, 1876, with an international exhibition. Technological displays caught the imagination of nearly everyone. The massive Corliss steam engine—throbbing as if it were the heart of a colossal beast—convinced the crowds of the magic of science as well as its material promise. The telephone and the typewriter, introduced to the public for the first time at the exhibition, promised to revolutionize communication as steam and the line shaft had industrial production.

At the same time, Hoosiers, still reeling from the deflationary cycle following the panic of 1873, were hosting the Greenback Party convention. Hesitant, the economy was slowly gaining momentum that would accelerate with the natural gas boom of the 1880s. Towns in the central part of the state such as Anderson would soon double in size as manufacturers were lured by the promise of free energy and building sites. In Indianapolis, where construction had lagged as a result of the devastating losses of the 1870s, many commercial buildings were begun in the following decade, including a new Union Station. Electric street cars replaced mule-drawn wagons and hastened the outward sprawl of the city, often in the form of opulent residential neighborhoods such as Woodruff Place. The capital strove to set the cultural pace for the rest of the state with four daily newspapers, several well-known bookstores, and the even better known Circle Hall and Plymouth Institute on the circle downtown. The latter were the venue of famous lecturers such as Henry Ward Beecher.[4]

The rapid material progress brought with it an uneasiness in the minds of some over moral decay and, in the minds of others, a sense of vulnerability. This, in turn, spawned the creation of a plethora of institutions. Fraternal organizations, women's clubs, religious and secular societies, and public institutions such as orphanages and reform schools proliferated. The working classes formed unions, the Grange, fraternal clubs, ethnic organizations, and political parties in response to a sense of diminished individual autonomy and personal meaning. As early as 1870, Indianapolis had an Agricultural and Mechanical Association, the Turnverein, and the Free-thinkers Society. All levels of society found themselves confronted with contradictions between their professed values and the realities around them. Ordinary folk combined to compensate for the psychological and social damage of an increasingly fragmented society.[5]

Whether organized for personal relief or societal salvation, and usually the two were combined, Hoosiers were duly caught up in the various reform movements. Community activists, churchmen, women's clubs, civic organizations, public philosophers, journalists, politicians, and other organizations and individuals sought to ameliorate social tensions and economic woes by exposing backward or corrupt practices and promoting institutional and legal reform. In spite of their manifest differences, these groups were united in a belief that republican virtues of independence, self-sufficiency, morality, and practicality could be combined with science, efficiency, cooperation, and institutional reform. Indeed, it was hoped that these attitudes and approaches would be mutually reinforcing and powerful enough in combination to overcome the all-too-obvious dangers of modern society.

Not least among reform efforts were those directed at the schools, particularly with regard to the curricular offerings of the expanding system. Why, in the face of so many external problems and internal arenas of contention, was school reform predominently centered on a battle between schoolmen over whether German should replace Latin or whether the needs of the students could be met without offering woodturning? The answer lies in the mindset that spurred and celebrated increasing materialism and self-interest while abhorring the results and that promoted skill and social responsibility while working feverishly to create a system that would run efficiently without these characteristics. The enthusiasm with which the business community, through commercial clubs and other associations, promoted the virtues of skill and responsibility was little affected by the fact that shop floor craft skills were being eliminated and responsibility separated from reward by the division of labor and accompanying managerial reform.[6]

In Indiana during the last three decades of the century, the leading industries requiring skilled trades declined slightly, while those relying on unskilled labor grew. Perhaps what mattered in this context were yet more generalized traits associated with "skill and responsibility" that would discourage unionism and sublimate the alienation inherent in new work processes. And what mattered most in school reform was developing a curriculum that would ostensibly create the "right" attitudes and put the imprimatur of rationality on what was inherently muddled. The result of this powerful rationalization was the phenomenal growth of public schooling and the location of a Promethean social struggle in the unlikely arena of school curriculum. On one side was an economic and ideological juggernaut, on the other a growing army of schoolmen, educational theorists, and the "child of the republic," the ever-expanding population of public school students. They, by studying the "right" subjects, would make the system work—efficiently.[7]

So, while school reform after the 1870s followed many paths—teacher education, administrative realignment, consolidation, and school tax legislation—curricular reform more than any other issue occupied professional schoolmen and educational theorists. Invariably, it was also tied to and used as justification for these other reforms. In the early years, as specified in the state school law of 1865, the state's schools, city and rural, required only a handful of subjects: orthography, reading, writing, arithmetic, English grammar, and good behavior. In 1869 geography, physiology, and U.S. history were added by virtue of their "practical" nature. These were the "common branches" which constituted the curriculum of the first eight grades. Other subjects such as German, music, and art were offered according to local preference. The spirit of this early legislation was absent in later decades as impetus for the enlargement of the curriculum came from an upward expansion into the high school accompanied by demands for courses that were "practical" in very different ways.[8]

"Practical" was the adjective most often attached to the "new" education. But by whatever label it was promoted, the "new" involved various elements of the theories of Pestalozzi, Herbart, Froebel, Spencer, and others interpreted by a gaggle of American theorists—notably Francis Parker and, toward the end of the century, John Dewey. While the resulting changes took myriad forms from object lessons to lesson plans, they almost always shared two key concepts: a conscious connection to the "real" and a related emphasis on the use of the hand or, more generally, on the active involvement of the student.

The connection between this broadly theoretical approach and the social and economic angst mentioned previously is direct and pervasive. By acquainting students with the processes and rationale behind social and industrial organization, those students would be made to understand how they were to fit into the system and, therefore, avoid alienation. Another factor that cut across the new education was a universal condemnation of the old, classical, or "bookish" education. Not without its defenders, the old education, surrounded and seemingly overwhelmed, persisted even as the new flourished. The battle, while often ferocious, was not to the death, and indeed evolved into a symbiotic relationship that tended to mask rather than resolve the basis of the original conflict.[9]

While the Corliss engine pulsated at the Centennial exhibition, a Russian educational exhibit no less powerfully captivated American educators. Centered on the theories of Victor Della Vos, this exhibit instantly resolved a dilemma perplexing John Runkle, president of the Massachusetts Institute of Technology. Having noticed that his engineering graduates who had previously been employed in trades attained positions more readily than other classmates, he pondered the means of giving all students such an experience. The Russian system solved that problem by putting the students through a set of graded manual exercises that represented the skills necessary for a given trade. This condensed trade training gave the prospective engineers insight into the processes that lay behind their designs. It had the additional virtue of being contained within the school curriculum, thus avoiding the taint of the vocational, which Runkle considered antithetical to sound educational practice. Runkle and others enthusiastically promoted the value of this manual training, which gained popularity throughout the nation. It promised to resolve not only the educational deficiencies of engineering students, but also the pedagogical weaknesses of the old education, the moral laxity of a nation wracked by political scandal, and the alienation of an industrialized and fragmented society. In the minds of many, manual training constituted an educational panacea.[10]

The pragmatic spirit supporting the manual training concept blossomed in Indiana after the Civil War. A resolution adopted by the Indiana State Teachers Association in 1877 asserted the right of every child to receive an education of "mind, heart and body" that would prepare for vocation as well as citizenship and offer "industrial" education as well as scholastic. The reference to vocational and "industrial" education at such an early date is noteworthy. For decades to come citizens debated whether this was indeed the purpose of manual training.[11]

In these early years the vocational, aside from teacher preparation, was generally limited to bookkeeping. Before a meeting of the State Association of School Superintendents in 1869, State Superintendent George Hoss proposed bookkeeping for all boys, a position supported by Abram Shortridge, the recently appointed superintendent of the Indianapolis schools, although by this time girls had been included in the suggestion. Indianapolis experimented briefly with a course in the "Science of Dress," a "scientific" approach to sewing and fashion, in the 1870s. Agriculture, included in the college curriculum with the formation of Purdue University, would not enter the public schools until after the turn of the century. Hoosiers were not about to be stampeded too far. Josh Billings, native wit, mirrored this cautious attitude toward educational extension in his advice to older boys who contemplated schooling beyond the eighth grade: "Git schoolin' and cloas both, if you kin; but if you can't git both, get cloas."[12]

Nevertheless, bookkeeping for middle-class urbanites, color coordination for future socialites, and agriculture for rural youth failed to satisfy the larger concerns expressed by manual training enthusiasts and educational reformers precisely because these subjects did not satisfy the "needs" of non-middle-class, non-rural youth. However broadly interpreted, manual training was intended primarily for the working classes, even when logical consistency extended its theoretical application to all youth. The *Indiana School Journal* in 1882 included a story originally printed in *Scientific American* of a boy applying for a job at the Indianapolis Rolling Mill. The president of the company reluctantly turned him down because being an American youth, rather than German, Irish, or French, he didn't know how to *do* anything. In a nation increasingly inhabited by shopkeepers, middle managers, unskilled laborers, and corporate employees, it seemed obvious to many that the youth needed a thorough grounding in eye-hand coordination and instincts of self-sufficiency. When the question was raised as to why this should be the case, the answer, paradoxically, was less often closely linked to the "real" world from which the theory claimed derivation than to the inadequacies of the existing school curriculum. The recognition and irony of this theoretical inversion has proven to be persistently elusive.[13]

Manual training enthusiasts provided an increasingly embellished rationale for its inclusion in the school curriculum at all levels. For approximately thirty years following the centennial exhibition there was a vague thematic unity, although no absolute consistency, to its particulars. Manual training was variously claimed to aid in the forming of conceptions, provide a broader culture than the merely "bookish" subjects, lessen selfishness and build character, inoculate against anarchistic tendencies, avoid mismatches between the individual and the job, increase efficiency, create knowledgeable consumers, engender an appreciation of utility, encourage a respect for property, train the senses, increase artistic skills, bring to the producer a larger share of the product, open new paths among the synapses of the brain, and give dignity to labor. Charles Emmerich, the first principal of Manual Training High School in Indianapolis, deserves credit for advancing the most far-reaching claim for the new subject: "Through the cooperation of brain and hand, as the active coadjutors of the passive senses, we have advanced, spiritually, towards the very limits of time and space."[14]

Manual training, more than any other of the "new" subjects, became the vehicle by which modern educators hoped to reform and enlarge the schools and thereby save the republic. Play in the kindergarten, drawing, and physical education shared many of the theoretical justifications of manual training, but it was manual training that most uniformly excited the passions of nascent progressive educators. It alone carried the weight of social and economic necessity that could be redeemed for radical pedagogical reform. In the end the reform was not radical, the necessity ill-explained, and the original justifications so egregiously violated in practice that manual training's most thoughtful early theorists disowned it as if it were a wayward and incorrigible stepchild.

Perhaps it was because the promise was so great that the concept spread so rapidly among educational theorists as well as lay enthusiasts. Since before the Civil War there had been a widespread lament that the workforce was losing its ethical underpinnings as well as its skills. Since jobs had become less skilled and rewarding, the inherent dignity of labor was a concept undergoing obsolescence. As a result, it was alleged, workers possessed less drive and determination to get the job done. This was seen first and foremost among the poor and their children. Hence, educational efforts in orphanages and the newly created "houses of refuge" or reform schools emphasized manual-labor-related activities such as chair caning, shoe repair, plastering, brickmaking, collar starching, and laundering. Reports from the superintendents of the Boys' School in Plainfield and the Girls' School in Indianapolis are laced with policy statements about encouraging the inmates to be "bread earners" and to avoid becoming lazy. Why they should also have acquired a sense of the dignity of labor from many of the same activities that the theory postulated were destroying a sense of dignity in labor in the larger world is a contradiction never addressed.[15]

Efforts to inculcate a restored work ethic were not limited to "bad" boys and girls. George Dealand, superintendent of Vermillion County schools, exhorted his teachers to be more businesslike, to remember that "knowing is not doing." The teacher who doesn't know only *about* things, but rather how to *do* them was a desirable "General Grant" type. Others were mere "tongue-giants." The *Indiana School Journal* throughout these years is peppered with anecdotal stories exhorting the value of hard, simple work. One short essay entitled "Work" ended with this stark admonition: "Don't be afraid of killing yourself with work, my son." There was a realization among all segments of society that industrialization, corporate concentration, and the accompanying division of labor were wreaking havoc on an individual sense of responsibility and vocational calling. Manual training enthusiasts hoped to restore these virtues by proxy through the school.[16]

Addressing Indiana teachers in 1889, A. H. Kennedy listed the standard pedagogical arguments in support of manual training but emphasized its curative powers with regard to the disappearance of dignity in labor. He cleverly pointed out that menial labor has always been despised and that education was implicated in this state of affairs: "The watchword all along the line has ever been 'Excelsior,' which means—get an education and escape drudgery. What teacher has not heard it? But while one reaches the summit, there are nine disappointed ones in the valley below. The spirit of education thus points ninety percent to a goal that they can never hope to reach, and gives them no special training for the vocations which they are

Curricular Reform in an Industrial Age

Manual Training for Truant Boys, Indianapolis, 1901. Source:
*Twentieth Biennial Report of the State Superintendent of Public
Instruction* (Indianapolis, 1901)

compelled by necessity to follow. Thus the spirit of education does not
satisfy the demands of the spirit of the age." Kennedy further explained
that since associations between personal values and labor are formed in
the schools, the inclusion of manual labor would engender a sense of its
dignity both in those nine-tenths who will practice it and in the favored
tenth who will escape it. Aside from the difficult question of how that
dignity was to be elicited, he does not anticipate, nor do any of the other
early enthusiasts, its certain destruction in the years following through the
differentiation of the curriculum and a corresponding assignment of the
masses to the vocational and the middle classes to the academic.[17]

Although the promise of manual training to solve deeply embedded
social problems was alluring, its star would never have risen had it not
been for a wider debate in the educational community over the methodology and purposes of schools. Anticipating and encouraging a burgeoning
and less homogenous school population, educators turned to a curriculum now thought to be inadequate. Nicholas Murray Butler, influential in
the creation of Columbia University's Teachers College, argued that the
curriculum must change with the times. In short, it must become "practi-

cal." Industrial education according to his argument was true education and had to be termed "industrial" only because the more general term "education" had been usurped. He was careful to note that it had nothing to do with training students for narrow occupational roles and therefore perpetuating a class-based society. Indeed it represented "mental democracy" as opposed to "mental oligarchy—the rule of a few faculties" on which the old education was based.[18]

According to Butler, education consists of two basic components, the expressive and the receptive. The problem with the old education was its reliance on only one mode of expression—language. It was not only limited, it actually separated people from reality by the interposition of a barrage of words. Manual training would supply the missing elements in "expression" and reconnect students with the "real" world. He supplemented this theory with several other common contentions of manual training enthusiasts: it exercised the nerves, developed executive capacity, trained the eye, and encouraged accurate observation—a cardinal trait of one who hoped to be scientific as well as "efficient," the highest ideal of the modern educator. It was only reluctantly that he added his last argument, the final blow for traditional education. While cautioning that this argument falls outside the educational, Butler felt obliged to point out that manual training did, in fact, engender a sense of the dignity of labor—*and*, if it happened to train for a job, all the better.[19]

Even in its early stages, opponents of the new education and manual training in particular had warned of its undemocratic potential in training for specific occupations; hence Butler's hesitation to encumber his argument with that aspect of the theory. More often attempts to reform the curriculum were based on the inadequacies of the old system. One of the new education's most thoughtful and dogged opponents was William T. Harris, a Hegelian philosopher, St. Louis schools superintendent, and eventually U.S. commissioner of education. As early as 1870, in an address before the National Teachers Association, this student of the dialectic turned the tables on new education advocates by suggesting that its highest-claimed values were in fact the province of the old education and that the object lesson approach, a seminal aspect of the new education, committed the very pedagogical sins that it was intended to overcome. Specifically, Harris suggested that these new techniques encouraged cramming, parroting, and imitation. It was the old, "bookish," textbook-based curriculum that stimulated critical thinking, independent scholarship, and a propensity to "dive into hidden essences." The book, he said, made the student independent of the teacher, the highest goal of education.[20]

Hoosier educators entered the fray over the new education, some with gusto and others with ambivalence. W. N. Hailmann, a nationally prominent theorist of early progressive education, incorporated many of its aspects into the La Porte schools while he was superintendent there. The editor of the *Indiana School Journal,* visiting the La Porte schools in 1886, while generally supportive, qualified that appraisal by adding that the attempt to secure "expression of thought" had not resulted in the *best* expression. Similarly, when State Superintendent John Holcombe addressed the National Education Association in 1885, he began rather defensively by pointing out that the state was no longer the educationally backward one portrayed in *The Hoosier Schoolmaster,* but ended by warning that we should not attempt to make education too pleasant. Hard work and duty should come before the pleasant.[21]

John Earp of Depauw University, in turn, warned against the tendency of the practical to become narrowly vocational. Before we teach children how to earn money, he warned, we should imbue them with foresight, honesty, and judgment. He concluded with the lament, "Is life never to reach beyond the raising of corn and hogs?" It would be a mistake, however, to conclude from objections such as these that all Hoosier educators were skeptical of the modern and newly practical. A volume written by Charles Hamm in 1886 advocating the adoption of manual training in all schools received a favorable review in the *Indiana School Journal.* The editor concluded by warning critics that too hasty a condemnation of such approaches ignored the reality that the educational system was failing to cure the evils of society and that this new approach deserved a fair trial.[22]

While the pressure to adjust the school curriculum and program has its roots in broader societal concerns over work, pedagogical theory, and a growing acceptance of education as a panacea, the immediate precipitating issue was often termed "The High School Question." The "question" had various aspects but centered on the need to make high school available to a broader cross section of American youth, to extend upward the school-leaving age, and to adjust the school curriculum in a way that would encourage these goals. In an address dedicating a new building for Indianapolis High School, State Superintendent Holcombe advocated these reforms in a rhetorical flourish that was clearly intended to startle the audience and disarm critics. After suggesting that high school education should be extended to all, he said, "In this we are communists, but we are a practical people, and do not take fright at names. A communistic practice that proves to be of general advantage we adopt."[23]

To describe an enterprise that pertained to such a small percentage of high school–age youth as communistic took considerable literary license. He was undoubtedly spurred by a determined opposition to what some, including the *Indianapolis Daily Journal,* considered expensive frills for an educational system that failed to confer an eighth-grade diploma on thousands of its school-age youth. These critics repeated a reasoned objection to publicly funded high schools that had persisted throughout the century. Such a policy, they claimed, while appearing to be democratic and egalitarian, was in fact the opposite.[24] It provided lavish high school education for the elite at public expense while most in the lower classes received a partial elementary school education at best.

Advocates of extended education, in order to avoid this sensible criticism, would require proof that they, not their critics, were the representatives of democracy and the common man. They often sought that high ground in an advocacy of the new education variously defined. The essence of the argument, repeated by many Hoosier educators, can be briefly outlined. Its variations and adaptations would grow with each new decade of the twentieth century and range from the obvious to the impenetrable. Education, so the argument goes, is inevitable. It is better, therefore, that it take place in the school where it can be controlled and made efficient and socially desirable. Traditional or classical education is suitable in some ways for some students, but the mass of students especially and all students more complexly need a new, broader education that goes beyond mental discipline. It should, through the mechanisms of the child's own interests and strengths, mold the child in a way that maximizes his potential and, therefore, value to the community. By scientifically encouraging such character development, children will learn to appreciate their differences and various social roles. This will help to avoid social, especially class-based, conflict. It's not what the workingman does that defines his character, it's the character that he brings to his work.[25]

Readers of educational history will recognize that the heart of this proposal, character formation, is in no way novel. Nor is the expressed intent to extend it downward to the lower classes while extending it upward in duration. What is new, perhaps, is a burgeoning faith that new routes, more scientifically determined, could be found to the promised land— modern highways rather than classical goat paths, with capacity for more travelers, at higher rates of speed, and with fewer fatalities. Peter Kropotkin, a Russian anarchist and inspiration to many of the new educators, minced no words in this regard: "Not only are we taught a mass of rubbish, but what is not rubbish is taught so as to make us waste as much time as possible." Perhaps Laura Donnan, a beloved teacher of American government at Indianapolis High School, had Kropotkin in mind when she warned fellow teachers that a great task lay ahead in freeing the republic of the "leprous disease" of anarchism.[26]

Even though few educational reformers were as blunt as Kropotkin, many felt that by the 1890s there were too many of the wrong courses producing too little competence. By then intense industrial competition with Germany, Japan, France, and Great Britain added the urgency of supposed national interests to the litany of pedagogical complaints. In this country an economic downswing and labor unrest added weight to the "democratic" arguments for reforming education. Charles W. Eliot, president of Harvard University, had delivered a speech before the NEA in 1888 advocating major changes in the high school program, including the relaxation of college entrance requirements so that schools could reform their curricula. In 1893 the NEA called upon Eliot and nine other educators to form a Committee of Ten that would look into the secondary curriculum and articulation between elementary school, high school, and college. Nine subcommittees or conferences were formed in the existing disciplines: Latin; Greek; English; modern languages; mathematics; physics, astronomy, and chemistry; natural history (biology, botany, and zoology); history, civil government, and political science; and geography.[27]

Few expected the Committee of Ten, even though a major undertaking, to receive the attention or achieve the influence it ultimately did. Eliot partially succeeded in his personal preference to include electives and a greater emphasis on science—largely at the expense of Greek. Nevertheless, the committee's findings, while ardently debated, were strikingly nonradical. Indeed they tended to contradict the broader progressive sentiments building in the educational community. Convened partly in response to the growing resentment against collegiate, and therefore purportedly elitist, influence on the high school, the committee concluded that the best high school preparation for life (the rallying cry of the new educators) was a college preparatory curriculum. In fact, they specifically condemned any attempt to differentiate the curriculum according to the presumed occupational goals of the students. Every student, the committee said, should be taught in the same way. Four courses of study were outlined: the Classical, Latin Scientific, Modern Languages, and English. Electives were to be available within courses only and most of the "new" practical subjects were to be accommodated by their inclusion in more traditional ones. For example, bookkeeping was to fall under the auspices of algebra. The committee emphasized mental and moral training and curricular cohesion in preference to the informational and idiosyncratic. Concessions to the new education were strictly limited. Grammar and Greek were de-emphasized. Math was to be more accessible and less concerned with mental puzzles.[28]

While these findings were anathema to many progressive educators, businessmen, and social reformers, Hoosier educators took the committee's report in stride. In fact, they had been debating many of these topics for some time. While failing to arrive at firm conclusions, their suggestions were compatible with if not identical to those of the Committee of Ten. The need for a uniform course of study in the high school already had been suggested on numerous occasions. Richard Boone, chairman of a curriculum reform committee of the state teachers' association, devoted himself to this question in 1885 and achieved only a consensus favoring a model course. Following in his footsteps in 1887, Hailmann's committee, while declining to prescribe a uniform course of study because of varying local conditions, partisan politics, and a weak profession, nevertheless made many suggestions that anticipated the conclusions of the Committee of Ten. Articulation was seen as crucial to the determination of curricula, as was a thoughtful coordination of subjects. The high school was not to stand apart from the grammar school, but rather to complete the course begun there. The high school course was to prepare for life, but the course that would accomplish this bore close resemblance to that which would prepare for college. The student intending to go into business could find sufficient practical instruction in related fields such as mathematics. Marie Dunlap, principal of Salem High School in 1894, echoed the conclusions of the Committee of Ten, saying that the best prep school is the best finishing school. Others in her discussion group cautiously embraced electives, but shunned a wholesale acceptance of utility as a guiding principle.[29]

Maxims of the new education appeared side by side with the prescriptions of the old. John Coulter of Wabash College reminded the high school teachers that colleges wanted "mental muscle." At the same time George Bass, a manual training teacher in Indianapolis, cautioned that the cultivation of common sense applied to teachers also and, if they exercised it, they would not teach "by rule." D. M. Geeting, in his superintendent's report for 1895, admonished Hoosier teachers to avoid cramming material into students' heads and to keep the pupil, not the course of study, foremost in their minds. The teacher was to set before the pupil "pure ideals of life and cause him to love them, to be dominated by them."[30]

Outside of the larger Hoosier cities, where manual training and domestic science began to appear in the nineties, the curriculum in the last three decades of the century remained almost exclusively academic, if not classical. Latin not only remained in the curriculum but also flourished well into the twentieth century. For most educators in this period an offering of algebra, Latin or German, composition, bookkeeping, and English (grammar, spelling, reading) in the first year; English, arithmetic, Latin or German, U.S. history, natural history, and geometry in the second year; and electives from among geometry, trigonometry, physiology, Latin, German, world history, philosophy, English, grammar, botany, physical geography, French, chemistry, and astronomy, with composition and rhetorical exercises required, constituted a typical and appropriate high school course. A similar mixture of subject matter had been standard fare as far back as 1870. In that year William Holloway emphasized its practical nature and the fact that it "is not designed, primarily, to fit our youth for the regular classes of a college course; but to give them the greatest amount of practical and useful knowledge adapted to their wants in *any* position in life." Clearly the prevailing conception of "practical" included much of what would constitute a college preparatory course, even if some subjects such as Greek were omitted. In 1886 Indianapolis had a very similar course, with additional offerings in Greek, civil government, drawing, and physics. This course closely resembled the uniform course of study discussed by a committee of the State Teachers Association in 1885.[31]

The controversy over the "practical" and the classical centered largely on whether Greek and to a lesser extent, Latin, were to be required. Indiana University relaxed its admission requirement for Greek in 1873 and for Latin in the 1880s. In both cases, however, full admission was made only after completing work for these subjects within the university itself. The Reverend Cyrus Nutt, D.D., of Indiana University warned against an overemphasis on the practical and even suggested that more, not less, of the classics should be taught. In Franklin county, parents in Nineveh township filed suit over the establishment of a high school there in 1872 in order to obtain Latin instruction for their children. Even after entrance requirements were relaxed, the emphasis on Latin in college undoubtedly affected its place in the high school curriculum. Greek, logic, moral philosophy, and rhetoric declined in importance as the twentieth century approached. English, science, and modern languages tended to take their place as representatives of the modern and practical in a trend that spanned the Midwest.[32]

While the concept of practicality as defined by correspondence with specific occupations would soon dominate the curricular debate, in the last decades of the nineteenth century this notion applied to the curriculum more in terms of general educational expectations, preparation for college, and the limitations of the schools themselves. The provision for "higher" learning had only recently been added to the common branches of the first eight grades. In 1874 the state had seventy-eight high schools, with a total of 168 teachers. Many of these schools, especially in the townships, were mere appendages to the lower grades and were taught by only one or two teachers.[33]

The battle over the curriculum in these years often represented a larger struggle to bring these local schools under the jurisdiction of state authorities. The first and most prevalent means to achieve this end was through the granting of commissions that would allow graduates of "commissioned" high schools to enter the state colleges without examination. The agenda of the state board of education in granting commissions included extending the term of the high school (to eight or nine months of the year and to a full four years), ensuring that teachers in the high school course had training in the subjects that they taught, and encouraging the consolidation of schools on the township or county level.[34]

By 1896 the state board had become determined to bring the newly formed high schools under their control. They clamped down on the extension of commissions by requiring minimum, uniform courses of study. The following year the state superintendent expressed pleasure over the success of the various efforts to enlarge and consolidate the schools. That the curriculum of township high schools basically resembled that of urban schools is not surprising considering the presence of three of the largest cities' superintendents on the State Board of Education. The establishment of county superintendencies and the Association of County and City Superintendents also hastened the achievement of uniformity. In 1884 there were thirty-eight commissioned high schools in the state. By 1890, the number had grown to 109. By 1907, the state legislature mandated the abandonment of the smallest township schools.[35]

Control over textbook selection and teacher certification rounded out the effort to bring about curricular uniformity in the high schools. In 1896 Superintendent Geeting decreed that all teachers and principals of high schools should be examined in the subject that they were to teach rather than in the common branches. Not until 1913, however, did the state board obtain legislation wresting control of textbook selection for the high schools from the counties. This legislation is especially representative of the desire for uniformity in view of the fact that the textbook industry had long since been an effective homogenizer of school studies rather than a source of diversity. There was a close linkage between the suggested curricula and the contents of well-established textbooks. In 1892 the suggested uniform course of study designated the amount of work in each subject in commissioned high schools as equivalent to that found in the texts selected by the best high schools.[36]

By the turn of the century, despite the rhetorical barrage accompanying the "new" education, what separated smaller township high schools from most of their urban cousins was not a different conception of what knowledge was of most worth but rather the resources at their disposal. Reporting with pride in 1903 on the progressive nature of Benton County schools, County Superintendent Levi McKnight highlighted his effort to boost the salaries of teachers so that they could pursue further qualifications. He boasted that the "trustees began the advance at once and kept it up until they had reached a point almost as high as that established by the minimum wage law before that law was passed."(!) Recognizing that they could not meet the necessary requirements for commissions in some of their high schools, the county board established their own uniform course of study in 1903. Although only three years in duration, this course resembled the core of urban plans. Music, modern languages, agriculture, manual training, and other "new" subjects were entirely absent. Nevertheless, as if reading from the script of manual training, the superintendent emphasized that the students should value hard, purposeful labor, and that schools should be a "place of preparation for the affairs of life."[37]

Within the next few years this pattern would begin to change even before state and national legislation provided funds for vocational subjects. The "enriched" curriculum, one of a string of euphemisms for non-academic subjects, was soon a part of consolidated and township as well as urban high schools. In fact, by 1910 the urban schools were lagging behind their consolidated neighbors in introducing manual training, domestic science, agriculture, and other "practical" subject matter. This was not true of the smaller rural schools, which still lacked the resources for such innovation. It should also be noted that their offerings were meager in comparison to the urban schools especially created to highlight the new subjects, such as Indianapolis Manual Training High School, established in 1895. Manual training and domestic science were soon propelled to the center stage of school reform in a transformation that must have heartened some early enthusiasts by its dimensions if not its shape.[38]

Even though advocates of the new education in Indiana failed, to the extent that they in fact tried, to loosen the grip of more traditional subjects, their rhetorical forays helped to pave the way for major curricular additions and a new mission of public schools. The lure of the new subjects proved irresistible as well as functional for public school promoters. Rather than displacing the old, they came to stand side by side with the traditional. The debate was resolved not by a consensus over what knowledge was indeed of most worth, but rather by gradual fragmentation of the student body into constituencies for the new courses and subjects. The solution had surreptitiously come to resemble the original problem.

"The school, like the factory, is a thoroughly regimented world." This description of the schools in Muncie in 1924 epitomizes what some progressive educators perceived as a failure of the school system to adapt itself to changing conditions. Others would recognize that the school had adapted all too well. The new education, especially as expressed in the manual training movement, had begun as an attempt to utilize the schools to inoculate their students against the alienating effects of modern industrial life. Now, according to many observers of the educational situation, the public schools had come to adopt and promote an acceptance of the same materialistic, undemocratic values most feared by many school and social reformers forty years earlier. By mid-decade into the new century, school reformers in Indiana, as well as the nation at large, were unabashedly speaking of the need to rapidly expand vocational offerings in order to meet the needs of a new population of students. The previous argument that the burgeoning high schools required a new curriculum that would continue the tradition of the common schools in training for citizenship and thoughtful individuality now disappeared before the tacit assumption that many of the new high school students sought only a job and that the schools should so prepare them.[39]

Ernest Kent, supervisor of manual training in Indianapolis in 1899, argued for the location of the original manual training goals in the grade schools since the high schools had already become involved in trade training. In the same year, Emmerich, Indianapolis Manual's principal, stated that "manual training's aim is purely educational: it is valued as culture element." How could such a contradiction have existed? Surely

Kent and Emmerich communicated. Had extravagant justifications for the inclusion of manual training in the curriculum reduced the movement to a convenient excuse for any proposed reform? Emmerich provided a good example of this convenient ambiguity when he later stated that, if in pursuing the "purely educational," the student also learns how to make a living, so much the better. While some, such as Butler, had earlier claimed this bonus, others had vociferously warned against the slippery slope of this educational rationalization. After the turn of the century vocational momentum would accelerate and earlier arguments tying manual training to an expansion of social empathy and mental capacity would fade if not disappear. The simultaneous discrediting of industrial unions and the concept of transfer of training rendered these parallel notions unpopular, in fact detrimental, to educators determined to enhance their professional credibility, especially among the socially and scientifically respectable. The curricular path from the classical to the practical/academic to the vocational was perfectly captured by the Muncie school board president in 1924 when he said, "For a long time all boys were trained to be President. Then for a while we trained them all to be professional men. Now we are training boys to get jobs!"[40]

Insofar as the Indiana Educational Policy Commission in 1924 was worried about the failure of the schools to meet the needs of "children of varying types," perhaps they were unduly pessimistic. The schools of Indiana for the previous twenty years had labored mightily to meet the needs of immigrant children, black children, poor children, rural children, and orphaned children, as well as those children who could afford to attend high schools in the nineteenth century. The question was rather one of who would define those needs and in what way. The answer to the question is embedded in the steady rise of vocationalism after the turn of the century. Earlier manual training exercises purported to stimulate the industrial imagination, serve as a focal point for the correlation of studies, and intermingle the rich with the poor became expressly vocational, progressively menial, and largely lower class.

In addition to Indianapolis, Fort Wayne, Bluffton, Evansville, South Bend, and other Hoosier cities would soon have courses in manual training and domestic science. Gary would become world famous in its attempt to incorporate the new subjects into a broad-based reform effort that introduced a variety of innovations, including the platoon system and widespread community involvement. Indianapolis Manual would be followed in 1912 by Arsenal Technical High School, which became one of the nation's first and largest comprehensive (including complete academic and vocational courses) high schools in the 1920s and 1930s, offering at its peak more than 400 courses to 7,000 students. While both Manual and Tech maintained excellent reputations well into the twentieth century, the larger reality of vocational education over the long run was its

Curricular Reform in an Industrial Age

Vocational Education in Fort Wayne, 1906. Source: *Twenty-Third Biennial Report of the State Superintendent of Public Instruction* (Indianapolis, 1906)

demise into a hodgepodge of lackluster, dead-end courses for the very students that the broadened curriculum was intended to benefit.[41]

When pondering how ideological movements such as manual training and the new education could so easily become convoluted and in the process transform our most powerful public institution, one is tempted by the accurate but overly simplistic recognition that education has always been vocational. Educators touting the practicality of academic subjects in the late nineteenth century intuitively recognized their vocational utility for themselves and their offspring. It is only logical from this point of view that vocationalism be extended to include other subject matter corresponding to new occupations. Such an interpretation, however, ignores competing views. Many educators in this period clearly felt that the schools had a more important mission than preparing some students to puddle iron and others to sell insurance. They were not concerned so much with students understanding how iron was puddled or insurance sold, but why either should occur, whether one should—as an individual or citizen—engage in such activities, and how to make such decisions intelligently and with social imagination. Interestingly, goals of this kind were as often claimed by the old line educators as the new.

The tradition represented by these educators, progressive and traditional, has persisted, but always in the shadow of a more pervasive ideology powerfully thrust to the forefront in the early years of this century. Dewey, writing for *Manual Training* magazine in 1902, prophesied that arriving at the right curriculum for the schools was the solution to all other social problems. The primary spokesperson for the new education and an early advocate of manual training, Dewey maintained that the curriculum should be broad enough for anyone's interest, that its connection to a supposedly narrow "calling" was not the problem. The problem lay in the society at large, in social and economic isolation and denigration of any worthwhile calling. He hoped that schoolchildren imbued with a sense of cooperation and occupational empathy would create a new society that would not rank occupations.[42]

Driven by this profound faith in the healing power of education, Dewey began questioning the new direction of manual training after the turn of the century. He bitterly denounced narrowing influences on this most promising of curricular reforms in a speech before the Eastern Manual Training Association in 1906. By then he surely realized that school reform as promoted by some members of this organization had gone astray. Soon a large faction would follow Charles Richards, professor of manual training at Columbia University, into his National Society for the Promotion of Industrial Education. Yet, as if the captain of an oceanliner, Dewey can be seen struggling with the rhetorical wheel in an attempt to avoid destruction on an iceberg of vocationalism and narrow business values. He understood that the most dangerous part, capable of ripping the bottom out of meaningful educational reform, lay submerged, invisible or a matter of indifference to those stoking the boilers. Alternately supportive and critical, optimistic and ominous, he attempted to finesse the ship onto a new course.[43]

Dewey, no doubt to the satisfaction of many in the audience, likened academicians to tamed parasites ensconced in their studies and thus unwittingly serving the forces of social and economic darkness. One wonders if murmurs of assent had died down enough for the audience to fully appreciate his next words:

> Meantime unconsciously if not consciously, by force of conditions if not by intention, the ideals and methods that control business take possession of the spirit and machinery of our educational system. If there is to be any result save blind conformity, passive reproduction, it must proceed from facing the overlordship of industry in modern life, with all that it imports. The question as respects education is how the school is to secure the good and avoid the ill of this sovereignty; how it may select and perpetuate what in it is significant and worthy for human life, and may reject and expel what is degrading and enslaving.

Dewey and others of like mind would go on to champion progressive education well into the twentieth century. Nevertheless, the course had been charted and subsequent formulations too often resembled salvage efforts rather than the bold, if problematic, new education of Dewey and the late nineteenth century.[44]

Although the dust of curricular battles has never settled, one result stands out clearly: the steady introduction of more subjects into the curriculum. In this respect Hoosier schools have long been in the mainstream. That this curricular expansion failed to deliver the optimistic results projected by nineteenth-century enthusiasts is not surprising, especially considering the contradictory demands placed on teachers and students as the new century progressed.

What began among some as an effort to vaccinate the young against the worst aspects of industrial society, to render them immune via a deep understanding of the social and economic structure, too often ended in intensifying the disease, especially for those most vulnerable. Whereas earlier calls for the "practical" implied that which was relevant to life in its broadest and deepest sense, later use of the term usually meant that which met the demands of the moment, whether personal or social. Whereas earlier calls for the restoration of dignity in labor implied a respect derived from universal personal experience, later application of the term was clearly directed toward those "to the broom born." And whereas earlier calls for the joining of mind and hand suggested, if somewhat vaguely, a profound psychological connection, later efforts were limited to marketable skills most often at the lower end of the pay scale.

By the 1950s in Indianapolis, as well as in other Hoosier cities, manual training, once the centerpiece of the new curriculum, had become trade training of the most menial kind. Emmerich's "coadjutors of the passive senses" that had taken us "towards the very limits of time and space" now were bounded by the limits of catering and shoe repair. The contradictions and logical inversions, while inherent in the original curricular formulations, were not, however, inevitable. Competing forces were at work. Whereas Dewey and others had hoped that schools would redirect society, more often the same pressures that had stimulated the original reforms overwhelmed the process and replicated societal problems in the schools themselves. The seriousness of curricular debates is not surprising when one realizes the long tradition of making school subjects surrogates for broader societal contests.

NOTES

1. *Public Education in Indiana: Report of the Indiana Educational Commission* (New York, 1923). The principal representative of the General Education Board was Frank P. Bachman. For a discussion of the influence of the GEB, see James H.

Madison, "John D. Rockefeller's General Education Board and the Rural School Problem in the Midwest, 1900–1930" in *History of Education Quarterly* 24 (Summer 1984): 170–85.

Among the many criticisms the committee offered on the state of affairs in Hoosier schools, none was more emphatic than its condemnation of a school financing process based too heavily on local taxation, thereby creating gross inequities in educational opportunity. The committee would not have been cheered had they recognized how this discrepancy would persist not only in Indiana, but across the nation.

2. Ibid., 117, 106.

3. Ibid., 107. Edward C. Kirkland, *Dream and Thought in the Business Community, 1860–1900* (Chicago, 1964), 138.

4. James H. Madison, *Heartland: Comparative Histories of the Midwestern States* (Bloomington, 1988), 173. For a more detailed description of the gas boom and economic prosperity at this time, see John B. Martin, *Indiana: An Interpretation* (Bloomington, 1992 [1947]), 75–101.

5. William R. Holloway, *Indianapolis: A Historical and Statistical Sketch of Railroad City* (Indianapolis, 1870), 278–79.

6. Kirkland, 26; David Montgomery, *The Fall of the House of Labor: The Workplace, the State and American Labor Activism, 1865–1925* (Cambridge, 1987), 112–70.

7. Clifton J. Phillips, *Indiana in Transition: The Emergence of an Industrial Commonwealth, 1880–1920* (Indianapolis, 1968), 271–322. See also John D. Barnhart and Donald F. Carmony, *Indiana from Frontier to Industrial Commonwealth*, vol. 2 (New York, 1954), 244. Bernard Wishy, *The Child and the Republic: The Dawn of Modern Child Culture* (Philadelphia, 1968). Wishy maintains that child rearing and national consciousness come together in this era. Aware of the dramatic changes in American society, social reformers turned their attention to the children in the hope that necessary republican virtues could be instilled in them, a likelier task than it would have been in the adult world. Kirkland, 55: "In 1877 the Commissioner of Education was in a put-up or shut-up mood. 'All the powers' of the child, he wrote, 'must be developed to resist misfortune and wrong. Capital, therefore, should weigh the cost of the mob and the tramp against the expense of universal and sufficient education.'"

8. Logan Esarey, *A History of Indiana from 1850 to the Present* (Indianapolis, 1918), 941–43. The only other subject to be specified in the last quarter of the nineteenth century was "scientific temperance" and it was short-lived.

9. Oscar Findley, "The Development of the High School in Indiana" (Ph.D. thesis, Indiana University 1925), 76. "The subjects selected should be aids only in calling on the responses that will enable the pupil to be at home in his new sphere instead of a stranger in a strange land." Edward A. Krug, *The Shaping of the American High School, 1880–1920* (Madison, 1969 [1964]), 216. In describing the memorable NEA debates of 1894–95 between DeGarmo, Harris and others, Krug suggests that the spectacle had the air of a sporting contest that the participants would look back on over the years with a sense of fondness and camaraderie that sets them apart from more recent combatants.

10. Charles A. Bennett, *History of Manual and Industrial Education, 1870–1890* (Peoria, 1937), 321.

11. Minutes of the December 1887 Indiana State Teachers Association meeting in the *Indiana School Journal* 23 (February 1878): 66.

12. Findley, 149–50. William O. Lynch, "The Great Awakening: A Chapter in the Educational History of Indiana" in *Indiana Magazine of History* 41 (June 1945): 126. Nevertheless, there's an appealing irony in the possibility of a naked enrollee in "The Science of Dress"! Harry Holt's *Historical Autobiography of a Hoosier Hillbilly* (Oxford, Ind., 1967) is an interesting account of one who used the public schools to climb out of impoverishment and marginalization. Holt took advantage of the growth of vocational agriculture by becoming a teacher in that field. Much interesting information on high schools and college in Indiana can be gleaned from this book. In 1915 there were only seven schools, with 122 pupils, offering full-time programs in vocational agriculture. By 1931 there were 143 schools with 3,914 students. See *Bulletin 109* of the State Department of Public Instruction, Division of Vocational Education: "Some Historical Data on Vocational Agriculture in Indiana" (Fort Wayne, 1931).

13. *Indiana School Journal,* 27 (November 1882): 578–79.

14. Charles E. Emmerich, "Manual Training" in the *20th Biennial Report of the Superintendent of Public Instruction of the State of Indiana* [1899–1900] (Indianapolis, 1901), 692–96. For a contemporary defense of manual training as the best way to enhance creativity while at the same time diminishing greed, see F. Gardiner, "Utilizing Boy Waste" in *Cosmopolitan* 26 (February 1899): 461–63.

15. 18th *Biennial Report* (1895–96), 565–67.

16. 15th *Biennial Report* (1889–90), 129–31. *Indiana School Journal* 45 (January 1900): 42.

17. A. H. Kennedy, "Educational Value of Manual Schools" in *Indiana School Journal* 34 (February 1889): 89.

18. Nicholas M. Butler, "The Reform of High School Education" in *Indiana School Journal* 39 (March 1894): 131–42.

19. Butler's argument seems strikingly similar to postmodern critiques of traditional studies! Nicholas M. Butler, *The Argument for Manual Training* (New York, 1888), 374–93.

20. William T. Harris, "The Theory of American Education" in *Proceedings of the National Teachers Association* (1870): 185–90.

21. *Indiana School Journal* 31 (April 1886): 201. John W. Holcombe, "Good Words for Indiana" in *Indiana School Journal* 31 (January 1886): 19.

22. John E. Earp, "Practical Education" in the *Indiana School Journal* 31 (April 1886): 174–76. *Indiana School Journal* 31 (1886): 247.

23. 13th Biennial Report, pt. 1 (1885–86), 86–91.

24. For a treatment of this argument, see Michael B. Katz, *The Irony of Early School Reform: Educational Innovation in Mid-Nineteenth Century Massachusetts* (Boston, 1968) and William J. Reese, *The Origins of the American High School* (New Haven, 1995).

25. Lacie Edmonds, "Education and Its Relation to Industry" in *Indiana School Journal* 33 (December 1888): 699, 702.

26. Peter Kropotkin, "Brain Work and Manual Work" in *The Nineteenth Century* 27 (March 1890): 461. Laura Donnan, "The High School and the Citizen" in *National Education Association Addresses and Proceedings* (1889): 519. For a description

of Donnan, see Walter B. Hendrickson, *The Indiana Years, 1903–1941* (Indianapolis, 1983), 131. Hendrickson is one of many students who subsequently paid tribute to this teacher—her insistence on equal treatment of blacks, her determination that her students would memorize significant portions of the Bill of Rights, etc. She is one of those teachers whose influence is incalculable. She, in fact, had probably never heard of Kropotkin and was confounding labor unrest and theoretical anarchism as reported in the newspapers.

27. Butler, "The Reform of High School Education," 133. Harold Rugg, *Curriculum-Making Past and Present* (New York, 1969 [1926]), 37–40.

28. Herbert M. Kliebard, *The Struggle for the American Curriculum, 1893–1958* (New York, 1987), 16. Butler, "The Reform of High School Education," 135.

29. W. N. Hailmann, "A High School Course of Study for the State" in the *Indiana School Journal* 32 (June 1887): 340–42. *Indiana School Journal* 39 (February 1894): 77. *Indiana School Journal* 35 (February 1890): 85, 88.

30. *18th Biennial Report* (1895–96), 36.

31. Holloway, 174–76. *13th Biennial Report*, pt. 1 (1885–86), 80–81. While a uniform course of study was sought for the high schools in this period, it was only in the first eight grades that such a course could be agreed upon by the Association of County Superintendents in 1884. See the *12th Biennial Report* (1883–84), 102.

32. Findley, 63, 66, 99. Patricia A. Graham, *Community and Class in American Education, 1865–1918* (New York, 1974), 58–59. Even though they disagreed on the precise nature of mental discipline, Eliot and Harris agree that the value of Latin lay in its rich cultural content, not in its mental disciplinary value. John E. Stout, *The Development of High-School Curricula in the North Central States from 1860 to 1918* (Chicago, 1921), 69–75. Science and English had now come to include subjects that had previously stood alone, such as astronomy and grammar.

33. Boone, 302–303.

34. *15th Biennial Report* (1889–90), 51.

35. *Public Education in Indiana*, 115. By 1921 commissioned high schools were designated as first, second, and third class. Noncommissioned had become "accredited" according to how many years of work would transfer to the commissioned high school. *12th Biennial Report* (1883–84), 110, and *15th Biennial Report* (1889–90), 56.

36. *18th Biennial Report* (1895–96), 233. Geeting urged the township trustees to pay more attention to the scholastic qualifications of their high school teachers since so many qualified graduates were available. Phillips, 394. This had occurred earlier for the lower grades—see the *16th Biennial Report*, 62. *16th Biennial Report* (1891–92), 44.

37. Levi A. McKnight, *Progress of Education in Benton County Indiana* (Benton County, Ind., 1906), 47–49. The statistics in the Superintendent's Report of 1899 present a clear picture of the status of high schools, commissioned and noncommissioned. Out of 717 high schools, 156 were commissioned. They produced approximately three-fourths of the total number of high school graduates, 3,899. On the other hand, total enrollment in the noncommissioned schools lagged only 15% behind the commissioned high schools, indicating that rural youth were more likely to attend but not graduate than their urban cousins. The percentage of high school–age youth enrolled grew as the size of the community declined—

from 3 to 7 percent for the largest cities to 10 to 32 percent for the smallest. In the largest cities rhetorical exercises were rapidly falling out of favor (presumably to be included in the specific courses)—a contradictory move *away* from coordination of subjects—while in the smaller communities they persisted, typically two to four exercises per month. There was little pattern in the nature of elective courses—either Latin, English, German, or science, although the availability of science courses tended to be limited to the larger communities.

38. Lester B. Rogers, *A Comparative Study of the Township, District, Consolidated, Town and City Schools of Indiana* (Menasha, Wis., 1915), 78–79.

39. Robert S. Lynd and Helen M. Lynd, *Middletown: A Study in American Culture* (New York, 1929), 188.

40. Ernest B. Kent, "Manual Training in the Grammar Schools of Indianapolis" in the *Indiana School Journal* 44 (July 1899): 406. Emmerich, 692. Lynd and Lynd, 194.

41. Richmond added drawing in 1885 and manual training in 1900. By 1912 they had three distinct courses of study—academic, commercial, and industrial. *Report of the Richmond, Indiana Survey for Vocational Education* (Indianapolis, 1916). Fort Wayne built a new high school with manual training facilities in 1904. In 1907, out of a total enrollment of 676, there were 401 students enrolled in at least one course in domestic science and art, applied art, or manual training. *Report of the Public Schools of Fort Wayne, Indiana* (Fort Wayne, 1908). South Bend had by this period established five courses of study including "General Culture, College Preparatory, Teacher's Preparatory, Commercial, and Vocational." *Biennial Report of the Superintendent of Schools of South Bend Indiana* (South Bend, 1914), 36.

42. John Dewey, "Current Problems in Secondary Education," *Manual Training* 3 (April 1902): 161–64. Unfortunately, Dewey's hope that entrenched attitudes of occupational elitism would be cured through the schools was violated by the structure of schooling itself. In this matter especially, progressive educators had the short end of a very long stick.

43. Just as Nicholas M. Butler was finally able to enter the ranks of the Columbia University professoriat through the creation of a new department (education), so too did Charles Richards create a niche in Teachers College by means of a new discipline. Curricular and professional expansion have been dynamically linked.

44. John Dewey, "Culture and Industry in Education," *Proceedings of the Eastern Manual Training Association* (1906), 21. Dewey goes on: "We know that our present scheme of industry requires a large supply of cheap, unskilled labor at hand. We know that this precludes special training; that the education which should develop initiative, thoughtfulness and executive force would not turn out facile recruits for our present system. And, if we are honest, we know that it is not intended that these qualities shall be secured more than is required to take charge of running the machinery to which the masses are subordinate" (p. 24). Unfortunately, "initiative, thoughtfulness, and executive force" were not destined to be the hallmarks of vocational education as it unfolded in the twentieth century.

ALEXANDER URBIEL

Civic Education in Indianapolis during the Progressive Era

B etween the late nineteenth century and the United States' entry into World War I in 1917, civic instruction in the schools became a promi-nent issue among educators. Although belief in the connection be-tween education and the survival and stability of American democracy was as old as the nation itself, the social stresses and strains of the late nineteenth and early twentieth centuries not only strengthened faith in this connection but led to a widespread discussion about how to improve it. Civic instruction became key to the emerging progressive education agenda nationally and in Indiana. In the years immediately preceding World War I, the public schools of the capital city of Indianapolis were held up to the nation as models of modern civic instruction. This resulted largely from the pioneering efforts of Arthur W. Dunn to define and institute a new form of civic education that was responsive to the changing realities of American urban life.[1]

The idea that public schooling strengthened the republic by nurturing democratic citizenship gained renewed vigor in the late nineteenth and early twentieth century, when the nation was transformed by economic changes often seen most visibly in urban areas. Labor unrest such as the 1886 Haymarket Riot in Chicago, the economic depression beginning in 1893, and the growing concern over the rising tide of immigration to American urban areas led educators to believe that schools needed to assume more responsibility for inculcating good citizenship among an increasingly heterogeneous population. On the national and local level, educators devised curricular plans that emphasized the making of good citizens. Their approaches varied in different communities, but educational reformers everywhere wrestled with common concerns.[2]

Although not a center for heavy industry or a destination for large numbers of recent immigrants, Indianapolis experienced many of the problems associated with growing urbanization. The city grew because of its dual role as a governmental and rail transportation center. Educators like Dunn were distressed by what they saw as the result of urban growth. Poor urban planning had tarnished the reputation Indianapolis held as "a city of homes." Dunn considered it a "pity" that a city "with all creation to expand in, should have become so possessed of the 'flat' habit." The concentration of cheap housing for the "poorest and most ignorant . . . without proper regulation by wise building laws" rapidly became "a menace to the beauty and to the physical and moral welfare of our city." Dunn observed that "[c]ontagious and infectious diseases spread from such localities, partly through the medium of the public school." Disease was just one of the many threats posed by urbanization. Immorality, like disease, was spread in the same manner, Dunn believed, and was incubated in the poor housing districts, then spread throughout the schools. "Vice and crime," Dunn continued, "are nursed in these dismal areas and prey upon society as a whole." The size of the slums did not matter for "[t]he safety and beauty of an entire community may be endangered by the existence of relatively small number of unwholesome homes."[3]

David Warren Saxe offers a useful framework to understand the philosophical tendencies of turn-of-the century educators as they redefined the role of public schooling in citizenship education. Emerging theories of social science "posited two opposing views of change that were relevant to education. Both strands of thought acknowledged change as phenomenon. The amount and speed of social progress, however, divided social scientists." One school followed the ideas of Herbert Spencer, especially as popularized by William Graham Sumner, who argued that social progress was inevitable; attempts to control or direct it were futile. For the followers of Spencer, education was at best a conserving agent to filter the harsh realities of change: it was not a core or central institution of society.[4]

A second group of educators championed the ideas of Frank Lester Ward, one of the founders of American sociology. Ward defined sociology as the study of how citizens consciously use the power of government to realize society's best interests. For them, progress could be directed and shaped and, therefore, education was vital in guiding social progress. These underlying views of the role of education in social change would help shape curricular reform during the first two decades of the twentieth century. Both strands of thought were evident in the school curriculum in

Indianapolis, especially in parts of the curriculum that sought to instill proper citizenship traits—such as history and civil government courses. However, those who believed that schools could be positive vehicles for directing social change held sway by 1916.[5]

The earliest organized national efforts to provide guidelines for the schools' roles in developing citizenship came from two sources. First was the 1892 Conference on History, Civil Government, and Political Economy held in Madison, Wisconsin. This conference was part of the larger National Education Association's (NEA) Committee on Secondary School Studies, or the Committee of Ten, as it was commonly called, led by Harvard President Charles Eliot. The second national attempt to guide citizenship education came from the 1896 Committee of Seven of the American Historical Association (AHA). Leading the Madison Conference was Charles Kendall Adams, president of the University of Wisconsin. Seven of the ten members of the Madison Conference were college professors, including Professor Woodrow Wilson of the College of New Jersey, later to become Princeton. The remaining three members were schoolmen. The Madison Conference reflected the dominant influence of the academics and the overall thrust of the Committee of Ten, which was attempting to strengthen academic instruction for the growing number of students who did not plan to attend college.[6]

The Madison Conference, in effect, sought to bring rigorous historical instruction into the schools. Courses in civil government, political economy, and especially history would provide students with much-needed intellectual skills that would result in sharper-thinking citizens. The Conference *Report* recognized that "[h]istory has long been commended as a part of the education of a good citizen." One objective of these courses would, of course, be the "acquirement of useful facts," but the chief object of more rigorous and widespread courses studying history would be "the training of judgement, in selecting the grounds of an opinion, in accumulating material for an opinion, in putting things together, in generalizing upon facts, in estimating character, in applying the lessons of history to current events, and in accustoming children to state their own conclusions in their own words." Schoolchildren, especially high school students, should examine history in the same manner as college students.[7]

To realize these objectives the Madison Conference recommended that the last year of high school and grade school instruction should include courses in American history and civil government—a schematic look at the structure of governmental organization. Half of the year would be devoted to each. Although these courses were being taught in many school systems, the Madison Conference urged that they be more widely adopted. They also recommended a change in methodology for these courses. A textbook was still considered necessary, but more creative use should be made of outside readings, assigned reports, immediate observation of the workings of local government, and comparisons of the American form of government with that of foreign nations.[8]

As Saxe points out, however, even though the Madison Conference provided a structural framework for uniform history instruction in schools, and in particular the high schools, its "vague language and generalities" led to a "lack of commitment to a particular program." The basic idea of more and better history instruction in the schools as a method of providing solid and meaningful citizenship education caught the attention of the AHA, which soon provided a more detailed plan of action for the schools.[9]

The AHA appointed a Committee of Seven in 1896 to provide a more complete history curriculum for the schools than that proposed by the Madison Conference. After two years of study the committee published its report. More detailed curriculum guides for a four-year sequence of courses starting with ancient history and proceeding through European history, English history, and, finally, American history and government, were offered as models on which local systems could implement a more meaningful history curriculum. This type of curriculum already existed in many larger urban schools. One of the goals of the AHA Committee and the previous Madison Conference was to promote a standardized curriculum for the more numerous small and rural schools. Aside from the more detailed course proposals, the most salient feature of the Committee of Seven's recommendations was that history and civic instruction should be combined. Like the Madison Conference, the Committee of Seven believed that through history courses students would gain the skills of democratic citizenship. The study of history and the development of citizenship were one and the same. The final report of the Committee of Seven stated that

> [t]he greatest aim of education is to impress upon the learner a sense of duty and responsibility, and an acquaintance with his human obligations; and that a manifest function of the historical instruction in the school is to give the pupil a sense of duty as a responsible member of the organized society of which he is a part, and some appreciation of its principles and its fundamental characteristics.[10]

Both the Madison Conference and the Committee of Seven argued for more academically rigorous history instruction in the schools. Putting history on a more intellectually challenging plane in the classroom would lead to better citizens because students would make correct and intelligent decisions in their public roles, thanks to the training that history gave them in weighing evidence, synthesizing information from diverse sources, and reaching logical conclusions based on facts.

Although one cannot make a direct link from the Madison Conference and the Committee of Seven to the curriculum of the Indianapolis public schools, the proposals brought forward by these two bodies surely must have been considered by local educators when drawing up curricular plans. Contemporaries recognized that the idea of reforming schools grew more popular everywhere, not simply in the meetings of professional organizations. Educational reform in the United States has never been exclusively national in scope because of the tradition of strong local school control. In the Progressive Era, however, as educators sought to become more professional, their ties became closer and the innovations they developed transcended traditions of locally controlled schools. While never dominated by a central bureaucracy, American educators in all parts of the country developed common agendas to reform the schools. Many of the changes recommended by the Committee of Ten and the Committee of Seven were already in place in the Indianapolis schools, as they probably were in other urban school systems. Like the entire Committee of Ten *Report*, the recommendations of the historians largely helped reshape existing course content and rationale in local school systems rather than provide blueprints for new courses or new pedagogical philosophies for local teachers to adopt.[11]

Between the mid-nineteenth century and 1903, the history curriculum of the Indianapolis schools expanded. In the 1860s U.S. history was the only history course offering at Indianapolis High School, later Shortridge High School. By 1873, the course offerings were expanded to include history, Constitution of the United States, Constitution of Indiana, and morals. Finer distinctions were made in the 1890s. By 1893, U.S. history was offered along with a general history course. Civil government, which in 1887 became a required course for graduation, and political economy probably assumed the functions of the courses on the Indiana and U.S. constitutions. In 1893, six years before the Committee of Seven *Report*, the history curriculum already resembled what the Committee later recommended: ancient history, medieval history, modern history, and civic government. Ten years later, U.S. history again appears as a distinct course. By 1903, separate courses on English history and civics were added to the curriculum.[12]

Whether these courses were attempting to promote a higher standard of academic historical study and, thus, a solid basis for informed citizenship, as the Madison Conference and the Committee of Seven recommended, is hard to ascertain. Probably both goals were sought. Certainly, the expansion of course content to include ancient, medieval, and English history exposed students to new worlds and ideas. But old habits of instruction were hard to break. Promoting solid historical inquiry in the schools was an uphill battle.

The courses more directly linked to citizenship training, civil government, and civics are even harder to evaluate. One contemporary student of citizenship training in the schools concluded after studying thirteen elementary and thirty-seven high schools that "[c]omparatively little conscious connection between school life and the community life as a whole was revealed." Historians of citizenship education, examining the growth of citizenship instruction around the turn of the century through courses that dissected the activities of local, state, and national governmental structures, are not very complimentary. Frederick Smith and John Patrick, while recognizing the wider adoption of these courses throughout the country in the late nineteenth century, criticize them for their reliance on the methodology of rote memorization of facts. "Pupils were required to know and regurgitate many dreary details about the structure of American government, while little attention was given to analysis that could lead to understanding of the American political process."[13]

Teaching the dreary formal details of government organization, however, was often preferred to exposing students to the more dreary realities of actual government operation. At the 1905 meeting of the history section of the Indiana State Teachers Association (ISTA), a discussion was held on the practicality and value of class city councils and moot courts in the schools as part of a larger discussion on "What Should a Course in Civics in the High School Be?" John R. Carr, a teacher of civics at Manual Training High School on the south side of Indianapolis, argued that these methodological devices were of little use because they tended to replicate the evils of real government. But, since these were popular teaching tools, "all questionable tactics of real legislatures should be omitted in the mock sessions. . . . The student should be taught nothing that will lead him to depreciate the majesty of the law," and "[t]eachers and pupils in the practical study of civics should steer clear of the questionable tactics of real legislatures." In other words, government, as it functions in theory, was the proper area of study, not government as it operates in reality.[14]

This approach underlines the dominant thrust of civics instruction at the turn of the century. Modern methods existed and were promoted, but objective analysis of government operations existed hand in hand with inculcating correct moral values in future citizens. As Professor James A. Woodburn of the history department at Indiana University and leader of the discussion on civic instruction at the 1905 history section of the ISTA stated, "The first aim of civics is to cultivate morality."[15]

Evidence on the actual content and pedagogical philosophy behind the courses in history and civil government in the Indianapolis high schools is lacking, but one can extrapolate from the evidence that does exist for the teaching of history in the grade schools of the 1890s. U.S. history was taught in both grades seven and eight. Teachers were urged to adopt methods supported by the Madison Conference and the Committee of Seven. Rote memorization from textbooks and mechanical, parroting recitations were discouraged. Although specific text material and required topics were outlined for grade school teachers, the *Manual of the Public*

Schools also urged teachers not to "require any part [of the text] committed to memory." Further, teachers were advised to "not consider the book as history; it is only a means, not an end."[16]

History instruction in the lower grades during the 1890s was a mixture of modern ways of interpreting the past and traditional emphasis on the past as moral lesson. Teachers were urged to use historical facts as the basis for broader generalizations and inculcated this way of thinking about the past in their students. Seventh-grade history stressed the development of "institutional ideas" established in the United States during the Revolutionary War period. Eighth graders focused on the entirety of nineteenth-century U.S. history with one general idea to be kept in mind, "the development of the spirit of nationality—or national freedom." Teachers were instructed to use the progression of nineteenth-century U.S. history to help students understand the growth of nationality "by noting (1) the phase under which it is shown, and (2) the process through which it was realized." Facts and events were not useful unto themselves. "Each event should be studied to understand (1) how it grew out of the movement of the general idea, and (2) how much it contributed to the movement of the general idea."[17]

However, placing history instruction in the grades on a more modern footing by promoting the synthesis of facts toward understanding broad generalizations and trends continued to exist concurrently with the older idea of history as moral instruction. Opening exercises for seventh graders consisted of "biographies of eminent Americans." Teachers were to "[t]ake moral themes from history" and, contrary to what would be considered scientific or analytical historical study, "[b]e careful not to introduce confusing details into moral instruction" based on these biographies. Eighth graders were also taught that "[t]he study of history rightly understood is but the study of the biography of morality. Many questions raised in history recitations can be discussed as moral problems at the morning lesson."[18]

Knowledge of formal government organization and an emphasis on morals characterized civic instruction in Indianapolis until the early 1900s. The influence of the Committee of Ten and the Committee of Seven on the history and civics curriculum appeared in calls to modernize classroom methods and to broaden relevant subject matter. At the same time, the moral lessons of history were entwined with a study of the pristine, schematic forms of government; a study of government in action provided few moral lessons and received little attention. What Saxe characterized as a Spencerian approach to citizenship instruction dominated Indianapolis schools. In this view, progress was marching on inevitably, and schools could do little but filter out harsh realities and negative effects. An orthodox approach that stressed tried-and-true morals and simultaneously allowed pupils to comprehend the growing complexity of government held sway. However, as schoolteachers and administrators carved out a professional niche and more educators viewed the schools as positive forces in directing and harnessing social change, the nature of citizenship education would change. In Indianapolis, civic instruction became, in the jargon of the times, more "progressive" beginning in 1903.

The drive toward professionalizing teachers and administrators profoundly affected school organization and curriculum. David Tyack has demonstrated how "administrative progressives" sought to rationalize school organization along the lines being adopted by other large bureaucratic organizations such as government and industry. The need to absorb growing student populations into city school systems required the skills of professionals trained in the art of both education and administration. Professionalization also meant breaking away from a perceived dominance by college educators and the requirements they established for college and university entrance. Therefore, school educators pushed for a curriculum that was not dominated by academic subjects designed to prepare students for higher education. Often this translated into stressing and developing subjects that carved out a larger role for the schools in developing social and vocational skills. Obviously, civic education was part of this phenomenon. The professionalization of teachers and administrators was concurrent with the broadening of the school curriculum in the early decades of the twentieth century.[19]

George W. Benton, principal of Shortridge High School, revealed the interrelationship of professionalization and the promotion of civic education in a 1905 article in the *Educator-Journal*, a publication for Indiana schoolteachers. Benton argued that the schools were failing "to develop in the child those high ideals of citizenship which the public has a right to expect." This failure, however, was not the fault of the schools. Rather, the overbearing nature of college entrance requirements had forced the schools to ignore more important goals. Citizenship must be promoted and taught, irrespective of other courses required for college entrance by specific institutions. These requirements "crowd out courses in civics, political economy and ethics, which should be the cornerstone of public education." A subservience to college requirements was, argued Benton, "medieval." It was "imbecile in light of present conditions, for it does not require acute sense to see that while college has raised its requirements, it has done so by requiring more mathematics, more language, more of this and more of that, along ancient lines and has entirely overlooked the revolutions in social needs, brought about by the tremendous development in community life."[20]

Part of the cadre of new professionals trying to establish themselves and their sense of importance, Benton believed that the only hope for youth was to free their education from the tyranny of college requirements. In fact, "[t]he greatest factor for good lies in the continued association of the youth of the land with strong men and women in our high schools whose wisdom, sense and skill are employed in bringing the impressionable and plastic mind into lively sympathy with right views of civic life." Benton, like others, used the supposed interference of institutions of higher education as a scapegoat to explain the shortcomings in schools, to expand enrollments by appealing to the non-college bound, and as a means to further carve out a more important role for people like himself in the growing urban school systems. This dynamic opened the way for changes in the curriculum that attempted to fill the supposed void in students' lives caused by urbanization.[21]

A self-promotional quest for professionalization and recognition does not entirely explain the changes that swept over the civic education curriculum in Indianapolis in the Progressive Era. Individual educators, influenced by the writings of pioneers in the fields of sociology and social psychology, brought to local school systems the belief that schools have the ability and the imperative to train students in active citizenship. Theorists such as Edward A. Ross, Albion Small, and George E. Vincent sought to transform schools into institutions promoting social efficiency, institutions that would resolve the growing tension between the individual and the group caused by the rise of cities and the growth of corporate capitalism. Ross argued that the "common life" that enabled "mates, kinsfolk, neighbors, and comrades to love and understand one another, to yield to one another, and to observe those forebearances and good offices that make associate life a success" had been eroded by industrialized and urbanized America. For Ross and others, the schools could be not just filtering agents to shield malleable young minds from the evils of modern urban life. Rather, the schools would train students to actively meet modern life and direct its course, making it manageable, democratic, and moral. This would require a new form of civic education from the one in place at the turn of the century.[22]

Dunn (1868–1927) led the effort to reform civics instruction in the Indianapolis public schools. Born in Galesburg, Illinois, Dunn received his A.B. in 1893 at his hometown Knox College. From 1893 to 1896 he was a fellow in sociology at the University of Chicago, receiving his A.M. in 1896. Dunn served as an instructor in English and lecturer in sociology at the University of Cincinnati from 1896 to 1900 before coming to Indianapolis as the head of the department of history and civics at Shortridge High School in 1900, a position he would hold until 1910. During his ten years in Indianapolis, Dunn transformed the civics curriculum of the schools and gained a national reputation that eventually took him to Washington, D.C., as a specialist in civic education for the U.S. Bureau of Education.[23]

Although not as famous as some progressive educators, Dunn was a crucial figure in the transformation of the emerging theoretical ideas of social science, and sociology in particular, into practice. Dunn's civics textbook, *The Community and the Citizen* (1906), written for the civics course he designed for Indianapolis schoolchildren, went through numerous printings and was adopted by various school systems throughout the country. In the preface to *The Community and the Citizen,* Dunn acknowledged his theoretical debt to John Dewey. In a lengthy quotation from Dewey's 1897 essay, "Ethical Principles Underlying Education," Dunn laid out the justification for his work.

According to Dewey, the schools narrowly interpreted the meaning of citizenship education and reduced it to developing the "capacity to vote intelligently, a disposition to obey laws, etc." Such a myopic view of citizenship education ignored other crucial aspects of the individual's role in society. Preparing citizens did not mean only imparting the meanings of laws and a working knowledge of government organization. Rather, citizenship education should include all the social roles that individuals assume. Therefore, civic education needed to concern itself with family, occupational, and community life. Along with enlarging the definition of citizenship training, Dewey argued for changing the method of citizenship education from one of memorization of facts and figures to a more engaging method of analysis and observation. "Training for citizenship is formal and nominal unless it develops the power of observation, analysis, and inference with respect to what makes up a social situation and the agencies through which it is modified." To Dunn, as for Dewey, training for citizenship in the schools needed to move far beyond the traditional civics curriculum.[24]

In the community civics course Dunn developed, citizenship training took on a much broader meaning than preparing students solely for political participation. Dunn criticized the "commonly prevalent idea of the subject of civics" that "it consists of a fund of information regarding the mechanism of government." While desirable, this information was not of the "greatest importance in the cultivation of citizens." Agreeing with many theorists, Dunn considered the re-creation of a sense of community, a concept eroded by urbanization and industrialization, paramount to the goal of civic education. In his 1909 report as the director of civics in the Indianapolis schools, Dunn emphasized his central goal: to strengthen a sense of community in schoolchildren. "What is being attempted in the eighth grade civics," he wrote, "is to develop in the maturing child a consciousness of the nature and meaning of community life, and of his relations to it; to help him form habits of thinking in terms of community life; to cultivate . . . community relations; and to develop . . . habits of intelligent action with reference to matters of community interest." If the meaning and relationship of the student to community life was developed, the more traditional and narrow goals of civic education would also be accomplished. "If this interest and these habits of thought and action [toward community life] can be established, a knowledge of the details of the mechanism of government may be safely left to take care of itself."[25]

Details of the mechanism of government, however, remained secondary to Dunn's purpose in creating a community civics course. He was "more concerned about the interest that the pupil shall develop in the life of the community and in his relation to that life, than about the amount of systematic knowledge that he shall gain regarding the forms and working of government." More important than imparting facts to the student was the desire to "stimulate a questioning attitude on the part of the pupil, and to leave him with an eager desire to know more. . . . To set the question in the mind of the pupil is the important thing." Building awareness of community functions was more important than memorizing facts about how those functions are accomplished. "It does not matter so much, after all, whether the child can describe the details of the water system or the organization of the school board, but it *is* important that the coming citizen should have a consciousness of the magnitude of the work the community does for him to supply him with pure water and with an education."[26]

Developing the ability in students to comprehend the complexities of the modern urban community would also further the process of social efficiency. In describing the citizenship education work of the schools for the city's business community, Dunn wrote, "[w]e are trying to make the idea clear to the children that the community is giving them an education, not as a benevolence, nor even as a right, but as an investment in expectation of returns in the form of increased efficiency in the various relations of community life. . . ." The proper form of citizenship "is not merely a matter of efficiency in public office, or in voting, or in mere obedience to law," rather, it involves all aspects of life including home, school, and community relations.[27]

Dunn promoted the application of progressive educational psychology theories as the best way to accomplish his goal of establishing a "consciousness" of community on the part of the student taking civics. These theories placed great importance on using the natural interest of the child in certain things to spur on other interests and stimulate more advanced thinking. This type of "child-centered" pedagogy, rather than "subject-centered," was a hallmark of progressive educational thinkers.

Two "well-known principles of educational psychology [were] indispensable in the teaching of civics" for Dunn. "The first of these is that the pupil's interest must, first of all, be secured," he wrote. "It is far better to stimulate interest and to impart very little detailed information than to fill the mind with more or less well-understood facts at the expense of interest. Interest, once killed, is hard to regain; while with the interest thoroughly kindled, the facts will easily follow." Securing a pupil's interest was also important for reasons other than aiding the learning process. Dunn, like Dewey and other progressives, believed in education as a training ground for social involvement. "[I]t is the individual's interest, and not his knowledge, that leads to action. The right kind of interest behind a very few facts will lead to good citizenship, while any number of facts without the interest will fail to do so."[28]

The second progressive educational principle that Dunn considered crucial to civic education was the use of the child's own experience to kindle and maintain interest. Civic education teachers needed to "build on [the students'] own experience, passing constantly from the facts of his experience to related facts just beyond his experience, and back again to his own experience." The teacher needed to use skill in tying increasingly complex concepts to what the student experienced in "his daily life at home, in school, or as a member of the community."[29]

The community civics course instituted in the Indianapolis schools was structured like a series of concentric circles of social activity. Each circle was larger than the previous, took in more people and more social activities, and was more complex in function. Not only would this method build on student experiences, it would emphasize that "good citizenship is a matter of the home, of the school, of the street, of business; and that good citizenship is, after all, only efficient membership in the community in all its relations." Students first studied family relations, moving on to school, neighborhood, municipality, state, and, finally, national community life.[30]

From 1906 to 1909, community civics was required of Indianapolis students in the second half of the eighth grade. By the 1909 school year, the course had been in use long enough for Dunn to make some evaluations of its effectiveness. In his 1909 report, Dunn wrote that if "the work in civics is really accomplishing the end desired, viz., the creation of an *interest* in community relations and the formations of *habits* of civic thought and action, the results ought to begin to show" in four different areas. The conduct of the individual pupil, the life of the school, student interest and participation in community activities, and student home life should all be affected by the community civics course. Dunn gathered reports from teachers of civics, school principals, parents, and the children themselves and found that "the study of civics has been, and is increasingly effective" in all of these areas.[31]

The conduct of individual pupils, according to Dunn's findings, improved through the study of civics. Teachers reported "numerous incidents" where the conduct of students changed in positive ways because of, they believed, civics work. For example, Dunn relates the story of a boy who was "addicted to the habit of carving his name on every telephone pole, or other convenient place." After studying the chapter on civic beauty, this practice stopped. Another student reported to his teacher, "I took water and soap and scrubbed our house on the outside, and I tell you it looks nice." The teacher asked the pupil why he did this and the response was, "I never would have thought of it if it hadn't been for civics."[32]

The study of civics also affected the life of the school. One teacher reported that students taking civics "have been influenced to a better school attitude, and to a greater sense of personal responsibility in school affairs." As examples, the teacher noted that civics students were "distinctly superior in the matter of self-government. Fewer rules [were] needed, and in many small points of discipline they can be safely left to manage themselves." Secondly, the teacher continued, many of the civics students took an increased interest in the cleanliness and overall appearance of the school and its grounds. "Committees see to it that the desks are kept free from ink stains, initials, and disfiguring marks of all kinds; and individual pupils of their own accord have helped to clear the yard of scraps of paper, and to keep it clear." Other teachers reported similar activities that they attributed to civics instruction. Good Citizen clubs were formed in a number of schools to protect the appearance of school grounds and regulate the conduct of children on the playgrounds. Teachers in other subjects noted that civics students often "show[ed] a well-defined sense of responsibility for the conduct of the classes" and assumed a "sort of guardianship over the welfare of the younger pupils."[33]

Dunn saw civics affecting the life of the school in the choice of programs for graduation exercises. Numerous schools, from 1906 to 1909, designed and carried out programs that had a civic education theme. It is difficult to reconstruct just what these graduation exercises may have meant to students; probably the sheer joy of graduation and a sense of celebration overshadowed the themes used in the actual ceremony. Nevertheless, the themes used in the graduation exercises are important indicators of what was being emphasized in student instruction. The graduation programs of the Benjamin Harrison School for the year before Dunn's civics course was fully implemented and the year after highlight the different approach given civic education. For the graduating class of 1906, traditional themes prevailed. Historic individuals were held up as models for the graduates to emulate and derive inspiration from. On the cover of their graduation exercises program was the famous quotation from Longfellow emphasizing the great benefit derived from studying the lives of great men:

> Lives of great men all remind us
> We can make our lives sublime
> And, departing, leave behind us
> Footprints on the sands of time.

The graduating program included student orations on Abraham Lincoln, Harriet Beecher Stowe, and Robert E. Lee.[34]

A year and a half later, the eighth-grade graduation program from the same school reflected the change in emphasis in civic instruction. On the cover of the program was the class motto: "He serves himself best who serves others." Orations at the commencement did not celebrate the lives of heroes and famous Americans but concentrated on the individual and his various roles as a citizen. The titles of the speeches are indicative of the new thrust in civic education: "Ideal Citizenship—What Is It?" "The Citizen of the Home," "The Citizen of the School," "Citizenship as Exemplified in: The Commercial Club, the Charity Organization Society, the Humane Society, and the Civic Art Association," "The Soldier of Peace," "The Citizens at the Polls," and, finally, "The City Beautiful—As Transformed by Its Citizens." Clearly, the topics of this program were influenced by the emphasis in community civics on citizenship being closely intertwined with all phases of community life including home, school, municipality, and nation.[35]

The third area in which Dunn evaluated the effect of his civics course was in the amount of student interest and participation in community affairs. Such activity in community affairs underlined the necessity for cooperation in the urban industrial world. Cooperation became more important than individual action in securing civic betterment. Taking an active part in movements for the community "is part of the method by which habits of civic action are formed." Dunn believed that "[t]he line along which children most easily work is that of beautifying the community; but opportunities also occur to participate in movements for the benefit of the public health, and in other movements." Staying in school, a major concern of educators appalled with high drop-out rates, was also promoted as an integral part of community participation. "[Students] are being trained in the idea that in the very act of going to school they are doing what the community expects them to do, and that they are doing it for the community welfare, rather than for their own selfish ends."[36]

Evidence of community participation by civics students included community gardens started by numerous classes, cooperation with the Indianapolis Commercial Club in marking historic city sites with commemorative tablets, repairing neighborhood fences, and participating in clean streetcar, sidewalk, and alley campaigns. All of this work outside the school led Dunn to conclude that "the schools are rapidly becoming centers of civic influence, not merely in outward appearances, but in the moral life of the people." More importantly, the students "feel that they count for something in the life of the community; that they are working with the larger forces of the community toward a common civic end." By working on projects outside of the school, students also gained other valuable lessons such as insights into the complexity of city life, the value of collecting facts before pursuing action, and "to see their own apparently feeble, but earnest, efforts, when supported by public sentiment, result in prompt action by the proper authorities."[37]

The influence of civics work in the home and the attitude of parents toward it was the final area Dunn evaluated. Not surprisingly, he found that students were taking valuable lessons home and sharing them with their parents, which, in turn, "is having an appreciable effect upon the community life." Many of the pupils were quizzing their parents regarding topics discussed in civics class. Parents approved of this activity. One reported that "[w]e have lively times at our breakfast table discussing the questions put to us by our fourteen-year old daughter. Her older brother, who did not have the advantage of the study of civics during his course in the grade schools, has been deeply interested in the subject." Another said, "[o]ur child now is on the alert to keep the house and yard neat and tidy, and has become acquainted with our own city as she never could have done outside of a civics class." Students were learning at school what previously had been taught at home or by other institutions in the community. Dunn must have been pleased. The schools were picking up the slack in community formation that had been eroded by the coming of modern, urban society.[38]

Dunn's overriding concern with citizenship education, the improvement of civic conditions, and the establishment of community consciousness in Indianapolis is exemplary of a particular strand of progressivism that permeated American cities during the first decade of the century. William H. Wilson, in his study of the City Beautiful movement, describes these middle- and upper-middle-class reformers as wanting "to tame the apparently disorganized, wildly growing city and to establish or restore a sense of community—that is feelings of civic responsibility, of commitment to a common purpose, and of municipal patriotism." They "spoke to yearnings for an ideal community and to the potential for good in all citizens." Neither utopians nor revolutionaries, these progressives were "imbued with the courage of practicality, for [they] undertook the most difficult task of all, to accept [their] urban human material where found, to take the city as it was, and to refashion both into something better." Many concerned citizens in a variety of cities, including Indianapolis, were part of the optimistic progressive quest to embrace urban growth and economic change while concurrently shaping it to deflect the potentially harsh effects that such rapid and dramatic change could bring.[39]

Not content to reform only the civic education curriculum in the schools, Dunn worked closely with the Indianapolis Commercial Club as chairman of its Civic Improvement Commission. This type of interlocking network for community reform is often seen as a hallmark of the Progressive Era. Enlightened businessmen and professionals joined ranks in Chambers of Commerce, City Clubs, Commercial Clubs, and other organizations throughout the country to do battle with the evils of modern life. Their spouses were often equally active, joining women's clubs, auxiliaries, and other gender-specific urban reform organizations.

As described by Dunn, the Indianapolis Commercial Club "owes its origin to a keen sense of the inadequacy of the city government to meet the increasing needs of a community that was at that time rapidly growing industrially." A host of problems arose including disorderly city finances, unpaved streets, inadequate fire protection, and a "city government [that] was apparently incapable of meeting the situation and was the object of discontent and distrust." The Commercial Club was involved in many city reforms such as a new city charter in 1891 which "was built on lines of the most advanced thought in municipal government," railroad track elevation to make the city streets safer, sanitation, sewage, public health, and housing improvement, park and parkway development, and other projects in which the "welfare of the city in all its civic relations has . . . been the underlying motive."[40]

In describing the work of the Commercial Club, Dunn emphasized the importance of cooperative efforts between the club and the public schools as a factor in "civic betterment." There were strong links between the improvement efforts of the Commercial Club and their effect on the youth of the city. For Dunn, "civic education in the schools will be only partially successful unless the organized citizens of the community cooperate with the schools," by being supportive of the schools and "by striving to create conditions in this city that will be conducive to the healthy growth of the children in civic consciousness." Because the Commercial Club exhibited such support and did its part to create such conditions "it has been possible to develop a practical course of instruction in . . . community civics . . . and to do much to form in the children habits of civic thought and action through participation with the civic bodies of Indianapolis in enterprises for the betterment of the city."[41]

Dunn left Indianapolis in 1910, but civics in the Indianapolis schools continued to expand. By 1916, the study of civics was extended beyond one half-year's work in the eighth grade to all of the grades of the elementary schools. In the high schools, civic relations grew more prominent in almost all areas of the curriculum. Although formally part of the social studies curriculum, civics work was considered important to other subjects as well, especially vocational education. In 1916, the Indianapolis Board of School Commissioners highlighted the effort the schools were taking to balance "individualistic" vocational training with community obligations. "In vocational training particularly, we are likely to give the suggestion that the end of education is the good of the individual and that we are sending students out in the world to be efficient, selfish 'dollar-grabbers.' Here then is the real problem for vocational civics—to help the student to get the right relation in his mind of individualism on the one hand and collectivism as manifested in community and national life on the other."[42]

After a year as the secretary of the City Club of Philadelphia and three as the executive secretary of the Public Education Association of New York City, Dunn moved to Washington, D.C., in 1914 to take up his post as specialist in civic education for the U.S. Bureau of Education, a position he held until 1921. During his tenure in Washington, Dunn tried to popularize the community civics course he designed and tested in Indianapolis as a national model.

Through Dunn's work in the Bureau of Education and as secretary to the Committee on Social Studies of the NEA's Commission on the Reorganization of Secondary Education, Indianapolis was touted as the most innovative school system in the country in regard to civic education programs. In 1915, Dunn wrote an extensive *Bulletin* for the Bureau of Education that outlined the history and current state of civic education in Indianapolis and urged other school systems to adopt a similar program. As coauthor of "The Teaching of Community Civics," another Bureau *Bulletin*, with J. Lynn Barnard, F. W. Carrier, and Clarence D. Kingsley, the Indianapolis programs again received national attention. Finally, Dunn was the main compiler of "The Social Studies in Secondary Education, Report of the Committee on Social Studies of the Commission on the Reorganization of Secondary Education." In this final report to the NEA Commission, he emphasized that the addition of community civics courses would help place secondary education on a modern footing, where social efficiency would be a guiding principle.[43]

The transformation of civic education in the Hoosier capital prior to World War I is historically significant in a number of ways. First, it demonstrates the implementation of nascent progressive educational philosophy. Although Dunn is not a recognizable name in the pantheon of progressive educators, he was representative of scores of educators in other school systems who helped translate theory into practice, moving the ideas of university-based scholars into day-to-day life in local schools. Second, civic education in Indianapolis highlights trends that would become hallmarks of progressive education, namely a shift in focus from subject matter to student needs, a broadened curriculum to attract and retain a growing student population, and an overwhelming concern by many educators with the increased complexity of American society and faith that schools could promote positive change and adaptation. Finally, the changes in civic education during these years highlight a central puzzle facing educators during the Progressive Era: how to reconcile the traditional American belief in individualism and liberty with the concurrent growth of interdependence.

As American society moves toward the end of the twentieth century, this puzzle remains unsolved. Current educational debates largely ignore the need to develop cooperative civic involvement in favor of promoting individualistic basic attainments and skills necessary to function in the economic marketplace. Ironically, one's fate is often not self-determined

The Power of Tradition: Patriotism in Indianapolis, 1948. Source: *To Form a More Perfect Union* (Indianapolis Public Schools, 1948)

but is at the mercy of large bureaucratic and economic structures. The most thoughtful educators at the turn of the century recognized that this was already becoming true. The ongoing debates over educational policy and goals may benefit by actively reengaging the issues that confronted Dunn in the first decade of this century. To maintain liberty and individualism, it is necessary to promote active involvement, cooperation, and participation in issues of political and economic power. Can schools aid in the development of citizens capable of the preservation of liberties and, at the same time, contribute to the common good?

NOTES

1. For a detailed and illuminating discussion on the role education plays in the American democratic tradition, see Rush Welter, *Popular Education and Democratic Thought in America* (New York, 1962).

2. Morris Janowitz, *The Reconstruction of Patriotism: Education for Civic Consciousness* (Chicago, 1983), 81–82; David Warren Saxe, *Social Studies in Schools: A History of the Early Years* (Albany, 1991), 7; Edward A. Krug, *The Shaping of the American High School, 1880–1920* (Madison, Wis., 1969) I: 10–11.

3. Arthur W. Dunn, "Some Social Conditions in Indianapolis," *Commercial Club Monthly,* vol. 1, no. 4 (February 1908): 75.

4. Saxe, *Social Studies in Schools,* 8.

5. Ibid.; Lester Frank Ward, *Pure Sociology,* 2d ed. (New York, 1915), 15–20.

6. The best one-volume discussion of the Committee of Ten and its 1894 *Report* is Theodore Sizer, *Secondary Schools at the Turn of the Century* (New Haven, 1964). See also Krug, *The Shaping of the American High School,* I: 18–92.

7. National Education Association, History Subcommittee Report, "History, Civil Government, and Political Economy," as found in the National Education Association, *Report on Secondary School Studies* (Washington, D.C., 1893), 169–70.

8. Ibid.; Arnold W. Brown, *The Improvement of Civics Instruction in Junior and Senior High Schools* (Ypsilanti, Mich., 1929), 21; R. Freeman Butts, *The Revival of Civic Learning: A Rationale for Citizenship Education in American Schools* (Washington, D.C., 1980), 62–63.

9. Saxe, *Social Studies in Schools,* 50.

10. Andrew McLaughlin et al., *The Study of History in Schools, Report of the Committee of Seven to the American Historical Association* (New York, 1899), 67–68. On the Committee of Seven, see Brown, *The Improvement of Civics Instruction,* 21–22; Krug, *The Shaping of the American High School,* I: 353; and Saxe, *Social Studies in Schools,* 50, 67–68, 90–98.

11. On the "national" scope of educational reform, see Lawrence Cremin, *American Education: The Metropolitan Experience, 1876–1980* (New York, 1988), 228–30. For an examination of the debate over just how much influence the Committee of Ten's *Report* had on local school systems, see Krug, *The Shaping of the American High School,* I: 88–92.

12. Indianapolis Board of School Commissioners, *Manual of the Public Schools of the City of Indianapolis with Rules and Regulations of the Board of School Commissioners and the Public Library, 1894–1895* (Indianapolis, 1894), 133–34; Indianapolis Board of School Commissioners, *Twenty-Seventh Annual Report of the Public Schools of the City of Indianapolis for the School Year Ending June 30, 1888* (Indianapolis, 1888), 82; Indianapolis Public Schools, *Survey Findings, Senior High School Division, Second-*

ary Schools (unpublished typescript, 1934, Educational Services Center Library, Indianapolis), 17–19.

13. Henry W. Thurston, "An Inquiry Relating to Training for Citizenship in the Public Schools," *The School Review* 6 (October 1898): 597. Frederick R. Smith and John J. Patrick, "Civics: Relating Social Study to Social Reality," in C. Benjamin Cox and Byron G. Massialas, eds., *Social Studies in the United States: A Critical Appraisal* (New York, 1967), 106.

14. *Indianapolis Star*, April 29, 1905.

15. Ibid.

16. *Manual of the Public Schools of the City of Indianapolis with Rules and Regulation of the Board of School Commissioners and the Public Library, 1894–1895*, 124.

17. Ibid., 94–95, 124, 127–28.

18. Ibid., 123, 126.

19. David B. Tyack, *The One Best System: A History of American Urban Education* (Cambridge, 1974), 126–76. On the broadening of the school curriculum as a hallmark of emerging progressive educational thought, see Ronald D. Cohen, *Children of the Mill: Schooling and Society in Gary, Indiana, 1906–1960* (Bloomington, Ind., 1990).

20. George W. Benton, "The Wage Problem in High Schools," *Educator Journal* 5 (February 1905): 236–37.

21. Ibid.

22. Edward A. Ross, *Social Control* (New York, 1901), 432–33; Albion Small and George E. Vincent, *An Introduction to the Study of Society* (New York, 1894). For a more nuanced discussion of the various derivations of the meaning of social control, see Barry Franklin, *Building the American Community: The School Curriculum and the Search for Social Control* (London, 1986); Krug, *Shaping of the American High School*, I: chap. 11.

23. Biographical material on Arthur W. Dunn is scarce. A manuscript collection of his writings, both published and unpublished, exists at Knox College in Galesburg, Ill. Unfortunately, this collection contains mainly material written after his years in Indianapolis and nothing of his school years. See *Who Was Who in America*, I: 347.

24. On Dunn's importance in taking Progressive ideas into real world public school environments, see Saxe, *Social Studies in Schools*, 22–23; John Dewey, "Ethical Principles Underlying Education," quoted in Arthur W. Dunn, *The Community and the Citizen* (Boston, 1907), iii. Dunn explicitly tied his work to Dewey's. In the "Suggestion to the Teacher" section of *The Community and the Citizen*, vi–viii, Dunn tells teachers "[n]o better preparation can be made for the use of the text in the spirit in which it is intended than by a careful reading of Professor Dewey's 'Ethical Principles Underlying Education,' quoted in the preface, and 'The School and Society' by the same author."

25. Arthur W. Dunn, "Report of the Director of Civics," in Indianapolis Board of School Commissioners, *Annual Report of the Secretary, Business Director, Superintendent of Schools and Librarian, 1908–1909*, 164. On the importance of re-creating a sense of community among social science theorists, see Franklin, *Building the American Community*, 4–6.

26. Dunn, *Community and the Citizen*, iv, viii.

27. Dunn, "Some Social Conditions in Indianapolis," 74.

28. Dunn, *Community and the Citizen,* vi.

29. Ibid.

30. Dunn, "Report of the Director of Civics," 164. On the progression from family to national communities, see Dunn, *The Community and the Citizen,* passim.

31. Dunn, "Report of the Director of Civics," 165.

32. Ibid., 165–66.

33. Ibid., 166.

34. Ibid.; "Graduation Exercises of the Benjamin Harrison School, January 1906," in scrapbook, n.p., Austin H. Brown Papers, BV2629, Indiana Historical Society, Indianapolis.

35. "Graduation Exercises of the Benjamin Harrison School, June 1907," in scrapbook, n.p., Austin H. Brown Papers.

36. Dunn, "Report of the Director of Civics," 166–68.

37. Ibid., 168–69. Dunn, "Some Social Conditions in Indianapolis," 74.

38. Dunn, "Report of the Director of Civics," 169–71.

39. William H. Wilson, *The City Beautiful Movement* (Baltimore, 1989), 41, 302.

40. Arthur W. Dunn, "The Commercial Club and the Civic Life of Indianapolis," *The Ohio Architect and Builder* 15 (June 1910): 21–27. Dunn's Civic Improvement Commission worked closely with George E. Kessler, one of the leading figures in the City Beautiful movement, hired by the city's park board to design and implement a series of parks and parkways. Kessler also proposed plans, that were never implemented, for a civic center, one of the recurring design themes in the City Beautiful movement, in downtown Indianapolis. See Paul C. Diebold, "Kessler's Boulevard and Park System," *Encyclopedia of Indianapolis,* David J. Bodenhamer and Robert G. Barrows, eds. (Bloomington, Ind., 1994), 868–69.

41. Dunn, "The Commercial Club and the Civic Life of Indianapolis," 27.

42. Indianapolis Board of School Commissioners, *Annual Report of the Business Director, Superintendent of Schools and Librarian, 1916* (Indianapolis, 1916), 44, 67–68.

43. Arthur W. Dunn, *Civic Education in Elementary Schools as Illustrated in Indianapolis,* United States Bureau of Education Bulletin, 1915, no. 17; J. Lynn Barnard et al., *The Teaching of Community Civics,* United States Bureau of Education Bulletin, 1915, no. 23; Arthur W. Dunn, *The Social Studies in Secondary Education,* Report of the Committee on Social Studies of the Commission on the Reorganization of Secondary Education, National Education Association, United States Bureau of Education, Bulletin, 1916, no. 28. On the great emphasis given to the concept of social efficiency by the Commission on the Reorganization of Secondary Education, see Herbert M. Kliebard, *The Struggle for the American Curriculum, 1893–1958,* 2nd ed. (New York, 1995), 91–99.

LAURIE MOSES HINES

Community and Control in the Development of the Extracurriculum: Muncie Central High School, 1890–1930

I n writing *Middletown* in 1929, Robert and Helen Lynd captured a community in the midst of change, in its "metamorphosing" from an agrarian town to an industrial city. According to the Lynds, the 1886 discovery of natural gas below the soil of Muncie, Indiana, set in motion the modernizing forces that eventually led to the commercialization of town life, with its Rotary clubs, chamber of commerce, and trade councils. But, if Muncie was no longer an "island community" cut off from the networks of modernity, by 1930 it had yet to emerge fully into the new bureaucratic order that regulated urban-industrial life. Rather than completely embracing a new hierarchical, impersonal, and regulative framework, Muncie citizens held on to some elements of the prebureaucratic order.[1]

Robert Wiebe first articulated the distinctions between nineteenth-century "island communities" and the bureaucratic communities of the twentieth century. According to Wiebe, the forces of modernity (the transportation and industrial revolutions in particular) forever altered social relations. In the nineteenth century, people primarily structured their identities around locale, and a community was a relatively self-sufficient network of interdependent people. By the twentieth century, Wiebe continued, individuals, especially in the emerging new middle class of professionals, no longer thought of themselves in local terms or organized themselves around community institutions. A pattern of association and identity based on functional groups of individuals across the nation who shared a common professional interest replaced the informal and local networks of people in the "island community." This new middle class of experts valued scientific bureaucracy, rational progress, efficiency, and expertise. They gained ascendancy during the Progressive Era, in part because the agrarian populist movement of the 1890s was too diffuse, too local, and too traditional in its emphasis on face-to-face relationships to win a broad base of support and succeed in the twentieth century.[2]

Certainly, the bureaucratic order increasingly dominated some arenas, such as the professions, the business world, and even national politics. By the mid-1920s, doctors, lawyers, and other professionals in Muncie were slowly gaining acceptance for the new scientific basis of their authority and expertise. These professionals believed that they "ought somehow to assume more community leadership because we are the people who know the facts." Yet they were frustrated with the community's reliance on folkways to solve problems. Some Munsonians still relied on traditional methods of child rearing and government participation, while others began to "delegate their interests" to the experts of the new order. In their frustration, the Muncie professionals may have recognized, as the Lynds did, that "changes in the life of the city have put increased strains upon institutional devices originally framed to operate in a simpler culture." Traditional ways and values thus continued to exist as new ways of relating and doing business—ways that reflected the hierarchical and scientific order—structured life in Muncie. The schools were no exception to this phenomenon, and the development of the extracurriculum at Muncie Central High School between 1890 and 1930 illustrates how these two different value systems coexisted in the world of education.[3]

The schools in Muncie reflected both the old and the new—the nineteenth- and the twentieth-century—ways of ordering society. School maintained some traditions of the nineteenth century: remnants of the classical curriculum and the belief that American schools served a democratic function and helped unify the community. But curricular changes and other school reforms, most notably the entry of the educational expert into the system, reflected the new bureaucratic order.

Some educational historians, such as Joel Spring, have in the last thirty years stressed the increasing domination of bureaucracy and social efficiency over the schools. In such interpretations, the extracurriculum was developed as a means to control students and instill in them certain values that benefitted the corporate state. Other accounts, in particular Wiebe's, have the schools' extracurriculum acting as a surrogate community and giving a "comfortable illusion" of community, an illusion perpetuated by school administrators. Recently, historians atuned to the limits of social control have challenged such interpretations. Looking for other explanations, Thomas W. Gutowski, for instance, described the development of the extracurriculum in Chicago public schools as "a process of conflict and compromise . . . involving students, teachers, principals, school system administrators, and the school board." Gutowski's argument about the development of the extracurriculum and the one posited here do not deny the existence in the schools of institutional structures of control that reflected the bureaucratic order. Gutowski states that in the official acceptance of student activities by the school, students lost the control they previously had, but the extracurriculum was "not simply imposed from above."[4]

Qualifying historians' arguments, like Spring's, are important because in so doing we see that bureaucratic structures existed alongside other ones and were not all-powerful. Community and social historian Thomas Bender suggested that the traditional-modern dichotomy (as in nineteenth-century versus twentieth-century, and local versus bureaucratic ways of ordering the world) may not illuminate the "interaction and interplay of communal and noncommunal ways in the lives" of people. Citing the theoretical work of anthropologist Robert Redfield, Bender states that Middletown, like any other community, exhibited characteristics of both ways of thinking about the world: "two opposite kinds of living, thinking, and feeling" simultaneously can exist, and American society, Bender insists, is no exception. This study shows this interaction and how individuals were able to accommodate the bureaucratic order without relinquishing the values of local community relationships. The extracurriculum at Muncie is a good example of how the nineteenth-century value of local community remained important to modern Americans and became part of a bureaucratic institution governed by educational experts such as superintendents. The extracurriculum was absorbed into the hierarchical, administrative structure of the school, while at the same time it promoted community. Muncie citizens of all ages were "boosters" who believed in "community spirit," and Muncie Central High School and its activities were a focal point around which the community often rallied. Modern and traditional structures coexisted as Munsonians adapted new bureaucratic structures to serve older community values. Citizens maintained community-based sources of identity and overlaid the rational, bureaucratic order with elements of local community.[5]

The story of the development of the extracurriculum qualifies the argument of historians such as Spring and Wiebe and extends Gutowski's argument into a larger understanding of society by providing an example of how both the bureaucratic order and the localized sense of community simultaneously existed in the first part of the twentieth century. The extracurriculum developed from an unofficial aspect of the student's social life to a formal element in the school's hierarchy. Supporters of the extracurriculum drew upon ideas of child study, adolescent development, and practical education in justifying its importance to the school system. The extracurriculum itself became a very organized and formalized segment of the educational institution, with its own experts. Even so, students utilized the extracurriculum to serve their own social needs. The extracurriculum was not just an adult-controlled mechanism to extend control over students. A boosterism or school spirit developed among the students and the adults that could not easily or completely be manipulated by educational administrators, the school system, or the new bureaucratic order. Muncie citizens were maintaining a sense of local identity and unity through the extracurriculum and the school teams. By supporting their clubs, their team, and their school, Muncie youth were learning to be contributing and participating members of the adult community. In this way, Muncie youth were being socialized into both the local community and the modern bureaucracy.[6]

When, in 1927, Frank E. Allen, the superintendent of Muncie schools, wrote "that all curriculum, as well as all school activities, are only a means . . . of producing in the boys and girls the highest and finest type of citizenship," he revealed how much attitudes toward the extracurriculum had changed since 1890. But so had the mission of the school. In the intermediate forty years, the curriculum shifted from humanistic to practical, and ideas about child study and adolescent development infused discussion of the school's function. The development of the extracurriculum reflected these educational trends. Supporters of the extracurriculum based their position on social and pedagogical ideas similar to those used to support the special curriculum (vocational education, manual arts, domestic science, and commercial education), the junior high school, and the comprehensive high school, where students of all abilities and academic interests could attend. Ideally, the comprehensive high school would allow for students to mix socially while maintaining their curricular specialization, thereby reflecting a democratic society.[7]

Commissioned as a high school by the state of Indiana in 1891, Muncie Central High School provided its students with the uniform course of study suggested by the state. Algebra, geometry, trigonometry, physics, chemistry, Latin, rhetoric, literature, history, and botany composed the academic course offered to the ten girls and two boys who graduated in 1894. The previous year, the National Education Association's Committee of Ten, headed by Harvard University's Charles W. Eliot, recommended just such a humanistic program of study for all high school students, regardless of whether a student would continue on to college or not. Statewide, Indiana educators were aware of the debate over the function of the high school. They, like the Committee of Ten, debated whether high schools should be preparatory institutions for higher education or for jobs. At this time, though, the issue did not have far-reaching ramifications since Muncie Central was serving a small proportion of Muncie's youth. In 1890, the 170 high school students accounted for only 8 percent of the total school enrollment in the city; most youth did not continue their education beyond the elementary grades.[8]

Student activities in the school at Muncie were limited during the 1890s. If students did have social organizations, fraternities, or sororities, as did students in larger cities such as Chicago, they did not surface in the school records. After 1894, students could contribute to an early high school annual, the *Zetetic*, or join the Turemethian Society, a literary group, but overall Muncie Central was an academic institution.[9]

After 1900, the high school's purely academic atmosphere was beginning to change as the field of child study emerged. In 1904, G. Stanley Hall published his two-volume *Adolescence*, which had a major impact on how educators saw youth. "Youth" was now seen as a distinct stage of development that warranted differential treatment, as did each individual child. Turning their attention from the subject matter to the student, educators began to change the curriculum to reflect these ideas. In Indiana, the state superintendent's office concluded that the high school, with its "foundation in the psychology of adolescence," should assist the youth in becoming an adult. No longer was the Indiana high school just an academic endeavor in preparation for advanced learning or a terminal diploma; students would be prepared for adult life. Rather than taking its cue from higher education, the high school was to be responsive to "the community and its needs." The introduction of practical education would not only meet these needs, but it would also instill habits of industry in its pupils and would appeal to a larger number of youth. Muncie High School began to respond to such pronouncements by the state by expanding its curriculum to include vocational courses. Courses once purely academic also became more practical instead of just theoretical.[10]

If, by 1905, the beginning of vocational education in the guise of practical education was making its way into both Muncie's and the state's suggested curricula, educators had yet to realize the potential of the extracurriculum for educating and controlling youth, and many educators did not welcome additional student activities, especially when they competed with academics for students' time and attention. Many educators felt that students were socially but not academically overextended. Mimicking a collegiate lifestyle, high school students formed fraternities and sororities and had busy social lives. Outside interests such as football, track, debate, and basketball dominated the social calendars of students, and Indiana educators found it "hard to see how much time can be left for study." Rather than encouraging these activities, state-level educators in 1900 urged teachers to cultivate "wise public sentiment with regards to the social life of students." The high school, State Superintendent Frank Jones thought, could be the means to control these activities and "serve as a center for the organizations and control of the cultural agencies of the community." Many educators, though, still saw student activities as a threat to academics. A heavy social calendar, to educators, was the nemesis of schooling.[11]

Educators had many reasons for disliking the student preoccupation with social activities like clubs and athletics. Athletics, some thought, gave a boy a "false ideal" of what would win him popularity, while fraternities seemed inappropriate for high school students. Fraternities and secret societies, especially, incensed educators throughout the country in the first two decades of the twentieth century. Fraternity members were reportedly more often tardy, absent from school, and less academically successful than students not associated with secret or Greek letter societies. Some states, such as Indiana and Iowa, passed anti-fraternity laws banning secret societies from schools, but the laws were never totally successful in prohibiting boys or girls from forming and joining these social organizations. In its battle with Greek organizations, Muncie's school leaders used just such a prohibitive tactic to curb fraternal social clubs in the high school. As late as June 1916, the school board required all high school graduates to submit statements to the board specifying any relationship the student had with high school fraternities and sororities. The board eventually instituted a school rule forbidding student membership in secret and Greek organizations.[12]

By December of that same year, a situation arose that tested the school board's resolve to rid the school of the Greek organizations. Student Evelyn Laughlin was questioned and temporarily expelled from the high school because she had been socializing with Holly Harvey at a sorority function. To make matters worse, three teachers, Hazel and Marcia Hart and Olive Spurgeon, had also been present at the forbidden fête, and the board threatened these teachers with dismissal if they did not fully explain their actions. Apparently, Spurgeon disclosed what her relationship was with the sorority and was reinstated as a teacher, while the Harts resigned rather than divulge the requested information. Just as quickly as this incident entered the annals of the school records, it disappeared, leaving behind an awkward silence regarding the fate of the Harts and Greek organizations at Muncie High.[13]

Such actions by the school board, though, could not deter social organizations from forming and gaining popularity with youth. According to the Lynds, former high school fraternities and sororities, kept active by high school graduates, did survive to become the basis of the purely social clubs for teens in the mid-1920s. Historian William Graebner's work on youth culture provides clues as to why secret societies were so popular and important to youth: secret societies preserved elements of community life threatened by the modern bureaucratic order. Graebner argues that secret societies challenged the ideology of a homogenous, meritocratic society—

the ideology taught by schools during the Progressive Era. Members of these societies, Graebner writes, "held . . . a vision [of the good life] that was particular, local, and even antimodern, and that placed a high value on community and mutuality." As such, the persistence of youth in forming and joining Greek organizations helps illustrate the importance of community in the first half of the twentieth century.[14]

Since students' propensity for social activities could not be eliminated, educators were determined to replace social organizations such as fraternities with teacher-supervised activities such as debating and oratorical classes, clubs, and societies. Recognizing that students could organize themselves for good or bad ends, educators started seeing student organizations as educational possibilities that could be "elevated to a more dignified and worthy plane" and would "satisfy and direct the social spirit" of youth. Already by the middle of the second decade of this century, educators' attitudes toward the extracurriculum were softening. While educators still had concerns about student overinvolvement in activities or the existence of exclusionary (and therefore nondemocratic) secret societies, the extracurriculum was beginning to be regarded by some as a "more than desirable adjunct" to the academic curriculum.[15]

Changes in the way adults related to children and the popularity of Hall's views on child development helped justify the establishment of adult-sponsored activities like the extracurriculum as a means of exercising control and authority over youth. During the first three decades of the twentieth century, an intensification of age-consciousness and age-grading made age differences more significant. While the school's age-graded environment helped shape these distinctions, other reformers involved with movements such as the Boy Scouts or the playgrounds created formal institutions as a means to manage youth's spare time. Boy-workers, for instance, found Hall's theory suitable because it subordinated class, ethnicity, and religious differences to the universal idea of maturation. These peer group activities organized by reformers appealed to individuals concerned with a perceived weakening of traditional social institutions. Many believed that the peer group would fill the void left by a supposedly deteriorating family, church, and community. That these people perceived a need to fill such a gap in the social structure attests to the importance of these values in the lives of many Americans, but their view of the development of the child as a problem to be managed by both parents and experts also attests to the power and influence of the new bureaucratic order. With these ideas and examples, a developmental and social rationale helped justify the entrance of the extracurriculum into the schools.[16]

The ascendence of practical education by the 1890s provided the pedagogical and theoretical justification for the development of the extracurriculum in high schools just when educators were voicing concerns over secret societies and Greek organizations. Educators who felt it was their duty "to unite education and activity by the closest possible bonds" found the extracurriculum the perfect method to do so. The curricular tide had been changing early in the century; courses in manual arts, industrial education, and domestic science, for instance, were becoming usual if not standard offerings in many schools. Funds from the Smith-Hughes Act (1917) permitted Muncie Central High School, like others throughout the country, to offer a wider selection of vocational courses. Between 1916 and 1919, commercial, mechanical drawing, and electrical departments were added to the school. The Lynds attributed the growth of Muncie Central's vocational curriculum to the needs of the business community which, by the mid-1920s, provided many jobs. Large manufacturing plants numbered fifty-seven, including the Ball Glass Manufacturing Company and Durant Motors (later bought out by General Motors), which employed 3,000 and 1,500 people respectively. Other industries included foundries, clay pot companies, steel plants, and auto parts suppliers. Demand for machinists, cabinetmakers, and electricians was also rising. To its sponsors, vocational education at Muncie Central High School was preparation for one's adult work life.[17]

If the local economy and business community were the spur for the practical curriculum, it received its official validation in 1918 with the National Education Association's publication of the Cardinal Principles of Secondary Education. Meant to supersede the Committee of Ten's humanistic curricular recommendations, the Cardinal Principles Report dictated that the curriculum should prepare students for actual activities in which they would engage as adults. The aims included health, vocation, citizenship, and the worthy use of leisure, and the Commission on the Reorganization of Secondary Education that issued the report gave its support to comprehensive high schools—those like Muncie Central.[18]

The practical curriculum had already introduced activities programs to the school, but with the language of the Cardinal Principles, supporters of the extracurriculum could promote it as truly educative. The values ascribed to the extracurriculum by the most frequently mentioned literature mirrored those values deemed important by the Cardinal Principles. The extracurriculum would give training in civic, social, and moral relationships, help in the socialization process, prepare students for leadership, recognize adolescent nature, and improve discipline and school spirit. Inherently practical, the extracurriculum was seen as preparation for citizenship: the school, with its activities program, would model the social life of the community and, therefore, provide the best education for life beyond the classroom. The abundance of literature by extracurriculum experts expanded in the 1920s, and most agreed with these basic, underlying principles. Indiana educators were familiar with this literature and most frequently cited the 1926 *Yearbook of the National Society for the Study of*

Education and handbooks by Charles Foster and Harold Meyers as useful guides in planning and directing an extracurricular program.[19]

Indiana's own state-level handbook for administrators mentioned these ideas about the general aims of secondary education and the extracurriculum's role in meeting them. Like much of the voluminous literature on the extracurriculum, this handbook stressed the administrative aspect—or possibilities—of school activities. Muncie administrators were quick to use student organizations in their attempt to control and oversee the students. In 1916, when the enrollment of girls in the junior and senior high schools exceeded 500, administrators appointed Elizabeth Kackley as dean of girls. She immediately formed the Girls' Council which was a group of eighteen girls, each of whom was a leader of a group of approximately twenty-five students. The leader was responsible for "the conduct of each girl in that group." We do not know how the group leaders handled misconduct or whether Kackley's means of peer control was effective. The leaders, though, used the Girls' Council to the benefit of the female student body. "Immediately after the organization of this council, activities were begun" and the girls set about furnishing a much-needed girls' rest room. The girls held fund-raising activities to purchase furniture, lamps, and oil paintings for the room, suitably decorated with a Muncie Central High School pillow. For the female student body, the Girls' Council aroused a "spirit of usefulness, comradeship and helpfulness" among them. Although originally formed as a means of conduct control, the Girls' Council quickly became an outlet for student initiative and for strengthening student community.[20]

While extracurricular activities were to grow out of the curriculum and promote young people's emotional and practical training, administrators and educators began to bureaucratize the extracurriculum once it grew in importance. The "curricularization" of the extracurriculum, as one expert stated, was occurring faster than most Indiana educators imagined, and the best way to manage it, most administrators and extracurricular experts thought, was to appoint adult supervisors and develop a hierarchy for school activities with participants, student leaders, faculty sponsors, committees, councils, and boards to govern the extracurriculum. In the handbook, state-level educators even told local administrators that the school's and the principal's reputations were "dependent very largely" upon the extracurriculum's standards and its proper management.[21]

Many contemporary handbooks elaborately detailed how the extracurriculum and its administration should look and offered diagrams, charts, and classifications of student activities to show the efficiently organized activities program. In all models, student groups clustered at the bottom of the educational pyramid and led to the apex of school control, the principal. One of these extracurricular experts, Elbert Fretwell, a professor at Teachers College, Columbia University, was nevertheless concerned about the "over-strong administrative tendency" which prescribed students' activities. The growth of youth, Fretwell said, required "a freedom to choose" on the part of the students; too much administration limited those choices, freedom, and growth. Nonetheless, the bureaucracy and control surrounding the extracurriculum continued to grow during the 1920s.[22]

Muncie Central High School's extracurriculum began to expand at about the same time as its vocational curriculum, its overall enrollment, and its administration, and it developed bureaucratic features such as a hierarchy of sponsors and administrative control. In 1911, before enrollments jumped and the curriculum was enlarged, the high school graduating class numbered only 68—more than the handful of students who finished in the 1890s but not large either. By 1924, the high school graduated 254 students and together with a new junior high had an enrollment of more than 2,000. The school's administrative staff also grew to include an assistant principal, a dean of girls, and various department heads, and its extracurriculum received strong support from the school's principals. Principal Jesse L. Ward and his successor Allen, who later became the superintendent of Muncie schools, organized and acted as sponsors of a variety of clubs. Having his tenure during the war years, Ward founded many service-oriented groups, while Allen seemed to be associated with athletic and pep organizations. Their support of student activities more than likely played a role in the expansion of the extracurriculum. Muncie Central High School was becoming a truly comprehensive high school with the bureaucratic structure to match. The extracurriculum was subsumed within this structure as the high school started to establish clubs according to academic subject matter and to organize students into homerooms, a favorite innovation of the extracurriculum experts who saw it as an administrative device to teach social and moral manners, school spirit, and citizenship.[23]

All types of clubs and activities at Muncie Central emerged during this period. Purely academic subjects remained popular with students, and clubs formed around those areas. The students of Latin, the most popular and prominent language studied at Muncie Central, organized a Latin club, "Res Publica Romana," for the first time in March 1916. Students also wanted to resurrect an old German club until World War I discredited the study of German. Because many academic clubs required the student to be enrolled in the specific course and even to maintain a certain grade, students became segregated in the extracurriculum based on their academic transcript. The Latin Club and the Home Economics Club, for instance, were open only to students of those courses, and the Latin Club further excluded itself from other clubs by holding a socially prestigious banquet annually at a local hotel for its senior members. Other more social and character-building clubs, such as Hi-Y, the M Club (a boys' social and

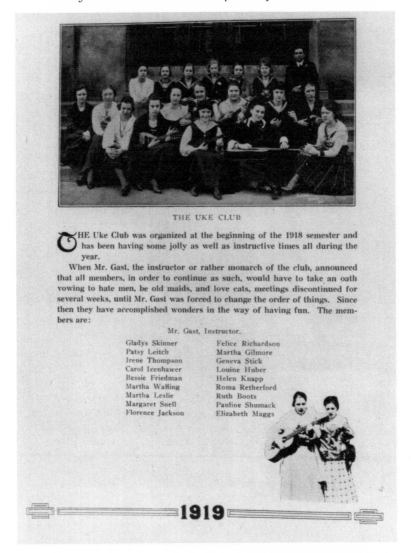

THE UKE CLUB

THE Uke Club was organized at the beginning of the 1918 semester and has been having some jolly as well as instructive times all during the year.

When Mr. Gast, the instructor or rather monarch of the club, announced that all members, in order to continue as such, would have to take an oath vowing to hate men, be old maids, and love cats, meetings discontinued for several weeks, until Mr. Gast was forced to change the order of things. Since then they have accomplished wonders in the way of having fun. The members are:

Mr. Gast, Instructor.

Gladys Skinner	Felice Richardson
Patsy Leitch	Martha Gilmore
Irene Thompson	Geneva Stick
Carol Icenhawer	Louine Huber
Bessie Friedman	Helen Knapp
Martha Walling	Roma Retherford
Martha Leslie	Ruth Boots
Margaret Snell	Pauline Shumack
Florence Jackson	Elizabeth Maggs

1919

Learning by Doing in Muncie. Source: *Muncie High School Annual* (Muncie, 1919). Courtesy Indiana State Library

booster club), and the Friendship Club (a club for girls associated with the YWCA), were both less exclusive and less prestigious.[24]

In Muncie, war efforts seemed to forge community solidarity at a time when many people recognized that society was changing and thought that the traditional structures of community life were weakening. One adult in

Be True to Your School. Source: *Muncie High School Annual*
(Muncie, 1919). Courtesy Indiana State Library

Muncie attributed a strengthening of community to the war that brought people together, "forcing men to learn to cooperate." Ellwood Cubberley, educational administrator and historian, noted the importance of the war in bringing citizenship to educators' attention. Commenting in the preface of an extracurriculum handbook, Cubberley stated that to many people, the war revealed the importance of education in a democracy, and, of course, the extracurriculum offered schoolmen and women the opportunity to train students to serve their community.[25]

During the war, as Edward Krug notes, educators saw service to the community as an extension of education's service and duty and associated it with the social aims of education. Cultivating solidarity and teamwork became one aim of the extracurriculum and, according to the extracurriculum experts, helped nurture good citizens. Leadership, initiative, "intelligent obedience to authority," and cooperation were among the good citizenship qualities that the extracurriculum was supposed to develop. A feeling of solidarity with the nation and the community entered Muncie Central High School, as it answered the calls of patriotism both symbolically (by dedicating its 1917 yearbook to the American flag) and practically (with war-related clubs and the teaching of patriotism in its academic courses).[26]

A bit of Wilsonian idealism infused the discussion about the extracurriculum and citizenship. In an article for the *Educator Journal* (Indiana's education magazine), State Superintendent Horace Ellis encouraged teachers—those self-sacrificing community servants who lead youth on their search for eternal truths—to be leaders in war activities as a means to defend and guarantee the faith in the future. Ellis encouraged both teachers and students to work in thrift stamp campaigns, liberty bond sales, and the Red Cross. A commitment to duty and service was visible in Muncie Central's clubs as youth took a direct part in the war effort. Members of Muncie's Junior Red Cross sold thrift stamps and participated in food conservation and preparation. This gave them "boundless joy and indescribable happiness," as they noted in the 1918 annual. The Home Economics Club made handkerchiefs for soldiers overseas and provided meals for the community during an influenza epidemic. No doubt overcome with patriotism, members of these clubs said they were "moved by conceptions of duty . . . replete with loyal service . . . [and] lovers of the Republic."[27]

Other wartime activities, for boys in particular, took on a more militaristic bent. Principal Ward formed a military drill company of fifty boys and trained them to be soldiers. Statewide, educators advocated military training in schools because, the *Educator Journal* argued, the boys would be future soldiers and soldiers with the most training are the best. These efforts by the school forged a connection between the youth and the community, and between the community and the nation. While youth had their own activities, the extracurriculum during the war involved them in the life and concerns of the adult community. The exceptional wartime pressures and needs inspired feelings of patriotism, duty, and service. These concerns for the commonweal—whether national or local—found an outlet and stimulus in the extracurriculum.

Even after the war, the idea of serving the community underlay many of the clubs' activities. The Drama Club, for instance, performed countless plays for Muncie residents, and the orchestras also performed for the community. School theater productions replaced more individual performance activities, as the high school sophomore, junior, and senior classes produced plays that attracted a sizable audience. These activities fostered connections between the students and the city.[28]

By 1930, there were enough clubs and student activities for practically every student's interest. Both boys and girls had debating clubs; students could work on the school newspaper (the *Munsonian*) or the annual (the *Magician*), or, if musically inclined, could participate in any number of activities such as the junior or senior band, orchestra, or chorus. Some activities, like the musical ones, even permitted students to earn credits toward graduation. Other activities mixed social and special interests, like the dramatic, girls' hiking, Pickwick (English), or Dauber (art) clubs. By 1927, these organizations and others had become a formal and accepted part of Muncie Central High School life. That student organizations even warranted a full section in the school's *Bulletin of Information to Assist Boys and Girls in Planning Their High School Courses* shows that student activities had come into their own. Muncie's extracurricular activities and educators may have been reaching into many aspects of the students' lives, but the extracurriculum also gave community members, both youth and adult, a place where their concerns, interests, and values could be expressed.[29]

Whatever motivated adults to organize school clubs, students learned to support them and, as adults, would sustain their support through community, civic, religious, or social organizations. Student clubs provided more than administrative control over students or even social distractions for youth. The Muncie Central High School club life prepared youth to become adults who became club and community members. Muncie's adult organizations promoted "those things which are for the best interest of the community." In 1924, Muncie boasted thirty-three secret societies, including the Masonic Order, Elks, Eagles, Knights of Columbus, Improved Order of Red Men, and Grand Army of the Republic. There were also thirty-two labor organizations and various civic clubs, such as Commercial Club, Rotary, Kiwanis, the Dynamo Club, and Business and Professional Women's Club. Through these organizations, Munsonians were "working hard to make Muncie one of the best cities of Indiana." Many Muncie youth probably had parents who belonged to these organizations and expected to join them as adults. As the Lynds noted, these organizations played a large part in community life. The high school invited these groups to participate in extracurricular activities and, in so doing, reinforced in the students the idea that involvement in and support of local organizations was dutiful and proper behavior.[30]

The extracurriculum and adult club life could have encouraged youth to structure their identities around separate groups: Latin student or business student, Elk Club or Moose Lodge member. Students could have developed separate, almost functional identities. Yet, students also developed broader, age-based identities, not only as youth (distinct from Muncie adults) but as age-divided youth who shared that same grade level with all other Muncie Central High School students throughout the community.

Within the school in the early 1920s, the senior, junior, sophomore, and freshman classes began to develop a sense of solidarity within their own grades. Each class held elections, chose class colors, and formed social committees that organized functions for their group, and the members seemed to pride themselves on the distinctions between their class and the others. Jokes about freshman getting lost in the building during the first week of school, about juniors being big-headed, or seniors being on top of the world abound in the annuals. Acting the part of wise veterans, seniors gave advice to their younger schoolmates, even if the advice was better unheeded. In a poem to the green freshman, seniors wrote: "Don't work. It is very bad for your health to tire yourself. Don't say anything when you talk. It consumes brain power. Don't study; it may affect your eyesight." Out of solidarity, the junior class of 1926 even referred to itself as an army, with their class president as the "commander-in-chief." Military "drives" were their dances and parties, and the juniors looked forward to the senior year when they would be "perfected" and at the top of the student hierarchy.[31]

Schoolwide solidarity and identity also emerged during this decade, with both students and community members identifying themselves as Muncie community members, as represented through the high school. This communitywide, school-based identity became most prominent when interscholastic athletics developed in Indiana high schools, although school administrators did not always support such school spirit. In 1905–06, the state superintendent's office thought that athletics were too highly developed in the high school and that class yells, colors, and excessive spirit were "frequent breeders of rowdyism." The trouble with this type of behavior, argued the administrators, was that athletics seemed to be the dominant force in the schools and that efficiency in work would decrease. School spirit would cause scholarship to suffer. As with the secret societies, though, the students' and community's valuing of athletics as a focus of school and community solidarity resulted in the eventual incorporation of athletics into the school system and the community's and school's life.[32]

Muncie students and adults rallied around their school and its athletic teams, especially the basketball team. In 1922, when a local newspaper first referred to the team as the "Bearcats," boosterism truly boomed, and students and adults had an image around which to structure a community identity. This school spirit embodied the entire school life and even adult

Hightops and Siss-boom-bah. Source: *Muncie High School Annual* (Muncie, 1919). Courtesy Indiana State Library

community life in Muncie. Bearcat spirit was athletics, organizations, and clubs; pep rallies, classes, the students, and their faculty also were part of what made Bearcat spirit. Muncie Central students realized that "the Bearcat spirit has permeated [their] high school . . . and pushed it to the prominence that it now holds." The student newspaper, the *Munsonian*, continually encouraged the further development of Muncie Central High School spirit, declaring that its motto shall be, "Boost the school and make it bigger and better than ever." By the 1920s, even school administrators encouraged such a fervent boosterism and community identification with the school. The extracurriculum experts believed that school newspapers and assemblies were good ways to create school spirit and unity, and Muncie administrators certainly used them as such.[33]

This type of boosterism led students to feel a strong sense of school and community identity. Students began to see Muncie Central High School as more than just an educational institution; students felt that Muncie was their community and the "Bearcats" their collective identity. In their informal interactions and relationships with others, female students even referred to themselves as "bearkittens," further embodying the school image, now made female, as part of their identity. Adults, too, began to associate a sense of community identity with loyalty to the school and the Bearcats. According to the Lynds, basketball dominated school and community life: "More civic loyalty," claimed the Lynds, "centers around basket-ball than any other thing." A school-based spirit existed, in part, because of the extracurriculum, though certainly not all people felt it equally. It would be simplistic to argue that school administrators could have controlled such spirit, channeling it to purely bureaucratic uses.[34]

Earlier in the century, pride in community and the school (apart from athletics) had existed, and the state superintendent's office had attributed the growth of the high school in Indiana to "the natural pride of one community" which had created "a sort of 'contagious high school spirit.'" By 1920, community pride was focused on the school—a bureaucratic structure in Muncie's modern world—but it was still a reflection of local community pride, commanding loyalties and shaping identities. While Munsonians adapted themselves to the new bureaucratic order and even accepted it, they also used those structures to sustain a sense of local community and identity.[35]

A combination of factors, then, made the extracurriculum appealing to schoolmen and women who realized that student social organizations could not be eliminated and who believed that guidance and control of such activities would be preferable to losing all influence over a student's social experiences. By the second decade of the century, adult-organized groups for youth provided a successful precedent for schools' involvement in such age-organized activities. With their emphasis on adolescent development, educators tried to shape youth's emotional as well as intellectual growth as one of their main duties and goals. Educators also saw extracurricular activities as a way to meet the practical ends of education, part of a national trend that was accelerated with the publication of the Cardinal Principles of Secondary Education. The extracurriculum also provided educators with a way of controlling and disciplining the students in a more subtle way than force. Joseph Kett argues that the transformation of the high school into a total adolescent environment (to encompass academic, vocational, emotional, and social experiences) between 1900 and 1920 led to "the virtual destruction of student autonomy." While Kett's interpretation is extreme, educators, nonetheless, stretched their authority over both academic and nonacademic student life.[36]

All these ideas coalesced to justify the organization of the extracurriculum as a formal part of the educational experience. Once accepted at Muncie Central High School, the extracurriculum quickly flourished. Not only did the number of clubs and activities expand, but the extracurriculum, including the athletic teams, became the focal point around which students, parents, and community members could rally. School spirit became synonymous with community pride and loyalty. Just before World War I, Muncie Central High School's curriculum and extracurriculum were expanding; with America's involvement in the war, community and national loyalty combined and the school became a site for the expression of these loyalties. The extracurriculum, in turn, was given an even more important place in education than it had had before, and its acceptance as part of the educational institution would not be questioned further.

By the end of the 1930s, though, radio, motion pictures, and government-sponsored programs such as the WPA emerged, which promoted a nationwide culture and possibly eroded the sense of local community that people in small towns like Muncie once shared. The institutional structures that once permitted people to bridge older, community-oriented values with the newer, bureaucratic ones still existed and were firmly entrenched in the modern world. After all, extracurricular programs still exist and are considered an important part not only of the school experience but of the adolescent experience in general. As William J. Reese and David G. Martin show in other chapters in this book, after 1930 people in towns like Muncie were unable to maintain their sense of local identity in the face of a national culture promoted by an emerging nationwide media and its advertising, which targeted specific audiences, whether by age or social group. The early part of the twentieth century, though, may have been a unique time when people were able to bridge the traditional and the bureaucratic values.

Extracurricular activities and clubs, in all their specialization and even segregation, share some characteristics of Wiebe's functional groups. Children learned to be certain types of participants in social groups and other groups that were organized according to academic interest and ability. However, the importance of schoolwide associations—not just juniors and seniors, athletes and academics, or Latin and home economics students—cannot be overlooked. As Redfield and Bender insisted, analyzers of community, whether historical or contemporary ones, should recognize both traditional and modern ways of ordering the world in any society. Bender encouraged historians to "probe [the] interaction" between "two patterns of human interaction"—such as between the traditional, nineteenth-century communal order and the modern, twentieth-century, bureaucratic one—and their significance in people's lives. As this study of Muncie shows, both ways of life were a significant part of the school. An identification with the entire school, as a "Bearcat," brought youth and adult together and was an expression of local community and collective identity. The extracurriculum taught Muncie youth the local importance of being a member and supporter of one's school, one's organizations, and one's community. Munsonians thus used the bureaucratic order and its institutions to bolster and sustain their sense of local community in the modern world.[37]

NOTES

1. Robert S. Lynd and Helen Merrell Lynd, *Middletown: A Study in Modern American Culture* (New York, 1929), 3–6; Robert H. Wiebe, *The Search for Order, 1877–1920* (New York, 1967), uses the term "island communities."

2. Wiebe, *The Search for Order.*

3. Lynds, *Middletown,* 434, 441–44, 427.

4. Examples of educational histories that stress social control are Joel H. Spring, *Education and the Rise of the Corporate State* (Boston, 1972); Edward A. Krug, *The Shaping of the American High School, 1880–1920* (Madison, Wis., 1969); and Robert H. Wiebe, "The Social Functions of Public Education," *American Quarterly* 21 (Summer 1969): 157–58 in particular. Also see Thomas W. Gutowski, "Student Initiative and the Origins of the High School Extracurriculum: Chicago, 1880–1915," *History of Education Quarterly* 28 (Spring 1988): 49–72, quotations on 50.

5. C. Warren Vander Hill, "Middletown: The Most Studied Community in America," *Indiana Social Studies Quarterly* 33 (Summer 1980): 47–57, quotation on 53. Herbert M. Kliebard, in the preface to his *Struggle for the American Curriculum, 1893–1958* (New York, 1986), briefly discusses the inadequacy of both the traditionalist's and radical revisionist's ways of looking at school development. Thomas Bender, *Community and Social Change in America* (New Brunswick, N.J., 1978), 28–43, quotation on p. 43. Robert Redfield, *The Little Community* (Chicago, 1955), 141–42, as cited in Bender, 42. I also attempt to avoid valuing the traditional community as preferable to the modern one. The dichotomous labeling of traditional society as good and modern society as bad hides how individuals saw elements of the modern bureaucratic order as beneficial to individuals and society.

6. Krug suggests that perhaps the extracurriculum and its clubs were in "imitation of and preparation for the complex club life of adults," in *The Shaping of the American High School,* 137. Joel Spring, though, in *Educating the Worker-Citizen: The Social, Economic, and Political Foundations of Education* (New York, 1980), states that

it is "naive to believe that social unity could be produced by extracurricular activities" and that "there is no evidence that extracurricular activities in the American high school created any sense of social service and unity" (p. 42). I suggest that the extracurriculum did create a sense of unity and community in Muncie. Wartime clubs and athletics, in particular, were rallying points for Munsonian youth and adults. The existence of a sense of community, though, does not mean that certain class, racial, or religious differences did not exist in Muncie. The Lynds noted the factors that affected community cohesion, especially the class divisions. But they also stated that at school events, "[n]o distinctions divide the crowds. . . . North Side and South Side, Catholic and Kluxer, banker and machinist—their one shout is 'Eat 'em, beat 'em, Bearcats!'" (Lynds, *Middletown*, 478–95; quotation on p. 485).

7. Muncie Board of Education, *A Bulletin of Information to Assist Boys and Girls in Planning Their High School Course* (Muncie, Ind., 1927), 5; Kliebard, *Struggle for the American Curriculum*, 30–58. On the comprehensive high school, see Edward A. Krug, *The Shaping of the American High School, 1880–1920* vol. 1 (Madison, Wis., 1969), 186, 276, 391–92.

8. *Muncie: Past, Present, Future* (Muncie, Ind., 1893), reprinted by Bob Stephenson and Bob Cunningham; State of Indiana, Department of Public Instruction, *Sixteenth Biennial Report* (1891–92), 43; *Seventeenth Biennial Report* (1893–94), 82; Robert and Helen Lynd, *Middletown*, 182–83.

9. Gutowski, "Origins of the High School Extracurriculum"; Muncie Community Schools, *History of Public Education in Muncie, Indiana, 1850–1990* (Muncie, Ind., 1991), 4.

10. State of Indiana, Department of Public Instruction, *Twentieth Biennial Report* (1899–1900), 464–66; *Twenty-Third Biennial Report* (1905–06), 724–33.

11. State of Indiana, Department of Public Instruction, *Twentieth Biennial Report* (1899–1900), 469–70; *Twenty-Third Biennial Report* (1905–1906), 731.

12. On secret societies, see William Graebner, "Outlawing Teenage Populism: The Campaign against Secret Societies in the American High School, 1900–1960," *Journal of American History* 74 (September 1987): 411–35. L. N. Hines, "Editorial Department," *Education Journal* 18 (February 1918): 316; Jesse H. Newlon, "High School Fraternities," *Educational Administration and Supervision* 7 (October 1921): 372–79, reprinted in *Readings in Extra-Curricular Activities*, ed. Joseph Roemer and Charles Forrest Allen (Richmond, Va., 1929), 573–82. Board of Trustees of the School, City of Muncie, June 2, 1916.

13. Board of Trustees of the School, City of Muncie, December 5, 1916.

14. Robert and Helen Lynd, *Middletown*, 215; Graebner, "Outlawing Teenage Populism," 435.

15. Jesse B. Davis, "Social Activities in the High School," *Religious Education* 8 (1913): 219–24, reprinted in Roemer and Allen, *Readings in Extracurricular Activities*, 81–87; State of Indiana, Department of Public Instruction, *Twenty-Fourth Biennial Report* (1907–1908), 16; *Twenty-Seventh Biennial Report* (1913–1914), 139; Krug, *Shaping of the American High School*, 136–37.

16. Howard R. Chudacoff, *How Old Are You? Age Consciousness in American Culture* (Princeton, N.J., 1989), 7, 72–78; Kett, *Rites of Passage*, 222–34.

17. *Magician* (school annual) (1916); Robert and Helen Lynd, *Middletown*, 196; Frank Allen, "A Survey of Central High School, Muncie, Indiana," (MA Thesis,

Indiana University, 1924), 21; Dwight W. Hoover, "Middletown Reindustrializes: The Case of Muncie, Indiana," *American Cities and Towns: Historical Perspectives,* Joseph F. Rishel, ed. (Pittsburgh, Penn., 1992), 96–108.

18. State of Indiana, Department of Public Instruction, *Twenty-Fourth Biennial Report* (1907–08), 123; Kliebard, *Struggle for the American Curriculum,* 113–15.

19. Leonard Koos, "Analysis of the General Literature on Extra-Curricular Activities," *Twenty-Fifth Yearbook of the National Society for the Study of Education,* 2 (1926): 9–12, 17–18; Charles R. Foster, *Extra-Curricular Activities in the High School* (Richmond, Va., 1925), 1–11; Harold D. Meyer, *A Handbook of Extra-Curricular Activities in the High School, Especially Adapted to the Needs of the Small High School* (New York, 1926).

20. *Magician* (1916).

21. State Department of Public Instruction, Bulletin No. 100, "Administrative Handbook for Indiana High Schools" (Indianapolis, 1928), 62; Franklin S. Lamar, "Extra-Curricular Activities," *NEA Addresses and Proceedings* 63 (1925): 609–14, reprinted in Roemer and Allen, *Readings in Extra-Curricular Activities,* 39–45; Elmer H. Wilds, "The Supervision of Extra-Curricular Activities," *School Review* 25 (November 1917): 659–73; Evan B. Clogston, "A Survey of Extra-Curricular Activities in the Public Senior High Schools of Indiana" (MA Thesis, Indiana University, 1930), 120.

22. Elbert Fretwell, *Extra-Curricular Activities in Secondary Schools* (Boston, 1931), 266.

23. Ernest J. Black, "History of Delaware County Schools," in State of Indiana, Department of Public Instruction, *Twenty-Eighth Biennial Report* (1915–1916), 271–74; Frank E. Allen, "A Survey of Central High School," 6–7, 44–45, 109. On the homeroom, see Krug, *Shaping of the American High School,* 138.

24. *Magician* (1916) (1923); *Munsonian* (school newspaper), 9 December 1921, 1.

25. Robert and Helen Lynd, *Middletown,* 484–85; Ellwood Cubberley, in preface to Fretwell, *Extra-Curricular Activities in Secondary Schools,* vi-vii.

26. Krug, *Shaping of the American High School,* 151; Foster, *Extracurricular Activities in the High School,* 1–7; *Magician* (1917). Academic courses reflected the emphasis on patriotism in 1919, and presumably throughout the war. For example, the history course's primary purpose was "to inculcate a love for country," while the English department claimed its courses would inspire patriotism. *Magician* (1919).

27. Horace Ellis, "The Patriotic Service of the War-Time Teacher," *Educator Journal* 18 (June 1918): 520–21; *Magician* (1918), 313; *Magician* (1919).

28. Dwight Hoover, *Magic Middletown* (Bloomington, Ind., 1986), 149–50.

29. Muncie Board of Education, *A Bulletin of Information to Assist Boys and Girls in Planning Their High School Courses* (Muncie, Ind., 1927), 26.

30. Allen, *Survey of Muncie Central High School,* 13–14; *Magician* (1919); *Munsonian* 9 December 1921, 1; Lynds, *Middletown,* 275, 286–87.

31. *Magician* (1912, 1923, 1925, 1926).

32. State of Indiana, Department of Public Instruction, *Twenty-Third Biennial Report of the State Superintendent* (1905–1906), 726–29.

33. *Magician* (1920), Dick and Jackie Stodghill, *Bearcats! A History of Basketball at Muncie Central High School, 1901–1988* (Muncie, Ind., 1988), 12–19; Hoover, *Magic Middletown,* 149; *Munsonian,* 28 October 1921, 2, and 4 October 1921, 2.

34. Lynd quotation from Hoover, *Magic Middletown*, 149. In the *Munsonian*, 28 October 1921, 2, a student writer referred to the high school as a community and made an analogy between the school and a town. The references to "bearkitten" can be seen in students' personal salutations to each other on numerous flyleaves to Muncie Central High School annuals.

35. State of Indiana, Department of Public Instruction, *Twentieth Biennial Report of the State Superintendent* (1899–1900), 436.

36. Kett, *Rites of Passage*, 187.

37. Bender, *Community and Social Change in America*, 43.

.6.

DAVID G. MARTIN

Gymnasium or Coliseum? Basketball, Education, and Community Impulse in Indiana in the Early Twentieth Century

A ngelo Pizzo's 1986 Hollywood movie, *Hoosiers*, gives a flavor of both the close, emotional relationship between the community and high school basketball in rural and small-town Indiana at mid-century and the conflict with academics that this relationship posed in the eyes of some teachers and others. In the movie, with the help of true love, both sides win. But, in real life, how did this conflict arise, how was it expressed, and what did the close link between the community and the school team reveal about the perceived role of public schools at the dawn of mass secondary schooling and the fundamental concept of community itself?

The association of basketball with Indiana, urban and rural, is pervasive today in the national sports media. It is central to the culture of schools and communities and is a source of identification and pride for the state and the region. This identification happened early, and it was accomplished through schools.

The phenomenon of tracking and the diversification of the curriculum into academic, commercial, and vocational programs in the early decades of the twentieth century was paralleled by a dramatic increase in extracurricular activities as high school changed from an elite to a normative experience and academics, the traditional justification for secondary education, was de-emphasized.

A principal justification for competitive team sports is their usefulness as a focus to encourage "school spirit" and community identification. And—since they involve lessons in competition, cooperation, and the relationship between the individual and the group—they are frequently lauded as contributing to "character." There is a parallel in the justification for teaching civics, which has also been seen as socially useful and morally beneficial. In the common experience of school, where social classes interact, the lessons of democracy can be drawn and children can learn to be "good citizens." But the ideology underlying loyalty to school and, through it, loyalty to community, is usually assumed and is less examined (both academically and politically) than the ideology linking schools to the reproduction of a democratic public. Nationalism, and the "patriotic" sense of belonging it engenders, require a degree of didactic pedagogy because the unit of nation is too large to be known directly. As one historian of the national idea recently stated, nations are of necessity "imagined communities."[1]

The community centered on a public high school, however, is not so large that it cannot be experienced directly. But what does that suggest about the insistence on the virtue of team, school, and community identity so well exemplified by the support for high school basketball in Indiana? Fundamental questions concerning the role of schools in the distinctly local expressions of regional culture are posed by the phenomenon of basketball in Indiana. While there is an abundance of literature on the national trends fashioning high schools in the Progressive Era, and the national debates over curriculum and the "articulation" of high school and college, there is less known about the variety of community adaptations. The urban model of a heroic superintendent as manager and system builder, a professional supposedly above politics and influence, is less than adequate when examining smaller cities and towns.

Writing about the 1940s, but clearly expressing a pattern that had developed in the preceding decades, historian Robert L. Hampel noted that

> frequent contact between small-town school administrators and the citizenry was an important aspect of school governance. The educational executives kept in close touch with their constituents. Of the superintendent's tasks, community liaison was particularly crucial. He worked with ministers, policemen, social workers, [and] town officials. . . . The tactful and sociable superintendent was much more effective than an administrator who closeted in an office and had no contact with local notables.

He goes on to note the particular importance of a winning basketball team, "especially in the Midwest."[2]

In the 1920s, when the "Hoosier hysteria" for basketball took on its essential characteristics, it was a phenomenon of modernity, not tradition. But in the popular imagination it quickly evolved an association with the moral values of rural and small-town life of an earlier era. Basketball seemed to stand apart from the stresses of economic development and bureaucratic institution-building that, ironically, made possible the system of state tournament and interschool rivalries, and the gratifications of the mass spectatorial gaze. Boys' basketball, while cooperative, produced heroic individuals who, having traveled afar to defeat foes, returned to the hearth to recount the adventure. Not unlike James Fenimore Cooper's *Leatherstocking Tales,* which were still popular, it recalled a nostalgic notion of the triumph of the frontier.

The game, in fact, is of no great antiquity. It was invented in 1891 at the YMCA-run School for Christian Workers in Springfield, Massachusetts, by doctor and educator James Naismith, to be played indoors during the winter months when outdoor sports were difficult. It was first played in Indiana at a YMCA in Crawfordsville in 1893 and was promoted at YMCAs around the state as an active, healthy, moral activity for youth. From its origins in YMCAs the game moved easily into schools during the rapid expansion of secondary schooling in the first decades of the century.[3]

Practical considerations contributed to basketball's burgeoning popularity. Unlike football, it requires relatively little space or special equipment. Indeed the "basket" came from the chance availability of peach baskets, which could be nailed to a wall. A team of five is easier to assemble than the larger numbers required for other sports. This was particularly important for small rural schools before the movement towards consolidation in the 1950s and 1960s. Basketball can be played indoors or out, a key consideration in areas of diverse and uncertain weather. Agricultural factors had long played a role in determining the American school calendar; and the convenience of the basketball season, starting as it did after harvest and ending before planting, contributed to the acceptance of the game by administrators and parents.

While there are distinct positions requiring particular skills, basketball is not particularly hierarchical or specialized. All players contribute to offense and defense, and everyone can score a goal. Communication, cooperation, individual quick judgment, and team strategy are rewarded. While overall physical conditioning is crucial, strength and size are not absolute advantages. Height matters, but quick shorter players have a role, particularly in the style of play typical in the early years. Physical contact and the risk of injury are less than in most team sports. The game can be played, or skills practiced, by boys and girls, alone or in groups, and well beyond the high school years. These are all attractions of the Greek gymnasium over the Roman coliseum—a distinction that would not have been lost on educators trained in the twilight of the classical curriculum. But there is nothing specific to Indiana about the above considerations, which could apply to schools throughout much of the country in the early decades of this century. While these factors doubtless contributed to basketball's popularity in Indiana, they do not explain the role that the game came to play in the state, a role perhaps most vividly demonstrated by the game's evolution beyond the humble gymnasia to the sort of coliseums, occasionally referred to as "temples," built and named by the Progressive Era boosters in cities throughout Indiana.[4]

In seeking to understand what basketball meant for the high schools of Indiana during the period of its rapid growth during the 1920s, it is useful to listen to the voices raised in opposition to it. While apparently popular with students and widely supported by the communities, the new sport was not unanimously popular. Alongside the rise of organized school sports in Indiana and in the rest of the country was a rise in voices warning of their drawbacks and abuses. The misgivings expressed by Pizzo's schoolteacher in *Hoosiers* that basketball was harmful to her pupils' academic endeavors are representative of the concerns of a broader national current that resisted the rapid growth of school sports. The most influential expression of this current was the Carnegie Foundation for the Advancement of Teaching. Its 1929 report was a major indictment of college athletics, which shook educators and received wide attention in the press and beyond as a significant critique of the emerging culture of schools.[5]

The decade following World War I was a period of rapid growth not only of high school athletics, but of college and professional sports as well. Increased concern with the ethics of sports organization focused on colleges where payments to ineligible players, the influence of gambling interests, and a host of other problems were rampant. This aspect of college life was satirized in popular entertainment such as the Marx Brothers' 1932 movie *Horsefeathers*. The Carnegie report is contained in two book-length volumes that systematically take up such questions as dangers in physical training and hygiene, alumni and fan influence on teams, recruitment, payoffs, bribery, intimidation, cheating, and the undermining of academics. The central criticism involves "commercialism," that is, the influence of money winning out over "love of the game." A major component of the philosophical discussion in the Carnegie study centers on an emerging conception of "amateur" as opposed to "professional" sport, with much attention being paid to the British experience of amateur sport and "fair play" as it evolved in the culture of elite boarding schools, such as Rugby School. Howard Savage, the author of the report and a full-time staff person at the Carnegie Foundation, had recently conducted such a study in British colleges and schools. Savage's American report includes a chapter on competitive high school sports and their relationship to physical education.[6]

The other volume is an exhaustive literature review and annotated bibliography of published and unpublished academic and governmental reports on school and college athletics from the previous three decades. A nine-point summary published in the *Journal of Higher Education* made these points starkly: "1. College athletics have a deleterious effect upon secondary schools. . . . 4. Coaches have an undesirable cultural influence upon their charges."[7]

The chapter on school sports pays particular attention to the often difficult relationship between educators and the community:

> It is normal for teachers of academic subjects to manifest active inter-
> est in the games and contests of their pupils and to serve as coaches or
> advisors of teams. . . . A similar interest is normal to the teachers of
> physical education. But not infrequently it happens that the proportion
> of victories won under such auspices does not satisfy the townsman
> whose interest is shown in selecting and paying a professional coach or
> trainer and donating his services to the school or its athletic association.[8]

That this phenomenon was seen as endemic and ubiquitous, at least by some in the educational establishment, suggests a profound cultural impulse. But the report's critique—couched as it invariably is in general terms of "townsmen" or "the communities"—leaves unaddressed the question of which layers of society were the driving force behind such boosterism, and for what ends. However, it can be inferred, from the financial form that some of the most worrisome involvement took, that local businessmen took the leading role: "Sometimes the professional coach is engaged by school authorities themselves because of the pressure exerted by town enthusiasts who desire winning teams, no matter what the cost. Even the openly professional coach is a more honest influence than the professional or semi-professional athlete hired covertly and given a position in a local store or factory in order to disguise his true relation to school athletics." And additionally the report warns:

> Town interests beyond school walls are making their influence increas-
> ingly felt in financial support to the association or to individual athletes,
> in procuring expert players, and in providing coaches, especially for
> football and basketball. In not a few towns, cities, and even states, school
> athletics have become less an affair of the school than an amusement for
> the community. . . .
> A community that finances the construction of a fine high school
> building out of the profits of basketball is in danger of capitalizing the
> excitement of the spectators and the notoriety of the players.[9]

Although teachers tended to support their school teams, there was an unease among a significant number with the glamour associated with school sports, a glamour not shared with academic achievement. This unease was fueled by the type of abuses revealed in the Carnegie report. In 1924, the *Indiana Teacher*, the organ of the state teachers' association, noting the popularity of basketball and the high attendance at school games throughout the state, had still been able to endorse the educational value of the sport for those involved: "The conduct required of the basket ball player is of the same kind as that required of the citizen." But in a 1930 editorial—reflecting stresses that were clearly building—the same magazine sounded this alarm: "Those who are interested in high school athletics might well read the Carnegie Report on Athletics in American Colleges and Schools. . . ." The editorial pointed out that the Carnegie report had found school sports to be "a highly organized commercial enterprise," in which "most of the initiative . . . has been taken away from the players and given to highly paid coaches." It cited such ill effects as diversion of attention from academic work, and the lowering of student "morale" by recruiting, subsidizing, and "over-grading" athletes.[10]

The *Indiana Teacher* also added, "The responsibility for the control of athletics should rest with the faculty and institutional head, and not with the fans, athletic associations, alumni clubs or paid coaches." This assertion is evidence that there was ongoing disagreement about who was in *control* of an area of school life that was already a big part of the new high school. The language suggests that "paid coaches" were not necessarily considered teachers. The article expressed concern that "Cases of professionalism, false grading, importation of players, toleration of gross immorality on the part of athletes, falsifying of school records and reports by the school administration, fan control of athletics, and even of the school board and administration, are to be found in Indiana public schools with apparently increasing frequency. . . ." The article concluded that "We must look for protection to the Indiana High School Athletic Association."[11]

The IHSAA had been founded in 1903 with 15 members, at a meeting of the state teachers' association. By 1928 it involved more than 800 schools, but some sense of the limited authority that this educator body originally wielded can be inferred from the fact that the state high school basketball tournament was first organized by the Indiana University Boosters Club in 1911 without its blessing. Given the IHSAA's initial weakness, it is hardly surprising that its attempts to curb local abuse were largely ineffective. An atmosphere of petty corruption seems to have been pervasive and widely tolerated. Calling amateurism "a sick joke," Phillip M. Hoose documents such practices as supporters giving cars to coaches, watches to players, and jobs to fathers—if they relocated and became resident in the school district. A former head of the IHSAA, Phil Eskew, observed that "The basketball players were important kids in anybody's town, and they could go anywhere they wanted. There were married and overaged kids playin' kids that hadn't passed a subject."[12]

Echoes of the Carnegie report can be found in high school yearbooks from the period, although (hardly surprisingly) yearbook sources are silent on any gross corruption or impropriety. A hint at some of the nefarious activities discussed in the Carnegie report, as well as the frustrations involved in functioning in this highly competitive sports environment, is contained in the 1930 Bloomington High School *The Gothic*, where, following the standard practice, each game of the year is recapped for posterity. "The season started off with a defeat by the strong Logansport team from the north, to the tune of 61–18. . . . The game was later forfeited to Bloomington." The forfeit was apparently the result of "ineligible players," an indication that there was both violation and enforcement of state association rules. The 1931 Bedford High School yearbook, *The Pioneer,* indicates that the Bedford coach, Charles Ivey, took that to heart to the advantage of his reputation: "He is a man who lives up to the laws and regulations of basketball even if it sorely hurts him. Ivey's frank, open-handed, clean game makes him foremost in popularity among Indiana's basketball coaches." It is revealing that in the eyes of the yearbook editors Ivey's reputation for eschewing corrupt practices apparently made him remarkable among coaches.[13]

Who were the coaches and how were they regarded as teachers? The extent to which coaches functioned as producers of winning teams—as distinct from educators of youth—was a subject to which Indiana educators gave considerable attention. Striving to maintain educator control over all the activities of the school, they sought for years to co-opt the "paid coaches," to bring them into the teaching profession, thus giving them responsibility for more than winning games.

Just prior to the Carnegie report, the *Indiana Teacher* ran an "evaluation" of the IHSAA, citing ten improvements they had been able to achieve in school sports ("it is a very rare occurrence now when brick-bats and rotten eggs are resorted to . . ."). But they also outlined six "avenues for progress," including "(1) The so-called physical director who is merely a paid coach; the physical director is first of all a teacher with a teacher's responsibility. We need to get away from the mercenary and commercial features of high school athletics."[14]

In 1927, the same magazine warned readers in a preface to a pro and con article on athletics: "He who raises any questions today about athletics is most certain to brand himself as a heretic." The following list, entitled "High School Coaches," consisted of summary data:

Small High Schools (1–150)

1. Average number of classes head coach teaches, 4.9.
2. Average tenure, 2 years.
3. Average tenure of predecessor of present coach, 1.3 years.
4. Average salary of head coach, $1,590.50.
5. Fifty percent of these men held degrees.

6. Sixty percent of these men could hold their jobs even if their teams were not consistently successful.
7. Most of these coaches do not have assistants.

Large High Schools (151–1,400)

1. Head coach on the average teaches, 4.1 classes.
2. Average tenure of head coach, 4.1 years.
3. Average tenure of predecessor, 3.2 years.
4. Average salary of head coach, $2,370.75.
5. Ninety percent hold degree. Highest, $3,200.00, lowest, $1,595.00.
6. Fifty-five percent could not hold jobs if their teams did not win consistently.
7. Ninety-one percent have assistants.
8. Average salary of assistant, $2,152.78.[15]

Data from the Bloomington High School faculty two years previously show that 56 percent had A.B. or B.S. degrees and another 10 percent had A.M. degrees. So, at least at large high schools, such as in Bloomington, coaches were equally or better credentialed than their noncoaching peers. For a teacher with a bachelor's degree, the maximum salary after four years was $1,580, or roughly the average for a head coach at a small school or the lowest-paid coach at a big school. For those with a masters, the figure was $1,800, considerably less than the large school average for coaches. Heads of departments, which as "director of athletics" most coaches were, would have received additional money under the Bloomington salary schedule. Although the search for a winning coach apparently led to considerable job insecurity, it would appear that coaches were among the better-paid teachers. The credentials of the coaches are an indication of the impact of the teachers' association's long campaign to integrate coaches into the teaching profession. Although it did not solve the problems it was designed to alleviate, an inadvertent consequence of the campaign was the tendency for successful coaches to be promoted to principals, and sometimes even to become superintendents.[16]

Clearly there was an effort at the larger schools to ensure that those hired to coach came with reputable teaching credentials and were expected to teach as well as coach. Whatever their academic credentials, coaches and assistant coaches are invariably described in yearbooks and newspapers by their sports pedigrees. The 1930 *The Gothic* gave this evaluation of the new athletic director and head coach (who arrived with two assistants of his own choosing):

This year opened the first year of the basketball coaching of Coach A. L. (Pete) Phillips at the Bloomington High School. In spite of the fact that from a won and lost stand point the season was not a great success, it is considered by most sports critics and fans a great success. . . . He came from Rushville where with only mediocre material he led two teams to the state tournament. Before that he had been at Wiley of Terre Haute, and before that at Angola, and had very successful years at these two places.[17]

A footnote in the Carnegie report suggests the extent to which Indiana was a particularly telling example of the phenomenon of high school athletics becoming dominated by community, as opposed to educational, influences:

> Some cases of "high schools built around basketball courts" may be found in Indiana communities, like, for example, Flora with a population of 1,441, a high school enrollment of 90, and a gymnasium seating capacity of 1,200; Martinsville, population 4,895, enrollment 500, seating capacity 5,000; Raub, population 258, enrollment 26, seating capacity 1,000; Veedersburg, population 1,580, enrollment 126, seating capacity 1,200. It is said that basketball is nearly as popular in rural Illinois, Ohio, and Utah as in Indiana.[18]

Other than New York City, these are the only public school systems mentioned by name in the entire chapter on schools in the Carnegie report. The national identification of rural and small-town Indiana with basketball had already been accomplished by 1929. Many in these communities would have been perplexed by the criticism of their new buildings. Paying for school construction has always been a contentious political issue. "Capitalizing" on local excitement and notoriety may have been seen as preferable to taxes, particularly for those with real estate. Some teachers might well have basked in the reflected attention gained for schools as centers of community interest and involvement. Corrupt or not, Indiana communities for most of this century have institutionalized the behavior the Carnegie Commission found troubling. Indeed, those concerned with the deleterious impact of the rapid expansion of high school basketball in Indiana cited the very practices condemned in the report. But the popularity of basketball facilitated the acceptance of expanded secondary education in communities otherwise suspicious of learned educational doctrine. By resisting other conceptions of Progressive Era school reform and emphasizing basketball, Indiana towns and cities were drawing on and maintaining a tradition of intense local control and direction of the use and purposes of schools. One advantage of financing gym construction through voluntary civic boosterism, outside overtly political and democratic scrutiny, was that local criticism was often subdued, repressed, or went unheard.

Today, seventeen out of the twenty largest high school gymnasia in the country are in Indiana, and twenty-eight out of thirty-six with seating capacities over 5,000 are in the state. Massive buildings had not always been deemed necessary for basketball. When the IHSAA began in 1903, and even when the state boys' tournament was launched in 1911, the venues for games were modest. Basketball was originally played in make-shift spaces, school auditoriums, Masonic halls, church rooms, barns, and stables—any space with high ceilings. The first gymnasia built specifically for school basketball were constructed around 1912–16. The push for ever-larger gym construction was a phenomenon of the 1920s.[19]

The structure of the IHSAA tournament is frequently credited with the community rivalries feeding the push for large gyms. Unlike most states, where schools are grouped into divisions based on size, the Indiana tournament was for eighty-five years, until 1998, organized on a strictly geographical "sectional" and "regional" basis. With nearly 800 high schools competing by the late twenties, small schools in small towns could always hope to go "all the way" and triumph over much larger institutions. This is the source of the drama in Pizzo's *Hoosiers,* inspired by the real-life story of tiny Milan high school's Cinderella triumph over Muncie Central in 1954. Any advantage that could be gained, including from the corrupt practices outlined in the Carnegie report, would be attractive and local accusations of corruption indicate that often no holds were barred in the efforts to bring glory to the home team. A legitimate "home court" advantage could be gained by having the elimination games played at the local school. Sectional and regional sites were selected on the basis of size. This accounts for increasingly larger gyms built in close proximity to each other but in rival towns, and such phenomena as regional games being played in tiny Huntingburg rather than in nearby, and larger, Jasper. Donald E. Hamilton compares this community competition to the nineteenth-century phenomenon of Indiana courthouse construction, where county seats built grander and grander courthouses in town squares, in an effort to establish themselves as regional centers dominating the surrounding hin-terland.[20]

The 1927 *Gothic* speaks at length about the new gym constructed in 1926. Citing Logansport, Vincennes, Washington, and Bedford, the *Gothic* explains that since "the movement for building larger gyms has started, it is only fair that Bloomington have the advantage held by other large schools." The gym was "finished in time for the Bedford-Bloomington game," which was preceded by a dedication ceremony. "The most promi-nent speaker was A. L. Trester, chairman of the IHSAA. He gave a very interesting talk and instilled a fine spirit in the crowd." (Despite the crowd spirit, Bedford won 29–22.) Trester's name is still on the state tournament award given today, and with good reason. Trester made a career out of keeping the regulation of high school basketball out of the hands of any-one but the IHSAA and in the process dedicated ever-larger gyms through-out the state. Under his leadership, the IHSAA evolved from a relatively weak body of educators seeking to regulate school sport to a remarkably

Gymnasium or Coliseum?

Hoosier Hysteria: Bloomington Panthers, 1930. Source:
Bloomington High School Annual, *The Gothic* (1930).
Courtesy Indiana State Library

autonomous and politically powerful body of athletic administrators
regulating each other. Trester did much to define basketball as a vehicle for
intercommunity competition and to promote it as a spectator sport. In
1925 he accompanied Naismith, the game's inventor, to the state championship played before a crowd of 15,000. Naismith found the new possibili-

ties for his game a "revelation." By 1927, Trester could report that the combined seating capacity of Indiana high school gyms had reached the one million mark, or one seat for every three people in the state.[21]

The language used in the Bloomington yearbook to discuss the school's new gym is typical. On occasion, the school had rented a gym from Indiana University, resulting in "a financial loss." Pledges were taken from the community to "guarantee" the new 4,500 seat gymnasium before construction began, when junior and senior high enrollment was 1,350. The community had responded and ticket sales were expected to "pay it back" in no time. After that a "profit" from basketball was expected for the school. The old gym had been built in 1914, and the team had won a state championship in 1919. "However," according to the 1928 *The Gothic*, "owing to the increasing popularity of basketball among the students and townspeople, the new need for a new gymnasium began to be felt." Construction reportedly cost $125,000.[22]

A 1927 thesis on the history of Bloomington High, by the head of the school's social studies department, remarked that despite being considered one of the "finest gyms in the state" at its construction in 1914, the twelve-year-old gym had recently been viewed as a "cracker box." That teacher viewed basketball and the need for a new gym as a measure of the growth and diversification of the high school. He noted that the faculty grew from twenty-nine in 1915 to seventy-five in 1926—including "the first coach to be hired to give all his time to physical education which, then, consisted largely of coaching basketball."[23]

The gymnasium for Bedford High School, one of Bloomington's main basketball rivals, had been built a year earlier in 1925, and also funded through the efforts of students, school officials, and community supporters. In 1930, Bedford's yearbook, *The Pioneer*, tells us: "Bedford High School's Athletic Association is the only organization of the school in which every student participates." "Sponsored" by the principal, who had also been the basketball coach, the association had already raised $40,000 towards the $80,000 construction. Making money to pay for itself was clearly a major concern for the basketball program. *The Pioneer* reports "$800.65 from the Sectionals and Regionals" but remarks that "at this time the proceeds of the season are not yet definitely known. The Association will endeavor to liquidate from 50 to 75 shares of the gymnasium stock this year. . . ."[24]

One indication of the amount of gymnasia construction taking place in the region is given indirectly in advertisements from the period by the Nurre Mirror Plate Company of Bloomington. The company sought to reach Indiana educators through large advertisements in most issues of the *Indiana Teacher* in the late 1920s and early 1930s, and also through advertising in the Bloomington yearbook. *The Gothic* ad for 1927 states that the "IHSAA suggests standardization of all basketball equipment" and lists by name fifty high schools in Indiana and neighboring states which had recently purchased glass backboards. By 1931 the list is well over one hundred high schools and a dozen colleges.[25]

The degree of student involvement in selling bonds for gym construction varied, as did the amount of money required for their purchase. In 1925 the Anderson Public School Athletic Association raised $100,000 towards construction of "the Wigwam" (home of the Indians) by selling $500 bonds to 200 people. This was a sizable sum in 1925, and it granted the patrons prominent season tickets for at least the period the debt was outstanding. A year later the Vincennes Public School Athletic Association sold 128 $1,000 bonds, giving a local bank enough confidence to lend an additional $100,000. A twenty-five-year lease agreement stipulated that all proceeds from events at the "coliseum" should go towards debt service. The school picked up the tab for custodial care, heating, and lighting. The Vincennes coliseum included 414 cushioned "theater seats" for "prominent boosters." The Kiwanis Club bought and installed an expensive organ, painted cream and blue, the Kiwanis colors.[26]

The 1929 sociological study of Muncie, *Middletown: A Study in Contemporary American Culture,* and the 1937 follow-up, *Middletown in Transition,* by Robert and Helen Lynd, provide an interesting contemporary account of the process of gym construction. The Muncie Central "Bearcats" were one of the most successful teams over several decades, but initially played at borrowed Ball State facilities. The city council had previously voted $100,000 towards a gym, while simultaneously rejecting a proposal to allocate an additional $300 to $1,500 earmarked towards securing an additional librarian at the public library. This decision was overturned "through an appeal by a small and unpopular group of citizens to the state authorities. . . ." But 1928 seemed the optimum time for a renewed effort to secure the Bearcats a home, given their victory in the state championship that March. Superintendent of Schools Frank E. Allen had previously been the team coach. Bypassing the city council, a "Public School Extension Association" was launched with pressure exerted on teachers to be among the 675 buying five-year season tickets at $50 apiece towards a $347,000 gym seating 7,500. Although the erection was euphemistically named the "vocational and physical education building," it was configured to allow large numbers to watch, not to play, basketball. Other purposes supposed from the title were obscure to the Lynds, and to some of the teachers with whom they spoke who referred to the building as a "white elephant." The $50 investment teachers were expected to make was equal to about two weeks' salary. Others in the community evaluated the gym in different terms. The Chamber of Commerce thought the gym worthwhile, recognizing that "thousands of dollars could not purchase the advertizing these boys have given Muncie."[27]

But 1929 would be the last year for such optimistic votes on the future, as the Depression fundamentally altered the process by which gyms were financed, at least for a while. Those in the Rushville High School Athletic Corporation who in 1925 lent the school corporation $27,000, interest free, toward an $80,000 gym were not paid back until 1944. The 1930s saw many Indiana towns using WPA and other New Deal programs to construct "community centers" for school basketball. Such public works did much to maintain skilled craftsmen throughout the state and produced many of the truly architecturally significant buildings from that period utilizing detailed stone and brick masonry. Examples include a gym in Peru with beautiful art deco lettering, and a combination auditorium and gym in Richmond with three immense entry arches and graceful Palladian windows.[28]

The 1950s saw a return in some ways to the pattern of the 1920s, at least in communities experiencing some of the sustained economic growth of the period. When the New Castle school board announced plans for a new high school, but not a new gym, in the early 1950s, "fans" formed an association to remedy the oversight and a new gym was completed in 1959. New Castle (now a town of 18,000) boasts the largest high school gym in the country, seating more than 9,000. Nearby Anderson's new $1.6 million "Wigwam," seating 8,996, opened in 1961 after the old one burned down in a mysterious fire. The decline of the American auto industry, the bedrock of Anderson's economy, and increasing construction costs, would make it difficult for Anderson to repeat their achievement in the 1990s.[29]

Local newspapers and radio did much to add to the community rivalry and boosterism that was the context for the growth of "Hoosier hysteria" in the 1920s, as did the relatively good system of roads and affinity to automobile transportation. The settlement pattern of evenly distributed towns and small cities, each in competition with but culturally similar to its neighbor, nourished the sort of boosterism memorably described by Sinclair Lewis in *Babbitt* (set in nearby Ohio). The local attention paid to basketball during the winter shifted at "March madness" state finals season to focus on the state capital. As recently as 1990, 41,000 watched the state finals in the Hoosier Dome, the largest live audience ever for a high school basketball game.[30]

One keen observer of the state tournament phenomenon in the 1920s and 1930s was William Fox Jr. of the *Indianapolis News,* who traveled the state by fast car at tournament time covering sectionals and regionals, building an understanding for his readers of the whole as it converged on Indianapolis. Writing for a national audience in the *Saturday Evening Post,* Fox remarked that "gyms are our nightclubs" with all the elements of that entertainment: a floor show, a band, and "bedimpled drum majorettes." Indeed the ritual, ceremony, and spectacle surrounding the games were integral to the thrill of attending the event as a fan. Although Fox writes approvingly, his comments underscore (and bring to life) the same enter-

Gymnasium or Coliseum?

"Buddy" Blemker [No. 45] and the Happy Hunters of Huntingburg.
Courtesy Joyce Blemker

tainment aspects of high school basketball that troubled the writers of the Carnegie report.[31]

In a controversial decision that suggests a sea change in the process of cultural production and consumption, the IHSAA radically altered the state tournament structure at its April 29, 1996, meeting. Rather than having all schools compete for one trophy, four classes were introduced, pitting schools of comparable size against each other in separate tournaments. This change, which brings Indiana in line with national practice, reflects increased reliance of television for entertainment, and the homogenization and commodification of culture; Indiana still loves a basketball hero, but increasingly that hero wears the colors of a college or professional team. The identity of community with school has been eroding since the consolidation of rural high schools in the 1950s and 1960s and since the introduction in many growing cities and suburbs of multiple high schools that compete for civic attention. Pointing to declining attendance at high school games over the last few decades and an aging of season-ticket holders, proponents of a multiclass tournament argue that allowing more opportunity for smaller schools to win—even if the win meant less—would increase community interest and identity. In a dispatch from Milan, Indiana, the *New York Times* noted, "The change is not going down easily among those Indianans old enough to remember Milan's victory [in 1954]." Matthew Moore, "a freshman basketball player at Milan High, sees it differently. Matthew is tired of playing bigger schools with bigger athletes, and he is tired of losing," although he acknowledges that "It's neat to have a movie about your town." In an example of how broader questions, such as generational differences in the meaning of community, can be expressed in Indiana in terms of basketball, Roselyn McKittack, the 61-year-old owner of a Milan antique store, asks "What are we doing wrong for them not to have pride in their home town?"[32]

It is noteworthy that the entertainment and community boosterism that basketball provided were benefits primarily enjoyed by adults. The use of the high schools as a vehicle for these purposes seems to have had little to do with the needs of the majority of students. Most of the educational and health-related justifications for sports involve playing them, not watching them. The Lynds stress that the school lives of Muncie's children were given importance in adult eyes through the school's team, the Bearcats. But the endeavors of the Bearcats represented only a small part of most children's real experience in school. It was, moreover, the part that was most mediated by adult concerns. The Lynds note that basketball was selected over "dance, dramatics, and other interests" also associated with the school. This is not just an aesthetic critique, because basketball preempted the schedule and affected attitudes and the dispersal of resources for the entire school. As the Muncie yearbook noted, "Friday night is basket-ball night." The Lynds are stark in their appraisal: "The relative disregard of most people in Middletown for teachers and for the content of books, on the one hand, and the exalted position of the social and athletic activities of the schools on the other, offer an interesting commentary on Middletown's attitude towards education." They then add "And yet Middletown places large faith in going to school."[33]

Among the striking features of the discussion of high school athletics in the 1920s is the fundamental nature of the options considered. The system of competitive team sports, at both the college and the secondary level, was new enough that one could conceive of radically altering it, or even doing away with it altogether. The Carnegie report survey of the educational literature reveals an elaborate discussion among educators at all levels about a system often perceived to be at odds with basic educational philosophy. While the system of school sports that was worked out in practice at most Indiana high schools demonstrates some attempt to avoid the worst-case scenario of no educational control, it represents a real compromise in terms of the educational philosophy of its day.[34]

Much of the literature on physical education cited in the Carnegie

report proposes a fundamentally different organization of physical education in the schools from the one provided by a head coach as "director of
athletics." For example, E. C. Cline suggests three major educational purposes that justify official support for school athletics: "(1) The health and
physical training objective, which call for a school athletic program broad
enough to include the whole school; (2) training in group activity—sports-
manship, team-play, . . . (3) providing a wholesome leisure-time recre-
ation. . . ." This last point is frequently tied to the idea of skills for lifelong
activity.[35]

One hint at the origins of the competing conceptions of sports appears
in an article reprinted in the *Indiana Teacher,* in which a professor of physical education from Teachers College, Columbia, makes this observation:

> For most of the nineteenth century, physical education both in Europe
> and America was viewed largely in relation to military goals. The drills,
> formations and mass effects were of the same garment out of which
> military tactics were fashioned. Whereas the military aspect has been
> more prominent in Europe than in America, many of the purposes of the
> school physical education here have been of military origin. Thus, we
> have had the notion that physical education was to develop obedience
> and discipline. Hence the emphasis on response-command exercises,
> exact execution of movements, and other forms of military procedure.[36]

The mass mobilization for World War I added weight to such military
considerations. The NEA Proceedings for 1918 included this exhortation
from Willard S. Small, speaking about the five million school-age boys in
the United States and referring to the opinions of commanding officers in
military training camps: ". . . above all, athletics must be utilized and
extended, must be made part of the training of every boy. . . . What of the
girls? Are they not to be thought of in this emergency? My answer is that
everything I have asked for the boys I ask for the girls. Racially the
educated vigor of women is more important than that of man."[37]

But, of course, girls did not receive the same treatment as boys. And in
light of more recent interest in gender equity in school athletics, the experience of the 1920s and 1930s provides food for thought. Girls' athletics
were a considerable part of the high school culture and, of course, winning
was not irrelevant. But, without the intense community pressure to produce winning teams that marked boys' sports, the school was able to
organize girls' sports along lines much more in harmony with the official
ideals of physical education as articulated by educators. A twelve-point
platform of "standards for girls' athletics" in the *Indiana Teacher* included
"1. Promote such programs of athletic activities for all girls and women as
shall meet their needs, and as shall stimulate interest in activities that are
suited to all ages and capacities." The introduction spoke of the "determination of women educators to keep their sports on a sane educational

basis, free from commercialization and over-emphasis and entirely wholesome," through an emphasis on intramural competition.[38]

At many schools this was accomplished by the Girls Athletic Association (GAA). In Bloomington, membership required "100 points" from
sports, or "for excellent work in physical training classes." The seventy
members in 1930 could earn additional points towards a "letter" by "making a [intramural] team," in gym class, and for outside activities. Extra
points were awarded for a diversity of physical activities. Organized
sports included basketball, track, baseball, soccer, dancing, clogging, and
hiking. (Boys had teams in basketball, football, wrestling, track, and for a
few years golf and tennis.) The sponsor of the GAA in 1930, Helen
Hodgman, was described in the yearbook as "a successful gym teacher,"
who encouraged "as many forms of physical activity for girls as time and
equipment afford. . . ." The justification advanced for the group's activity
was: "It is in high school that most girls lay the foundation for their future
life as the womanhood of America. Mental education alone cannot attain
the goal to which they aspire; it must be supplemented by physical education. . . ."[39]

The following year the yearbook paid tribute to Cora Purdy, saying
"Besides directing the regular physical education classes . . . Miss Purdy
has instituted a new department which has proved a great success. The
Corrective Department provides remedial exercises for all girls who have
a need for them, and a rest room is furnished for those not strong enough
to take any exercise [a euphemism for menstruating]." It is ironic that the
discriminatory attitudes that relegated girls' athletics to a low-profile
status seem to have allowed them to develop in a direction in which the
health and physical education of the female students was the overriding
priority.[40]

The gender-defined variations in how basketball was played in Indiana
schools suggests the role of ideology in sports. Girls played basketball
from the beginning of the game, although it had initially been conceived of
as a game too strenuous for them. Senda Berenson Abbott, physical education director at Smith College in Massachusetts, introduced basketball for
women in 1892 within months of its invention. Abbott was instrumental
over the next several decades in defining separate rules for women.
Among the adaptations deemed necessary were teams of six, rather than
five, and the division of the court into thirds, to reduce the amount of
running involved. Players of certain positions were restricted to designated areas of the court. As with the men's game, there has been an
ongoing evolution of rules and strategy over the years.[41]

Basketball was played by girls in Indianapolis schools as early as 1898,
with a first interschool competition as early as 1900, although such events
were rare. Abbott felt that too much emphasis on competition would
detract from the physical education and health purposes of the activity

and relentlessly discouraged interschool play while at Smith. A model of intramural play became the norm for women and girls.[42]

This thinking was very much in line with educational consensus on physical education for either sex, but it was only in the comparative backwater of girls' and women's athletics that such thinking could be implemented. Following a serious fight in 1907 after an interschool boys' football game, Indianapolis schools briefly tried the intramural path. Citing that example, an IHSAA official, G. T. Giles, proposed it for the state as a whole in 1912, saying of interscholastic sports "hero worship accorded participants is not in proportion to the intrinsic value of their achievement." He added that "the training for England's military victories was on her cricket fields, not their bleachers." Dale Glenn remarks that "there is little evidence that suggests the move to intramural sports was taken seriously state-wide." The virtues of the intramural remained reserved for girls.[43]

Much of the discussion of girls' presumed lack of physical and mental stamina, as compared to boys, strikes the modern reader as spurious, sexist, and downright silly. But it reflects the widely accepted medical opinion of the times, and much of it was written by women physical education professionals who were by their very examples carving out new opportunities and roles for their students and others in society.

And behind some of the discussions of what was suitable for women, there also appears an implied critique of the purposes and nature of sport in its male-defined manifestation. An example is a discussion in an essay, "The beneficial results and the dangers of basket ball," by J. Anna Norris. After discussing the virtues of the game and its educational value, and warning against overexertion and stress, she goes on to remark:

> It is quite possible for it to foster a spirit of boisterousness and mannishness, and this is especially likely to crop out if match games with other institutions are played, or if newspapers over-emphasize the event, or if games are played before audiences that treat them as spectacles. In such cases, not only is self-display likely to creep in, but rivalry may become bitter antagonism, so that good comradeship between opposing teams may be absent, and the lessons are lost that might have been learned by accepting the victory or defeat with dignity. The danger of the development of the wrong attitude is one of the strong reasons brought forward against permitting interscholastic games.[44]

Apart from the warning against "mannishness," it is hard to see why these concerns would not apply to boys' ball as well, as indeed they did. The concern that newspapers might "over-emphasize the event" is particularly revealing here. Apparently young girls needed protection from public salaciousness and display, but boys were to learn different lessons. It was not until 1976 that an IHSAA girls' state tournament was initiated, as the rules of the game and expectations of girls' athletic ability converged with those of boys.[45]

Throughout the 1920s, the social transformations driving the need for mass schooling were simultaneously undermining many traditional outlets for cultural expression and engagement. Basketball enthusiasm provided a new outlet and enabled residents of towns, no matter how small, to create a sense of "belonging" and continuity in a rapidly changing world—to imagine themselves as a community. This sentiment was important and enduring. In fact, after basketball was established as a central fixture of Indiana schools, it encouraged resistance to consolidation, a consequence of which became not simply losing one's school, but losing one's team, and thus one's sense of being part of a community. In a rather bizarre, but nonetheless revealing, episode the town of Onward (population 171) resisted consolidation in 1950 with nearby Walton (population 835), through civil disobedience. *Life* magazine featured a standoff that involved nearly seventy state troopers against fifty children in the barricaded school. They kept their team for two years, but lost accreditation, forcing attendance at the consolidated township school, which also soon disappeared into a larger unit. This is the stuff of legend and nostalgia for a vanishing rural lifestyle.[46]

The period in which basketball enthusiasm and hometown boosterism became established was also a period in which the Ku Klux Klan enjoyed tremendous growth in Indiana, a phenomenon that is not (now) normally associated with the positive community values commonly identified with supporting the home team. Historian Kathleen Blee remarks that "in 1920 Indiana was remarkably homogeneous. Ninety-five percent of the population was native-born, 97 percent white and 97 percent Protestant." Some historians estimate that as many as a quarter million Indiana women, or roughly 32 percent of white, native-born females in the state, were Klan members at one time or another during the 1920s. Male membership rates were likely just as high or higher.[47]

The racist, anti-Semitic, anti-Catholic demagogy of the Klan was, at one level, the opposite of the ideology of unity promoted by basketball support. The Lynds see the Chamber of Commerce, a prime team supporter, as a vehicle for promoting unity for the sake of business, quoting the president: "Merchants and farmers, Catholic and Protestant, bankers and working men—we're all living here together. . . ." But did the camaraderie of "all living here together" really extend equally to all residents? Parks were segregated and teams with black players were excluded from the YMCA. Jews were excluded from the Rotary Club, and the Lynds document the anti-Catholic hysteria that "ran like wildfire through the city" of Muncie in the mid-twenties.[48]

Revealing a somewhat romanticized view of the unity engendered through the experience of being a fan, the Lynds add: "An even more widespread agency of group cohesion is the high school basket-ball team. . . . Today more civic loyalty centers around basket-ball than around any other one thing. No distinctions divide the crowds which pack the school gymnasium for home games. . . . North Side and South Side, Catholic and Kluxer, banker and machinist—their one shout is 'Eat 'em, beat 'em, Bearcats!'" They tend to overlook the distinctions dividing the crowd—for example, the expensive seats reserved for those whose financial involvement in booster organizations gave them a powerful say in the running of the team.[49]

Nonetheless, the fervor of basketball support does seem to have been widely experienced as a fervor of (albeit illusory) civic unity, satisfying an apparent hunger for a sense of community. Broad town participation in the fan experience created an atmosphere of identity of community with school, an identity wider than the direct ties of student, teacher, and parent. While it was overlaid with differential perceptions by social class, a major attraction of enthusiasm for the home team was that it was perceived as transcending class divisions, and conferred on fans the gratification of feeling themselves to be part of a community.

But was the impulse that drove so many residents of small towns in Indiana to join the Klan really so different from the impulse that made them yell "Eat 'em, beat 'em, Bearcats!"? As the Lynds point out in a chapter entitled "Group Solidarity," the Klan couched its propaganda in terms of moral renewal, positioning itself as a vehicle to unite white Protestants otherwise divided by church, civic organization, or social class, in the face of blacks, Catholics, the foreign-born, and Jews. Its appeal was largely an appeal to community cohesion, a cohesion supposedly threatened by "alien-minded and foreign influence."[50] For what, after all, does "community" signify? As Ferdinand de Saussure pointed out with regard to linguistics, "There are only differences"—i.e., meaning is not inherent in a sign but is a function of its difference from all other signs. Likewise, in order for a community of "us" to really signify anything—to have a gut-level meaning for those who seek to experience it—there must be a "them" in opposition to which the community can define itself. Both basketball and the Klan spoke to this need. Intense rivalry with the teams of neighboring towns was indubitably a far less invidious manifestation of the urge to find self-definition through defining "the other" than the explicitly white, Protestant, nativist bigotry through which the Klan sought to define community, but the attractiveness of both were rooted in the same impulse to create a sense of inclusion precisely by excluding "the other."[51]

And, indeed, despite the wholesome image of the ethos of identification with the home team, it is significant that the "unity" that it seemed to embody was one based on racial and religious exclusion. Segregated black schools, such as Crispus Attucks in Indianapolis, were *excluded* from participation in the IHSAA and had to go as far afield as St. Louis to schedule a full season. Historian James H. Madison draws this conclusion:

> For much of the twentieth century the sport was largely the privilege only of white boys. Blacks played for a few teams before World War II but often faced barriers that limited their freedom to accompany their teammates into restaurants on trips. And the Indiana High School Athletic Association (IHSAA), . . . did not allow the state's all-black high schools . . . to join the association or participate in the state tournament. Nor were Catholic schools allowed to participate. In 1941 these restrictions were at last removed, though other schools were reluctant to schedule all-black schools. Change came with time and with the marvelous teams assembled at Crispus Attucks, which won the state championship in 1955 and 1956, and which featured the best player in the history of Indiana Basketball, Oscar Robertson.[52]

It is easy to forget, in the 1990s, that the Klan too once enjoyed a "wholesome" image. As Blee remarks in her extraordinary study of the Klan, "In the Indiana of the 1920s respectability lay in being a Klan member." As one ex-member told her, "Store owner, teachers, farmers . . . the good people all belonged to the Klan. . . . They were going to clean up government, and they were going to improve the school books. . . ." In Muncie, a "Klan stronghold, . . . many of the city's officials and business leaders" were reputed to be in the Klan. Spectacular Klan parades, replete with decorated floats and marching bands, followed by family picnics and fireworks displays, delivered excitement and entertainment throughout the state.[53]

While the Klan pageantry relished by so many Indiana residents has (fortunately) fallen into disrepute, the ritual, spectacle, and ceremonial aspects of school sports and associated fan activity that evolved so rapidly in the 1920s have proved enduring, suggesting that such spectacle serves a profound need for social interaction and for the celebration of a sense of community in which "internal" conflict can be at least temporarily submerged, as ranks are closed against the "external" enemy.

Competitive boys' basketball, and its enthusiastic support by communities across the state, was an integral part of the expansion of secondary education into a mass phenomenon, and facilitated its acceptance by diverse elements of the population. The adoption of basketball as a central element of civic life in small cities and towns throughout Indiana, and the commandeering of the new public high schools to lend shape and definition to the communities they served, had a deep and long-lasting impact on the problematic relationship of athletics to the rest of high school life, on the relationship of the high school to the town, and on each community's sense of its own identity. This impact has proved durable indeed, surviving depression, world war, television, and shifts in societal norms and (perhaps most notably the racial integration of teams), the defining features of high school experience and community life in Indiana remain, for better or for worse, profoundly affected by the innovations of the 1920s.

NOTES

1. Benedict Anderson, *Imagined Communities* (New York, 1991), 7.

2. Robert L. Hampel, *The Last Little Citadel* (Boston, 1986), 28.

3. Herb Schwomeyer, *Hoosier Hysteria (A History of Indiana High School Boys Basketball)* (Greenfield, Ind., 1990), 3.

4. Donald E. Hamilton, *Hoosier Temples: A Pictorial History of Indiana's High School Basketball Gyms* (St. Louis, 1993).

5. Howard J. Savage, *American College Athletics,* Bulletin Number Twenty-three of the Carnegie Foundation for the Advancement of Teaching (New York, 1929).

6. Ibid., 50, 52–76.

7. W. Carson Ryan Jr., *The Literature of American School and College Athletics,* Bulletin Number Twenty-four of the Carnegie Foundation for the Advancement of Teaching (New York, 1929). W. H. Cowley, "Athletics in American Colleges," *Journal of Higher Education* 1 (January 1930): 30.

8. Savage, *American College Athletics,* 63.

9. Ibid., 63, 60.

10. Henry Noble Sherwood, "Indiana Basket Ball," *Indiana Teacher* 69 (December 1924): 17; "High School Athletics," *Indiana Teacher* 74 (April 1930): 17.

11. "High School Athletics," *Indiana Teacher* 74 (April 1930): 17.

12. Dale Glenn, *The History of the Indiana High School Athletic Association* (Greenfield, Ind., 1976), 63. Phillip M. Hoose, *Hoosiers: The Fabulous Basketball Life of Indiana* (New York, 1986), 41–42.

13. Bloomington High School, *The Gothic,* 1930, 110–13. Bedford High School, *The Pioneer,* 1931, 144.

14. Norman J. Lasher, "An Evaluation of the Indiana High School Athletic Association," *Indiana Teacher* 74 (December 1929): 14.

15. *Indiana Teacher* 72 (November 1927): 22.

16. Kathryn Flanigan, "A Few Interesting Features of Bloomington Public Schools," *Indiana Teacher* 70 (September 1925): 8. Robert S. and Helen Merrell Lynd, *Middletown in Transition: A Study in Cultural Conflict* (New York, 1937), 291.

17. *The Gothic,* 1930, 95.

18. Savage, *American College Athletics,* 60.

19. Hamilton, *Hoosier Temples,* 4, 20.

20. J. Ronald Newlin, "'Middletown' & Hoosier Hysteria," *Indiana Basketball History: A Publication of the Indiana Basketball Hall of Fame* II (Summer 1994): 2. Hamilton, *Hoosier Temples,* 9.

21. *The Gothic,* 1927, 68. Glenn, *History of the IHSAA,* 90–145. Hoose, *Hoosiers,* 44. Hamilton, *Hoosier Temples,* 56.

22. *The Gothic*, 1927, 69. *The Gothic*, 1928, 66.

23. C. Roy Williams, "The Bloomington High School 1863–1927" (Master's thesis, Indiana University, 1927).

24. *The Pioneer*, 1930, 104.

25. *The Gothic*, 1927, 125. *The Gothic*, 1931, 129.

26. Hamilton, *Hoosier Temples*, 30–34.

27. Hamilton, *Hoosier Temples*, 32–33. Robert S. Lynd and Helen Merrell Lynd, *Middletown: A Study in Contemporary American Culture* (New York, 1929), 284. Lynd and Lynd, *Middletown in Transistion*, 291.

28. Hamilton, *Hoosier Temples*, 60. His beautifully illustrated book has an appreciative discussion of gym architecture generally.

29. Hamilton, *Hoosier Temples*, 69.

30. Drew Lindsay, "Hoosier Heartbreak," *Teacher Magazine* (April 1995): 38.

31. Quoted in Hoose, *Hoosiers*, 46.

32. Keith Bradsher, "Ending the Dream of Giant-Killing," *New York Times*, 9 May 1996. Lindsay, "Hoosier Heartbreak," *Teacher Magazine* (April 1995): 38–43. Kevin Johnson, "Hoosier Hoop Dreams," *USA Today*, 23–25 February 1996.

33. Lynd and Lynd, *Middletown*, 213, 218.

34. Ryan, *Literature of American School and College Athletics*, 203–39.

35. Ryan, *Literature of American School and College Athletics*, 208.

36. J. F. Williams, "Physical Education in the Elementary School," *Indiana Teacher* 73 (January 1929): 9.

37. Ryan, *The Literature of American School and College Athletics*, 232.

38. "Standards for Girls' Athletics," *Indiana Teacher* 75 (November 1931): 7.

39. *The Gothic*, 1930, 123.

40. *The Gothic*, 1931, 83.

41. Herb Schwomeyer, *Hoosier HERsteria (A History of High School Girls Basketball)* (Greenfield, Ind., 1985), 12–14.

42. Schwomeyer, *Hoosier HERsteria*, 113.

43. Glenn, *The History of the IHSAA*, 82.

44. Schwomeyer, *Hoosier HERsteria*, 43.

45. Schwomeyer, *Hoosier HERsteria*, 287.

46. Hamilton, *Hoosier Temples*, 98.

47. Kathleen M. Blee, *Women of the Klan: Racism and Gender in the 1920s* (Berkeley, 1991), 78, 125.

48. Lynd and Lynd, *Middletown*, 479–85.

49. Lynd and Lynd, *Middletown*, 485.

50. Lynd and Lynd, *Middletown*, 484.

51. Terry Eagleton, *Literary Theory* (Minneapolis, 1983), 101.

52. Indiana Basketball Hall of Fame, New Castle, Ind., exhibit on basketball at Crispus Attucks and other black schools. James H. Madison, *The Indiana Way: A State History* (Bloomington, Ind., 1986), 255.

53. Blee, *Women of the Klan*, 171, 2, 66, 136.

WILLIAM J. REESE

Urban Schools in Postwar Indiana

America's urban schools remained a faithful barometer of the major economic, political, and social changes that swept across the nation between the mid-1940s and early 1970s. Throughout the 1950s and early 1960s, public school administrators possessed a buoyant optimism, a familiar boosterism, reflecting the end of the Great Depression, the winning of World War II, and the dramatic expansion of the American economy. Public schools faced a steady barrage of criticism during this period, but school people also realized that their services were essential as the population boomed, suburbs grew, and increasing numbers of citizen consumers sought more educational credentials for themselves and for their children.[1]

By the mid-1960s, cities in Indiana such as Indianapolis, Gary, Evansville, South Bend, and Fort Wayne to different degrees faced a crisis of confidence concerning public education. Confidence weakened further as the economy deteriorated in the 1970s and suspicion of government grew following defeat in Vietnam and the scandals of Watergate. The hemorrhaging of economic life from central cities had begun in the 1950s, as economic investments shifted outside of downtowns and mostly white middle- and upper-class citizens moved further and further away from the poor, aided by federal housing loans, improved highways, and suburban development. Inner-city schools by the early 1970s came to serve predominately poor and minority group children, and their failure to do so adequately led to mounting public criticisms. For the first time since their establishment in the mid-nineteenth century, urban public schools were regarded as among the worst in the nation.

The years separating the end of World War II and of the war in Vietnam were obviously crucial to the making of America's modern urban school systems. For more than a century, citizens had regarded these schools as among the best in the nation, so their reversal of fortune in a relatively short period of time requires some explanation. By the late nineteenth century, cities were the first to build graded classrooms, to hire women in large numbers as elementary teachers, and to establish high schools; by the early twentieth century, they employed increasing numbers of educational experts to meet the various needs of young people. Urban school systems had become complex bureaucracies, highly consolidated and centralized and increasingly run by credentialed professionals. While poor and minority children attended urban schools, the majority dropped out before high school in the decades preceding the Great Depression; they often went to work to help their families survive. While concerned with the high withdrawal rate of students, educators accepted, however grudgingly, the reality that they had little impact or responsibility for the education and welfare of most poor teenagers. This also meant that urban schools were not equated as they are today so exclusively with the education of the economically disadvantaged.[2]

Before the 1960s, in Indiana as elsewhere, ambitious teachers often eagerly left rural and small-town schools for urban teaching positions, which offered higher pay and, they believed, better working conditions. Individual schools within cities varied in terms of academic quality, but the systems as a whole were often seen as centers of innovation. For example, lay people and professional educators in the early decades of the twentieth century literally came from around the globe to study the Gary schools, regarded as one of America's premier educational systems. Whether or not they agreed with the particular curricular philosophy undergirding Gary's approach to work, study, and play, many citizens realized that urban schools were often in the forefront of pedagogical change. Prominent educators almost uniformly called for the elimination of small rural schools, hoping to make innovations first tested in the city universal.[3]

The equation of growth with progress was common in American life generally in the twentieth century, and so it was within the schools. Given the paucity of jobs for teenagers in the 1930s, enrollments had even grown in hard times as high school attendance in particular skyrocketed. This reinforced the idea among educators that bigger was better, that with each passing decade more and more children would seek additional years of schooling, often in increasingly consolidated systems modeled after the city. In Indiana, the Gary schools were undoubtedly the most publicized across the state and nation, but various schools elsewhere also became very well known. Shortridge High of Indianapolis was long regarded as a premier academic institution for the college bound, and Arsenal Technical High School became a leading comprehensive high school, offering an array of high-quality curricula from the academic through the vocational.[4]

Such heady optimism and pride in things urban survived the depression and World War II, exemplified in a statewide educational study commissioned in 1947 by the Indiana State Teachers Association. Since the turn of the century, most of Indiana's organized teachers had fought for traditional bread-and-butter issues: pensions, better pay, and smaller class sizes. The leadership of the state teachers' association had a distinct urban bias. Its journal, the *Indiana Teacher*, traditionally had joined with administrators to urge the consolidation of smaller schools, which were especially prominent in rural areas and small towns, and the elimination of the power of the township trustee, whose control of schools in hundreds of districts blunted the authority of superintendents and autonomy of teachers. The organization's journal regularly emphasized that urban teachers enjoyed higher salaries, more job security, and better professional opportunities than anywhere else in the state.[5]

The newly appointed Indiana School Study Commission did its work quickly, releasing its preliminary findings in 1948 and issuing its final report the following year. A few dozen prominent lay people and professional educators served on the blue-ribbon commission, generously funded by the state teachers' organization. From the elementary grades through high school, said the commission, city schools were superior to those operated in towns and especially those run in more rural areas by township trustees. Since the years following the Civil War, city and town schools were governed formally by a small board of education, which to an increasing degree in this century delegated the responsibility of running schools to a superintendent and his administrative subordinates. In the jargon of educational leaders in the early 1900s, the board served a legislative function while the superintendent was the chief executive. Township schools, in contrast, were run by the local township trustee, who tightly controlled administrators, teachers, and the purse strings, an affront to the emerging educational profession.[6]

The commission reported that "on the whole, the city elementary schools are providing a much more adequate program than are the rural schools. These differences are to be accounted for by such factors as length of school term, training level of teachers, teacher turnover, school buildings and equipment, and administrative and supervisory services." Like many previous studies that compared rural and urban schools, the commission emphasized that "curriculum practices are more desirable in the larger administrative units, where research is utilized to a greater degree in curriculum planning and specialized leadership is provided more often to help with curriculum improvement. In the city schools, the curriculum generally is better adapted to local conditions and needs."[7]

The members of the commission, who were disproportionally drawn from the larger school districts, shared many of the guiding assumptions of urban educators in the first half of the twentieth century. That is, they assumed, for example, that consolidated schools offered the finest education, that large high schools were preferable to small ones, and that hiring more certified teachers and specialists would improve the schools. Removing as many lay people as possible from decision making—apart from parent participation in PTA's and citizen lobbying for bond issues—was sound educational policy; experts—whether superintendents, researchers, counselors, psychologists, or teachers—knew what was most appropriate for youth. And the most progress along these lines, of course, had occurred in the cities.[8]

Impressed with the efficiencies of scale in industrial plants, school reformers throughout the early twentieth century began talking the language of business efficiency and educational productivity. Schoolhouses in cities became "school plants," and the industrial model proved very influential. Business metaphors peppered the report by the Indiana School Study Commission, which uncritically assumed that small rural schools were inferior, anachronisms in a sophisticated world of large-scale organization. Characteristically, the commission noted that the size and character of high schools varied in different types of school districts. The median enrollment of high schools in townships was 78 but jumped to 183 in towns and 467 in cities. Township schools could not hope to offer youth large libraries, well-equipped science laboratories, or other urban advantages. Moreover, many teachers in small high schools reportedly taught subjects in which they lacked any mastery or credentials.[9]

Teenagers in township high schools also had fewer choices of study. Most enrolled in the traditional academic curricula; their city cousins, in contrast, chose from among alternative vocational tracks. Since wide access to common courses was standard there, small places also lacked sufficient counseling and guidance services and enough after-school activities. "Other than basketball," claimed the commission, "large numbers of small schools have no activity program to give pupils opportunities in social living in addition to the training received in course assignments. On the other hand, most large schools have a full program of activities in athletics, music, speech and dramatics, club organizations, and school publications."[10]

While the Indiana School Study Commission downplayed the achievements of small schools and exaggerated the benefits of larger ones, it reflected well the dominant perspective of leading citizens and educators, especially those who controlled the leading professional associations. This perspective prevailed at the annual meetings of superintendents, principals, and teachers, informed the leading pedagogical journals, and characterized the speeches and publications emanating from the office of the state department of public instruction and its many divisions. The commission recommended the elimination of small schools, the creation of more hierarchical systems, the hiring of more credentialed administrators and teachers, the expansion of vocational education for the non-college bound, the growth of more guidance, counseling, and testing programs to identify "individual" and "group" needs, and other familiar urban remedies for modern educational problems. In assuming that what was good for Hoosier cities was basically good for everyone, the commission reflected what leading school leaders and administrators throughout America believed at mid-century.[11]

It takes some imagination to realize that city schools, having fallen upon difficult times today, were held in such high esteem less than a few decades ago. With their concentrated populations, higher tax bases, and commercial and industrial advantages, however, cities were understandably seen by an emerging educational profession as the best hope for the public schools. Every census demonstrated that schools were growing in importance, with enrollments and budgets often expanding dramatically. Growth seemed endless. As the baby boom burst forth after the war, more systemwide growth seemed almost inevitable, expanding the authority of superintendents, principals, counselors, and teachers.

In the 1940s and 1950s, most leading school administrators in Indiana as elsewhere had been reared in a common tradition, one that elevated expertise over the opinions of lay people, that emphasized the benefits of intelligence tests and standardized exams, and that claimed that the largest units of supervision led to better schooling. Many of these educational leaders had grown up in and often previously worked in small communities and assumed that being commander of a city system represented the pinnacle of one's academic career. Coming of age during decades of school expansion, they had little to bequeath to their successors in the late 1960s and 1970s, who were ill equipped to know how to respond effectively or creatively when enrollments declined, when poor and nonwhite children became the majority in classrooms, and when rich suburban schools took center stage.[12]

As historians David Tyack and Elisabeth Hansot note in their history of educational leadership, most urban administrators in the 1950s worked out of an intellectual framework forged in the early twentieth century. They embraced science, expertise, models of business organization and efficiency, and bureaucracy and hierarchy. They could not have anticipated all of the criticisms they would face in the 1950s—that the schools were godless, or academically lame, or responsible for the decline of American scientific prowess after the embarrassment of Sputnik, or wrongly segregated by race. But they understandably thought as enrollments expanded and school construction boomed in many towns and cities that the decade would be marked by "business-as-usual." Prominent leaders within Indiana's urban systems confidently assumed that their school bureaucracies would grow and that public criticisms could be answered or downplayed through proper public relations. There were many signs after the war of a bountiful educational future.[13]

In 1948, as the Indiana State Teachers Association released its preliminary findings, Indianapolis was the state's largest school district, enrolling more than 56,000 pupils. Gary's once-famed system, which had lost its luster as its ideas became well known, enrolled more than 21,000, while Evansville had more than 17,000, Fort Wayne 15,000, with South Bend close behind. The School Reorganization Act of 1959 greatly stimulated the consolidation of schools in rural areas, as the number of school districts and township schools rapidly declined. In the cities, however, which were already fairly consolidated, enrollments grew because of the baby boom after 1946, because of their still robust industrial and commercial economies, and also in some cases because of the annexation of nearby townships. By 1960, Indianapolis enrollments had nearly doubled from the late 1940s to more than 96,000 students; Gary's did double to more than 44,000. Fort Wayne's student numbers exceeded 35,000, and Evansville's and South Bend's were more than 31,000.[14]

Administrators running these systems assumed that emerging demands for change could be addressed within the existing educational structures. Cities would build more schools, hire more administrators and teachers, extend the holding power of high schools to prevent juvenile delinquency, and thus realize the promise of equal educational opportunity for every child. Schools would do so mainly through a differentiated curriculum that met the "needs" of every individual and group. The population of nonwhite students grew in each of these cities after the war, but neither that fact nor the rumblings of the emerging civil rights movement, pressing for racial integration, seemed to dim the optimism of many educators.[15]

Evansville's educational leaders, like those elsewhere, were enthusiastic about rising enrollments and further school consolidation. Throughout the 1950s, the *Public Schools Bulletin*, the public relations organ of the superintendent, championed the cause of consolidation. Some neighboring townships voted against the opportunity to join their urban cousin in 1957, but Perry, Center, Pigeon, and Knight Townships finally consolidated with Evansville in 1957. Superintendent Ralph Becker proudly announced in January of 1958 that "the new corporation operates 41 separate school plants with a total pupil enrollment of approximately 28,000."[16]

The new Evansville School Corporation employed 1,634 persons, 1,119 of them teachers. With obvious pride befitting the booster spirit, Becker noted that through increased enrollment Evansville was now "the third largest corporation in the state, behind Indianapolis and Gary," and he believed that "the new corporation should be able to serve the educational needs of our greater community more efficiently . . . particularly as our city expands and grows." Becker feared not the dark satanic mills of school bureaucracy but welcomed the expansion, even stating that "we hope that in spite of our size, we will be able to maintain close personal relationships within our system. All of us want our new school system to be a friendly and democratic place in which to work." By 1962, all of the school corporations of Vanderburgh County joined together to form the Evansville-Vanderburgh County School Corporation, continuing the process of growth and consolidation. Herbert Erdmann, the new superintendent, could write as late as 1964 that, with a staff of more than 2,000 people, serving 32,000 students, "one of the rewards of working in the field of education is the opportunity to watch growth," in its many guises.[17]

This faith in bigness was universal in the cities. *The School City Trend,* which emanated from the office of South Bend's superintendent, applauded the passage of the School Reorganization Act of 1959 by the General Assembly, which accelerated the consolidation of township districts, and he also praised local efforts to absorb surrounding townships. Superintendent Alexander Jardine, who had previously been an administrator in Evansville, editorialized in 1960 that everything pointed with favor toward school consolidation. "Specifically, it is believed that larger districts can offer an educational program that will meet the needs and interests of all pupils. It is doubtful that a small one can," for little places lacked enough expertise, administrative supervision, vocational education programs, counselors, and the best teachers. In larger districts, "school plants are more adequate, school sites more extensive, and facilities more numerous." Despite reactions in some of the townships against consolidation in the early 1960s, Jardine happily announced the creation of the South Bend Community School Corporation in 1962, enrolling more than 33,000 pupils in 50 schools, taught by more than 1,300 teachers, governed by a centralized, appointed school board. Would growth have no end?[18]

Throughout the state, in response to the baby boom, towns and cities prepared for the increased enrollments by consolidating more districts in the interest of efficiency and by building or remodeling thousands of schools. Throughout the 1950s, experts in the School of Education at the state university in Bloomington were paid to advise local districts on how to respond to the rising enrollments. In 1962 the head of the Division of Schoolhouse Planning in the state superintendent's office noted that "a new school structure or an addition is now being completed every two and a half days in Indiana. . . . " That same year, the superintendent of the Vigo County School Corporation, newly organized in Terre Haute, boasted that the system now had 13 secondary schools, and he announced plans to reinvigorate and extend programs in vocational education. Consolidation was not welcomed everywhere, however. Late in the decade, Indianapolis, with a growing minority population, saw its school boundaries contained largely in historic Center Township, as Republican Mayor Richard Lugar and his allies merged county and city government in 1969, except for the schools. This relegated poor and minority students to the central city, allowing suburban development to advance without concern for those left behind in a worsening economic situation.[19]

Between the late 1940s and early 1960s, Indiana's urban school leaders often evoked an air of confidence about themselves and about the mission of the public schools. Such hopefulness evaporated in later decades. Educational leaders fretted about the recurrent criticisms lodged against the schools after the war, but they pressed forward with what seemed to them sound educational theory and practice. The economy was booming, and so were the schools. America was the most powerful nation on earth, her schools the most inclusive and expansive. The faith of educators in the capacity of the schools to adapt themselves to contemporary needs and criticisms sometimes seemed inexhaustible. Despite the saturation of the culture in the values of materialism and consumption, which the schools furthered, school leaders retained their missionary zeal and quasi-religious tone.[20]

Schoolmen after World War II prized the concept of equality of educational opportunity as central to their work. They defined the phrase in a particular way, emphasizing that only with the expansion of more guidance and counseling services, the application of more tests and measurements, and more emphasis on vocational education could the schools realize this lofty goal. When critics in the 1950s said schools needed to respond to man-power shortages, urban educators did not flinch, seeing this as only an extension of existing practices. Federally funded programs for the gifted in science, mathematics, and other subjects were welcomed. Linking schools to work was not in itself an especially novel idea. Since the turn of the century, urban schools had begun emphasizing more vocational and less academic subjects to students, especially those who did poorly in school and fared badly on standardized tests. Urban schools at mid-century remained committed to preparing youth for the world of work to help enable them to find their niche in an interdependent, democratic society, made more crucial because of the threats of communism and the Soviet Union.[21]

School people after the war strenuously denounced godless philosophies such as atheism and communism and praised the American free enterprise system and something called the "American Way of Life." Social studies textbooks lost the critical edge that, for example, had sometimes characterized them in the 1930s, joining in a patriotic, missionary crusade against the Soviet Union. America, said most spokesmen for the schools, was blessed by God with material prosperity, yet that did not make schools materialistic, as some critics claimed. School prayers and Bible reading were common in Indiana's urban classrooms during the 1950s and 1960s, backed by over a century of tradition and regarded as compatible with the schools' enhanced vocational orientation in an intensely consumer culture. America was a cornucopia of consumer goods and still God's favored nation.[22]

Postwar champions of the urban schools were confident, not complacent. Americans lived in propitious times, wrote Charles L. Farrington, president of the Indianapolis Board of School Commissioners in 1948, in a preface to an in-house volume entitled *To Form a More Perfect Union*. Many Americans had recently given their lives to secure freedom at home and abroad, and it was incumbent upon the schools to maintain and defend the "American Way of Life." As one unnamed contributor to the volume, probably the city superintendent, wrote, "If men are to be free, they must have free institutions which foster individual initiative, recognize potential leadership, and stimulate industry, courage, and self-reliance in individual citizens. The world around, knowledge, technical skills, and competent and wise leadership go hand in hand with human progress." Horace Mann had said it best: that public schools were the greatest discovery of mankind.[23]

However, unlike Mann's generation, whose missionary zeal had spread the gospel of free public education, urban schools—whether in Indianapolis or elsewhere—had long abandoned the idea of educating pupils in common subjects in common schools. Since the turn of the century, urban systems gradually adopted policies that effectively denied youth access to the same knowledge. Classroom teachers created ability groups, usually around student reading competence, in graded elementary schools; elaborate achievement and psychological testing, increasingly utilized in many towns and cities by the 1920s, helped track high school pupils into different curricular streams from the academic to the vocational. As readers were reminded in *To Form a More Perfect Union*, the modern American republic was a complex yet democratic society, and schools necessarily promoted the idea of equality of educational opportunity, which was not synonymous with the same education for everyone.[24]

"To establish justice, equality of opportunity, in the educational sense, does not mean that all children should take identical courses of study," continued the report. "On the contrary, it means that each child should be given the training most suitable for his needs." In the modern economy, a division of labor had produced a bountiful consumer-oriented, democratic culture, something schools had to nurture. Schools had differentiated programs because the "interests, aptitudes, and capacities" of individuals differed so dramatically. In Indianapolis, citywide testing for placement purposes existed for everyone in grades one, four, and seven, and various "standardized and departmentalized" tests in every high school grade helped guide teenagers into the right curricula. This faith in scientific measurement and in social engineering would continue through the early 1960s and stood in sharp contrast with the emerging belief that standardized tests discriminated against poorer children and racial minorities. Such faith would steel educators of the 1950s against critics such as Arthur Bestor, who said the weakening of academic course work in the high school had produced an "educational wasteland."[25]

The comprehensive high school, born in the early twentieth century, remained the favored approach to secondary education in most cities. Certain high schools emphasized more vocational education than academic subjects, but most tried to offer a range of curricula for what educators called the varying needs, interests, and capacities of individual teenagers. When James B. Conant produced his famous book in the late 1950s on the need for more tracking and differentiation in American secondary schools, school leaders in Evansville, Indianapolis, and other cities held forums on the subject and concurred that the differentiated curriculum remained the heart of sound secondary school practices. Conant's recommendations were hardly revolutionary but seemed to confirm local practices.[26]

The nation's larger urban high schools had pioneered in offering diverse curricula to different groups of students, and the Indiana School Study Commission like previous blue-ribbon panels praised them for their achievements and urged smaller high schools to follow their example. The social views and labors of Herman L. Shibler, superintendent of the Indianapolis schools in the 1950s, helps to illuminate the worldview held by urban schoolmen at the time. An inveterate Cold Warrior, Shibler was an outspoken defender of the mission of public education. He enthusiastically promoted the virtues of the free enterprise system, advocated additional vocational programs, solidified ties between the schools and local businesses, and imbibed the dominant ideals of administration of his generation. As head of an increasingly large and impersonal bureaucracy, Shibler strengthened the identification of schooling with vocational ends yet simultaneously applauded the teaching of traditional Judeo-Christian ethics.[27]

Shibler would have agreed with the main tenets of the earlier report, *To Form a More Perfect Union*, especially its emphasis on the civic goals of schools and its definition of equal educational opportunity. All education, said Shibler, began with the individual, the sacred unit in the school organization. Some individuals were blessed with high intelligence, motivation, and a favorable home life; others were less fortunate. About 40 percent of the graduates from Indianapolis high schools entered college in the early 1950s, roughly the national average. Like other administrators, Shibler denounced juvenile delinquency and worked diligently to lower the dropout rate, but surely, he claimed, the needs of the academically talented and well motivated and those who were not differed dramatically. All youth should learn the same civic values, such as respect for free enterprise, hard work, individual responsibility, and disdain for communism. The modern school, however, had to respect the rights of the individual and of society, which meant preparing various youth differently for the work force.[28]

Writing in the *Phi Delta Kappan* in 1953, Shibler emphasized that "the successful school administrator of today and of the future truly must be a human relations engineer." That meant publicizing well to the lay public the complicated world of the schools but also fitting every child into a proper educational and social niche. Armed with data from intelligence tests and the cumulative scholastic record of students, guidance counselors, teachers, and principals had to determine the appropriate curricula for every individual and to shape each student's future destiny within the capitalist system, which was increasingly governed by powerful corporations yet threatened by godless communism. A champion of American capitalism, Shibler persuaded local businesses to publish thousands of free pamphlets for teenagers on nearby opportunities.[29]

Shibler worked continually to expand the vocational emphases in local high schools and to broaden the counseling and psychological services in the Indianapolis schools. Organized into ability groups in the lower grades, pupils were also separated into "X" classes (for "exceptionally bright children") and "S" classes (for "slow learning children") in area high schools. In 1955, Shibler applauded the recent establishment of the Harry E. Wood School, a vocational secondary school, that promised to curb the dropout problem by offering such courses as barbering, beauty culture, personal service, and "cleaning and pressing" and an assortment of programs for "normal, mentally retarded, and socially maladjusted children." In 1958 the school commissioners approved Shibler's "Four Diploma Plan." For the first time, high school diplomas identified the vocational track to help prospective employers weed out applicants. Sneering at those who wanted high schools to offer only academic subjects, he said such nearsighted critics cared only about the college bound.[30]

Equating growth with advancement, Shibler was convinced that these various initiatives would allow the schools to continue their upward expansion and service to the community. With 70,000 pupils enrolled in the system by 1955, Indianapolis was already spending a quarter of a million dollars, out of a total operating budget of $22 million, on the salaries of five psychological consultants, thirty-eight social workers, and other counselors and advisers in the constantly growing system. Shibler realized that this was a fraction of the budget though crucial for student placement, and he favored more expenditures in the future. The more that experts were put into control, the more youth would benefit from schooling, the better the fit between the individual and the course of study, and the more likely that the socially immature or maladjusted could adapt to school and society.[31]

When Conant's studies appeared, emphasizing school consolidation, improved counseling and guidance, and a differentiated curriculum, Shibler proudly noted that most of these things were already common practice in the capital city, as they generally were in most urban systems. Heir to an administrative culture that accepted the wisdom of professionalism, hierarchy, and expertise, Shibler and his peers in other cities were part of a now irretrievable world, not a golden age but one when educational leaders believed in the certainty of their ideas and in the unassailable nature of the existing structure of schooling.[32]

While later generations would struggle with the issue of separation of church and state in the schools or intelligence testing and tracking or the presumed benefits of vocationalism, school leaders in the late 1940s and 1950s were not paralyzed by such concerns. Examples of such faith in educational certainties set them off from educators in later decades. A postcard from Elkhart depicted four nearby buildings—the public library, high school, courthouse, and a Presbyterian church—with the caption "The Corner of Education, Justice, and Religion." Superintendents in most school districts publicized local Christmas and Easter pageants; Evansville in the 1950s and early 1960s published school-by-school statistics on the percentage of pupils who attended church or Sunday school. The capacity of schoolmen then to merge religious and secular values into a coherent worldview was remarkable, though understandable when seen in context. The booming capitalist economy and material abundance seemed like the continuing work of a beneficent God. To adjust youth to this world of free enterprise seemed like sound educational as well as Christian policy.[33]

When some critics called the local schools godless because of the prevalence of secular values and focus on job preparation, Shibler of Indianapolis pointed out that nearly every teacher opened morning classes with prayer and Bible reading; indeed, most of the teachers were active, churchgoing Christians. In his writings and speeches, Shibler liberally quoted Scripture, showing the compatibility of deep religious conviction with the language of business enterprise and human relations. In the early 1950s, Shibler gathered a number of religious leaders together to plan a new course on America's religious heritage, which was first taught separately as a short course and then incorporated into the regular social studies curriculum in the seventh and eighth grades, receiving national attention.[34]

The impact of the Cold War upon the worldview of educational leaders was powerful in Indianapolis as elsewhere. Besides working closely with business leaders to advance vocationalism, Shibler gave many addresses and speeches that contrasted the horrors of godless communism with the wonders of free enterprise. He helped organize a presentation for teachers at the Murat Temple by some Soviet defectors who reportedly smuggled consumer goods to the United States, which were displayed to demonstrate the superiority of capitalism and the shoddy quality of communist production. The glory of America seemed like its capacity to treat its consumers well, perhaps an apt definition of citizenship at mid-century.[35]

The capacity of the Indianapolis schools to deepen respect for American capitalism went beyond speeches from the main office. Building a consensus around the superiority of the "American Way of Life" achieved noteworthy results. The Valley Forge Freedoms Foundation, which held annual prize competitions among public schools, emphasized the superiority of free enterprise and importance of civic education, meaning fairly uncritical love for America and capitalism, a goal in which the local schools excelled. Throughout the 1950s and into the early 1960s, Indianapolis was among the leading prize winners in national contests sponsored by the organization. Writing in 1956 in the local public relations bulletin, *Your Schools and You,* Shibler emphasized that Americans, adults as well as youth, were locked into a life-and-death struggle with the Soviet Union, and he told pupils to help hold "the line of freedom." By 1958 Indianapolis had won more awards from the Freedoms Foundation for promoting the "American Way of Life" than any other school system. As late as 1965 the local bulletin noted that the city was still in the lead![36]

All these developments after the war—the expanded enrollments, the faith in the power of expertise and centralized authority, and support for the Cold War—was not conducive to self-criticism, whether in Indianapolis or in other cities. Shibler and many citizens were obviously proud in 1957 when both *Time* and *Newsweek* named Shortridge High School, long the leading academic high school locally, one of the nation's premier high schools. The policy of emphasizing quality academic education for some pupils but not everyone meant that Shortridge and its many distinguished alumni had their day in the sun, and material advantages in the everyday world. Was there a downside to progress?[37]

Shibler and others buried or ignored data that called into question the costs other students, especially the poor and minority children, paid for the glory that was Shortridge's. The Harry E. Wood School, which was supposed to curb the dropout problem through vocationalism, in fact in 1959 had an 80 percent dropout rate, easily the worst locally. In 1965, local experts, with an obviously condescending attitude toward the poor, said that too many students and parents worried about the "prestige" of their high school degrees; in other words, those enrolled in vocational education well understood that they had lower status and fewer occupational choices but should not complain. Instead of rethinking their assumptions about the benefits of vocationalism, the experts responded by saying that "school personnel" needed to administer heavier doses of the same medicine, to "provide realistic educational plans for all pupils who are enrolled in the Indianapolis Public Schools." Equality of educational opportunity meant respecting individual differences and accepting one's educational fate.[38]

Certainly no one in central administration in the chilly atmosphere of the Cold War raised questions about mindless patriotism, the separation of church and state, the possible misuses of scientific testing, the slow movement toward racial integration, or the stigmas attached to nonacademic curricula. The public, of course, elevated these concerns to a more critical level of discussion by the late 1960s. Their virtual absence before then says something essential about the worldview of those previously in charge.

While Indianapolis, as the largest city in the state, was hardly a carbon copy of every urban area, the main trends there were unmistakably present to a significant degree in Gary, Evansville, Fort Wayne, South Bend, and other communities. Here, too, communities had often hired their first psychologists to administer and evaluate intelligence and other standardized tests by the 1920s, and faith in science was hardly shattered after the war. Initially most counseling for student placement into vocational courses was done informally by teachers, principals, and parents, a situation that continued in smaller towns even in the 1950s. The first high school counselors were appointed in Evansville after World War II. By the 1950s, counselors were already commonplace in most urban high schools, usually part of an administrative unit called "Pupil Personnel and Guidance." In 1962 South Bend reported that it had 20 counselors on the high school level and as many in junior high schools, where youngsters would sample some "prevocational" fare. Everywhere, said administrators, these counselors were overworked and spread too thinly, with one counselor sometimes serving several hundred or more students. But they were an essential part of the infrastructure in the maintenance of the multi-streamed comprehensive high school.[39]

To educational leaders since the 1920s, proper counseling and guidance for scientific placement in the comprehensive high school was an unquestioned good. It was the key to the schoolmen's dream of a fair, smoothly functioning, scientifically calibrated, and vocationally oriented school system. Everything was directed toward the proper adjustment of every pupil to a particular course of study. Students were labeled "normal" or "abnormal" and "special," and vocationalism was supposed to fix many educational maladjustments. Pupils in Gary were typically classified as "accelerated," "normal," or "retarded" from the first grade through the twelfth. Superintendents in most cities talked confidently in the 1950s about the capacity of counseling and guidance, vocational education, and mental health clinics to direct the poorly adjusted away from a fascination with sex and violence and toward healthier values and better study habits.

Writing in the *School Executive* in 1950, Superintendent Becker of Evansville offered the opinion that young George, a potentially maladjusted juvenile, became "a quiet and well-adjusted boy" thanks to the attention paid to his physical and mental health; otherwise "it is certain that George would today be a retarded delinquent."[40]

Defensive about the dropout rate, Daniel W. Snepp, Evansville's "director of pupil personnel," said that the schools were often not to blame. Many of those who withdrew were from a "bad home environment" and suffered from "socioeconomic maladjustment." And while participation in the extracurriculum—the joining of the right clubs or teams or membership on the Yell Squad—had become a surefire sign of sound mental health, the director dismissed critics who said that it was expensive to join the student culture on equal terms. "Many of our so-called high costs to students," wrote the director, "are self-imposed, such as high-school rings, historical trips, and expenses incidental to the extracurricular activities of the school." In the 1960s some writers would call this blaming the victim.[41]

In 1955, experts studying the Gary schools, which had the largest percentage of minority students in any Indiana school corporation, condemned the famous industrial city on the lake for failing to emphasize vocational programs enough. Again, educators claimed that more nonacademic courses would help keep working-class pupils in school longer. While sometimes stereotyped in earlier decades as having schools controlled by U.S. Steel and big business, Gary had a number of schools that housed students from kindergarten through twelfth grade, which critics said militated against the creation of strong vocational programs in the upper grades. Moreover, local educational leaders, including the prominent architect of the "Gary Plan," William Wirt, superintendent from 1907 to 1939, had often opposed narrow trade training popular in some circles, favoring educating all the city's children in the cultural aspects of industrial arts, woodworking, and the like. There were still many unskilled jobs for young men in particular in the steel mills and ancillary industries in the region, so a heavy emphasis on vocationalism also seemed superfluous to those administering the schools. Only when a citywide vocational high school opened in Gary in the late 1960s was the vocational lobby satisfied.[42]

Trust in science, testing, guidance, and tracking was fairly unchallenged in American educational circles in the 1950s, a period when prayer at school, increased enrollments, and defense of the "American Way of Life" seemed as certain as the laws of gravity. The faith of administrators in expertise, bureaucracy, and hierarchical rule had often been reinforced on the job, as the most ambitious and successful among them worked their way up the career ladder. And researchers in university-based schools of education only buttressed this worldview. At Indiana University, for example, the School of Education operated a research bu-

reau that sent experts into small towns to advise and counsel local superintendents. The advice they gave to towns in the 1950s and early 1960s was
invariably the same: to form little versions of big-city bureaucracies in
their own backyard.

By the 1950s, teachers, principals, and superintendents had increasingly become certified as professionals by attending a college or university. Various colleges and universities built strong ties with particular
school systems, whose principals interviewed and hired new teachers
upon the recommendations of their old professors in Bloomington, Terre
Haute, West Lafayette, or Muncie. There was also a relatively closed circuit
of ideas that moved back and forth between urban systems and the universities, as demonstrated by the dozens of school surveys of towns conducted from the campus in Bloomington.

While Indianapolis, Gary, and other cities had the largest systems in
the state, administrators in smaller communities such as Columbus,
Princeton, Peru, Wabash, and Decatur also turned to experts for advice in
the 1950s in anticipation of a student enrollment boom. Sometimes the
increase was smaller than anticipated, but the experts from Bloomington's
research bureau within the School of Education nevertheless often offered
stock recommendations to communities that differed markedly in industrial characteristics, size, and social structure. That further demonstrates,
however, the relative uniformity of thinking about school governance and
administration on every level of education after the war. Boilerplate suf-
ficed in lieu of critical thinking or diverse perspectives.

In the dozens of communities studied by the Division of Research and
Field Services, researchers focused on the common need to extend the
benefits of counseling and guidance, scientific testing, and vocational
education. School systems in little towns in fact in many ways had already
modeled themselves after the cities; their schools were also governed by a
relatively small board of education, which appointed a superintendent to
administer the schools, who in turn appointed some subordinate staff to
perform specialized tasks. To outside evaluators, the issue was how to get
town schools to hire more and more credentialed specialists, to make their
operations more professional and similar to the bigger cities.[43]

Researchers lodged a familiar complaint against the town of Madison,
on the Ohio River, in 1956. According to the 1950 census, Madison had
about 7,500 residents, roughly its population since the turn of the century.
Its school population had grown fairly dramatically after the war, noted
the researchers, yet the size of the administrative staff had not kept pace.
This was undoubtedly music to the ears of the local superintendent,
though the advice to hire more and more administrators and experts was
the stock response to local school boards that commissioned an external
survey. It was self-serving, of course, for the universities to claim that local
schools always seemed to need more of what schools of education had to

offer, but it remained a frequent refrain. Studying Peru's system in 1956, the university researchers complained that "the public schools are one of the largest corporations in the community and have an extremely small staff to operate the widely divergent specialized services of the corporation."[44]

Most of Indiana's small towns had high schools enrolling a few hundred pupils, and they nearly all offered a differentiated curriculum. In the 1950s Madison said it offered 5 different courses of study; Decatur, which had fewer than 500 pupils enrolled in grades 7 through 12, said it had 6. Peru claimed that its fewer than 900 pupils had access to 7 different courses of study: college preparatory, general, art, business education, industrial, vocational machine shop, and vocational home economics. Obviously these were not truly separate four-year curricula but rather concentrations, yet it shows how far the idea of the common school had retreated in the twentieth century. Logansport, which had a few more than 1,000 pupils enrolled in its high school in 1955, reported 9 separate secondary curricula.[45]

Those surveying these towns and others always applauded their ability to promote equality of educational opportunity by diversifying the curriculum. They never argued that schools might consider the possibility of a common curriculum for everyone, or that there were class biases in scientific testing, curricular tracking, and vocational education. Since even small-town high schools had different curricular streams, reflecting the modern notion of a division of labor, they were on the right track, the urban track, the one paved so well by the largest cities. Where town systems were mostly amiss, according to many researchers, was that scientific management of the life chances of pupils had not proceeded far enough. It was all well and good that school leaders had long gravitated, like ducks to water, to the idea of a differentiated curriculum. The difficulty was the lack of enough qualified experts hired locally to administer tests regularly, to interpret them accurately, and thus to guarantee the promise of equal educational opportunity. Educators in Columbus were praised in 1957 for their scientific testing programs in the elementary grades but chastised for their less systematic efforts in the junior and senior high school, a situation that the local "curriculum coordinator" and guidance staff hoped to correct. Other towns had too many teachers and principals rather than guidance counselors and trained experts administering tests and interpreting the results.[46]

University researchers criticized educators in Wabash in 1961 because they failed to recognize sufficiently the individual differences of elementary school pupils and to meet certain professional standards in counseling and guidance. In the junior high school, "guidance activities . . . are very limited. Apparently, individual counseling is infrequent and is conducted without systematic plan. A certain amount of information and records are available in the cumulative record folder kept in the principal's office. Some guidance is attempted through the health and physical education classes." The guidance program on the high school level was also criticized on many points. The recommendations, predictably enough, were that the schools needed to adopt more rigorous and systematic testing and evaluation policies and to then identify the proper curricular tracks for each individual.[47]

At every turn, therefore, educational researchers shared many of the professional values and perspectives of the big-city administrators; indeed, many professors of educational administration had formerly worked in urban bureaucracies or otherwise embraced the ethos of business efficiency, scientific management, and school consolidation. When criticisms of urban schools mounted in the 1960s, school leaders quickly discovered that conventional answers increasingly lacked legitimacy. The shared value system of urban school leaders and educational researchers disintegrated in the wake of the social convulsions of the 1960s, as poor citizens living in increasingly desperate circumstances lost their deferential posture toward authority. Those who once ruled urban schools were leaving behind a familiar world forever.[48]

When the members of the Indiana School Study Commission studied schools after the war, it categorized schools in familiar ways, according to their legal incorporation as urban, town, or township units. For over a century, reformers spoke of the great divide between the more urbanized districts and the rural township schools. Such comparisons lost their meaning as school consolidation proceeded rapidly in the 1950s and 1960s, leading to a drastic decrease in the number of school corporations and small township schools. Soon the great distinctions drawn in the educational world were between inner-city and suburban schools.[49]

Following the war, Indiana's cities, like those across the nation, witnessed a demographic and economic revolution. While downtowns had been the center of economic activity—home to major banks, financial services, and shopping—the movement of thousands of white middle- and upper-class families to expanding suburbs led to profound changes in inner-city life. Historian James H. Madison notes, for example, that in "the late 1950s six downtown Indianapolis stores accounted for 90 percent of department store sales in Marion County." By 1972 the percentage had shrunk to 18. The pace of economic and social change varied in different urban areas. By the 1960s most city school systems were nevertheless serving more and more poor students, often minority children whose families lived in substandard housing and faced dwindling prospects for steady or well-paying jobs.[50]

Even though enrollments continued to rise in many urban school systems through the mid-1960s, a sense of uneasiness about the future of urban schools was already apparent. Given the slow progress toward school integration, black citizens in particular understandably became outspoken critics of local schools. Most of Indiana's black citizens lived in cities, and their children's prospects for success were inevitably tied to the health of their public schools. As urban whites increasingly moved to the suburbs or attended private schools, the prospects of building well integrated public schools evaporated in many communities, as the proportion of poor and minority pupils rose dramatically. Neither administrators nor teachers usually had much knowledge about or experience in educating the poor effectively in academic subjects; it had not been a pressing concern in earlier decades, since the poor either dropped out, frequently before high school, or otherwise were disproportionately tracked into nonacademic curricula. As larger numbers of middle- and upper-class high school graduates, and even more working-class whites, prepared themselves for college, inner-city parents and youth witnessed yet another sign of the widening chasm between city and suburb.[51]

Despite the expansion of the economy in the 1960s, the fruits of capitalism were not distributed evenly, and the education of the urban poor became a matter of national debate. Conant had warned of the "social dynamite" that existed in a world divided into slums and suburbs, but simple appeals to the virtues of expertise, consolidated schools, vocationalism, and the nostrums of the past seemed ineffectual as the economies and schools of many cities began to deteriorate.[52]

Even before a plethora of educational reform programs of the Great Society—such as Head Start and Title 1—began to channel more federal funds to urban centers, local systems were grudgingly admitting that they were doing a poor job of helping those most in need. Teacher workshops to improve the education of the "culturally disadvantaged" were increasingly held in Indianapolis, Gary, Evansville, and South Bend, but they did not seem sufficient to dramatically improve the education of the poor. Federal monies helped enhance local school budgets, but it is unclear whether most of this increase was actually spent on the poor. Angry at the slow pace of change, many black citizens grew angry and frustrated at what were seen as white controlled, unresponsive school bureaucracies.[53]

A collapse of respect for teachers and schools was soon evident in many urban schools in the 1960s. In the 1950s, Evansville's officials happily reported that most of the windowpanes smashed in the district resulted from innocent accidents on the playground; by the 1960s, urban educators everywhere commented on the increase in wanton vandalism. "Malicious or mischievous destruction of school property—vandalism—has become a source of mounting concern for school administrators," said a contribution to the Evansville *Public Schools Bulletin* in 1965. Students in one single incident committed $8,000 worth of damage to a South Bend school that same year, and similar stories emanated from many urban systems. The pent-up hostility of poor children whose families were under severe stress produced much uncivil behavior; no matter what its source, it remained shocking to those who assumed that schools were orderly institutions and teachers were in control of their classrooms. By the late 1960s, contributors to professional journals such as the *Indiana Teacher* worried about how schools should respond to vandalism, drug abuse, and similar contemporary ills.[54]

As inner-city residents grew more angry and frustrated in the late 1960s, they worried less and less about the likelihood of racial integration and became increasingly concerned about improving the quality of their increasingly segregated schools. Their faith in the capacity of expert-run bureaucracies to enhance the quality of their children's education was not improved as the inner cities grew more isolated from the suburbs, as businesses moved, and the local tax base began to shrink. And, given the wider climate of cultural protest during the period, even those working within the system who traditionally defended top-down management styles and the authority of the school broke ranks.[55]

In the *Yearbook of Indiana Education*, published in 1970, a number of educational leaders from across the state shared their thoughts on current educational trends. Some of their views would have shocked any administrator working in the days of Shibler, revealing the widening gap between past and present. One contributor noted that the state had already seen "some teacher walkouts, work stoppages, and strikes"; the Anderson Federation of Teachers had even been held in contempt of court for violating a restraining order. Just as students lost their deference toward teachers, teachers were increasingly less deferential to the school board and central administration.[56]

John W. Vaughn, executive secretary of the Indiana Association of Elementary School Principals, noted that some teachers were finding creative ways to subvert the existing order. The building of large consolidated schools had been one of the presumed accomplishments of reform movements throughout the twentieth century, but Vaughn and other writers increasingly feared that individual pupils were lost in the bureaucratic maze. Teachers since after the war, he claimed with obvious hyperbole, had "devoted themselves to techniques of 'beating the system.'" They tried to group children in creative ways, hoping to undermine the lockstep of that other major urban reform, the graded classroom. They used learning centers and "enrichment groups," or taught in schools without walls and more open classrooms. Teachers worried about relating to their students. Vaughn added the heretical idea—at least for an administrator— that school marks were bad for pupils, and that competition for grades was unnatural and undesirable. Talking the hip language of the times, he added that "What turns some students *on* [at school] will almost assuredly turn some students off."[57]

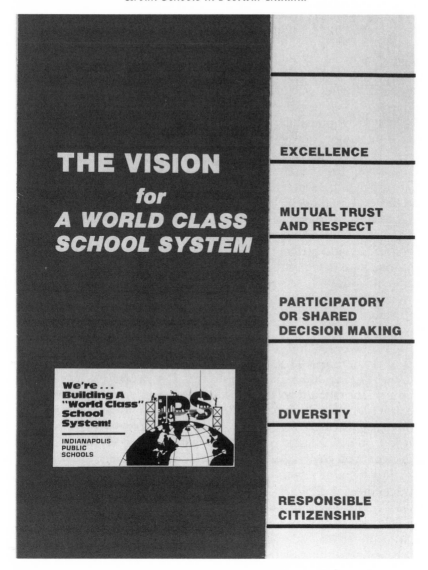

THE VISION

for

A WORLD CLASS SCHOOL SYSTEM

EXCELLENCE

MUTUAL TRUST AND RESPECT

PARTICIPATORY OR SHARED DECISION MAKING

DIVERSITY

RESPONSIBLE CITIZENSHIP

We're... Building A "World Class" School System!

INDIANAPOLIS PUBLIC SCHOOLS

City Schools and the Challenge of the 1990s. Courtesy
Indianapolis Public Schools

The majority of teachers were not radical pedagogues or outspoken critics of the major accomplishments of twentieth-century school reformers. They probably still wanted orderly schools and continued to give grades. But unquestioned support for key assumptions that administrators shared as late as the 1950s and early 1960s had disappeared. Some teachers as well as administrators had come to doubt that large-scale institutions were appropriate centers of learning; those who taught and studied there could be understandably repelled by the demands for mindless conformity and lockstep education. The graded school, which was supposed to offer a logical and rational approach to instruction, now seemed too rigid, ignoring how children of the same age differed emotionally and developmentally. And the urban superintendent, who had expected deference and often received it before the mid-1960s, now spent considerable time defending his actions before an often angry and contentious public. The complex of interlocking assumptions once shared by many urban leaders after the war about curriculum, testing and guidance, and respect for authority and hierarchy seemed to lack legitimacy.

Once-mighty urban school systems would continue to face severe problems after the fall of Saigon and scandals of Watergate. The economies of inner cities would further deteriorate because of deindustrialization. Any hope that local schools might offer poor and minority children a first-rate academic education seemed illusory. The Indianapolis schools, whose enrollments reached well over 100,000 in the 1960s, would decline by half well before the end of the century. Vacancies for big-city superintendencies—once the plum jobs in most states—became difficult to fill and the incumbent faced almost daily crises and controversies.

The strength of city schools had always been built upon a vibrant economy and sound public investment. That world has vanished. Its disappearance should not necessarily be mourned. Cities had never made the provision of high-quality academic instruction for the poor a priority, so their failures since the 1960s to educate them well is tragic but hardly shocking to the historian of urban education. The recurrent conservative claim, that you can't solve a problem by throwing money at it, does not explain why more advantaged suburbs spend on average three times as much money per capita on their children as is spent on the inner-city poor. That blue-ribbon groups such as the Indiana School Study Commission in the 1940s found urban schools superior to others seems almost incomprehensible to readers today. This, nonetheless, dramatically shows the distance now separating their world from ours.

NOTES

1. The best history of school governance and administration is by David Tyack and Elisabeth Hansot, *Managers of Virtue: Public School Leadership in America, 1820–1980* (New York, 1982), part 11-III. For contrasting interpretations of educational change in the postwar years, see Diane Ravitch, *The Troubled Crusade: American*

Education, 1945–1980 (New York, 1983), and Joel H. Spring, *The Sorting Machine: National Educational Policy since 1945* (New York, 1976). On suburban development, see Richard Polenberg, *One Nation Divisible: Class, Race, and Ethnicity in the United States since 1938* (New York, 1980), chap. 4.

2. See my earlier chapter in this volume.

3. See "How Does It Look for 1945?" *Indiana Teacher* 89 (December 1944): 101; and "Why Teachers Go to the City," *Indiana Teacher* 90 (May 1946): 277. On Gary, see Ronald D. Cohen, *Children of the Mill: Schooling and Society in Gary, 1906–1960* (Bloomington, 1990). A survey of the Gary schools in 1955 indicated that the city schools were studied far more than they were emulated; see *The Public School System of Gary, Indiana* (n.p., 1955), 5.

4. David B. Tyack, Robert Lowe, and Elisabeth Hansot, *Public Schools in Hard Times: The Great Depression and Recent Years* (Cambridge, 1984); and Jeffrey Mirel, *The Rise and Fall of an Urban School System: Detroit, 1907–1981* (Ann Arbor, 1993), chap. 3. On Shortridge High, see Laura Sheerin Gaus, *Shortridge High School 1864–1981: A Retrospect* (Indianapolis, 1985); on Arsenal Technical High, see Milo H. Stuart, *The Organization of a Comprehensive High School* (New York, 1926).

5. "The Object of County Unit," *Indiana Teacher* 69 (January 1925): 18; "The Basic Defect of Our Rural Schools," *Indiana Teacher* 73 (March 1929): 16; "Ten Advantages of City Schools over Country Schools," *Indiana Teacher* 73 (March 1929): 16–17; Harold C. Feightner, "Consolidation of Small Political Units in Relation to Education," *Indiana Teacher* 76 (February 1932): 7–9; Lewis S. Bowen, "Larger Units for Economy in Local Government," *Indiana Teacher* 79 (September 1934): 18–19; and "The Horse and Buggy," *Indiana Teacher* 80 (December 1935): 16.

6. Indiana School Study Commission, *An Evaluation of the Indiana Public Schools* (Indianapolis, 1948), the preliminary report; and the final report, *An Evaluation of the Indiana Public Schools* (Indianapolis, 1949).

7. *An Evaluation* (1948), 8–9. On reform efforts in the 1920s, see James H. Madison, "John D. Rockefeller's General Education Board and the Rural School Problem in the Midwest, 1900–1930," *History of Education Quarterly* 14 (Summer 1984): 181–99.

8. *An Evaluation* (1949), 441–48.

9. *An Evaluation* (1948), 18, 21–24; *An Evaluation* (1949), 85.

10. *An Evaluation* (1948), 20. On the importance of basketball in Indiana's schools, see A. Z. Christopher and W. L. Howard, "Cocurricular Activities in 200 Indiana High Schools," *School Activities* 25 (October 1953): 43–45.

11. Individual chapters in both the preliminary and final versions of the report by the commission contain numerous policy recommendations. Also see Tyack and Hansot, *Managers of Virtue*, parts II and III.

12. The best history of urban education is David B. Tyack, *The One Best System: A History of American Urban Education* (Cambridge, 1974).

13. Tyack and Hansot, *Managers of Virtue*, 223. On the reaction to Sputnik, read Barbara Barksdale Clowse, *Brainpower for the Cold War: The Sputnik Crisis and the National Defense Education Act of 1958* (Westport, Conn., 1981).

14. U.S. Bureau of the Census, *County and City Data Book, 1949* (Washington, D.C., 1952), 351; U.S. Bureau of Census, *County and City Data Book* (Washington, D.C., 1962), 507.

15. On school strikes and other community reactions to school integration, see James B. Lane's 'City of the Century': A History of Gary, Indiana (Bloomington, 1978), 271, 294.

16. "Consolidation," Public Schools Bulletin 33 (November 19, 1956): 1, 4; "Second Merger Try," Public Schools Bulletin 33 (April 15, 1957): 2; "Evansville School Corporation," Public Schools Bulletin 33 (May 13, 1957): 1; and "The Evansville School Corporation," Public Schools Bulletin 34 (January 13, 1958): 1.

17. "Superintendent's Editorial," Public Schools Bulletin 34 (January 13, 1958): 2; and "Superintendent's Editorial," Public Schools Bulletin 40 (June 1, 1964): 2.

18. "School Reorganization Act of 1959," The School City Trend 1 (November 1960): 2; Alexander Jardine, "School Reorganization in St. Joseph County," The School City Trend 1 (November 1960): 3; "Why Larger Districts?" The School City Trend 1 (November 1960): 4; and "South Bend Community School Corporation Begins First Year of Operation," The School City Trend 3 (September 1962): 1, 4.

19. Robert E. Martin, "From Concept to Concrete," The Hoosier Schoolmaster of the Sixties 2 (December 1962): 5–7; Max P. Gabbert, The Hoosier Schoolmaster of the Sixties 1 (January 1962): 13–15; and William J. Reese, "Education," in The Encyclopedia of Indianapolis, ed. David J. Bodenhamer and Robert G. Barrows (Bloomington, 1994), 84.

20. On the 1950s, see John Patrick Diggins, The Proud Decades: America in War and Peace, 1941–1960 (New York, 1988), 178–81; William L. O'Neill, American High: The Years of Confidence, 1945–1960 (New York, 1986); James T. Patterson, America's War Against Poverty, 1900–1960 (Cambridge, 1981), 82–85; and the comments by David Chalmers in And the Crooked Places Made Straight: The Struggle for Social Change in the 1960s (Baltimore, 1991), 2–5.

21. The manpower theme is developed most fully by Spring, The Sorting Machine.

22. On the controversies over the social studies in the 1930s, read Herbert M. Kliebard, The Struggle for the American Curriculum 1893–1958 (New York, 1995), 171–78. On consumerism after the war, see Karal Ann Marling, As Seen on TV: The Visual Culture of Everyday Life in the 1950s (Cambridge, 1994) and Stephanie Coontz, The Way We Never Were: American Families and the Nostalgia Trap (New York, 1992), 25. B. Edward McClellan makes the subtle observation that the crusade against communism drew its strength from multiple sources and probably became more important than traditional citizenship and character education, in Schools and the Shaping of Character: Moral Education in America, 1607–Present (Bloomington, 1992), 83.

23. To Form a More Perfect Union (Indianapolis, 1948), 3–4.

24. There is a voluminous literature on the testing movement; see especially Henry Minton, Lewis M. Terman (New York, 1988); Margo Horn, Before It's Too Late: The Guidance Movement in the United States, 1922–1945 (New York, 1989); Paul Davis Chapman, Schools as Sorters: Lewis M. Terman, Applied Psychology, and the Intelligence Testing Movement (New York, 1988); and Michael M. Sokal, ed., Psychological Testing and American Society, 1890–1930 (New Brunswick, 1900).

25. To Form a More Perfect Union, 11, 14; and Ravitch, The Troubled Crusade, 75–76. Carl F. Kaestle points out that Bestor had little influence on school practice, though pressures for improved school performance by some children increased after

Sputnik, in "Literate America: High-Level Adult Literacy as a National Goal," in *Learning from the Past*, 340.

26. James B. Conant's *The American High School Today* (New York, 1959) was widely discussed among school people in local communities. See, for example, "Public Meeting," *Public Schools Bulletin* 34 (March 10, 1958): 2; and "Indianapolis Stacks Up Well by Conant Checklist," *Your Schools and You* 9 (February-March 1959): 1, 3.

27. On the nature of the high school curriculum in the twentieth century, read David Angus and Jeffrey Mirel, "Rhetoric and Reality: The High School Curriculum," in *Learning from the Past: What History Teaches Us About School Reform*, ed. Diane Ravitch and Maris A. Vinovskis (Baltimore, 1995), 295–328.

28. Shibler wrote many editorials in the local public relations bulletin, *Your Schools and You*, and he was also a frequent contributor to educational periodicals. See Reese, "Education," 83.

29. H. L. Shibler, "We Invite the Public In," *Phi Delta Kappan* 36 (February 1953): 171; H. L. Shibler, "A Letter from the Superintendent," *Your Schools and You* 5 (November 4, 1955): 2; "A Letter from the Superintendent," *Your Schools and You* 6 (November 1956): 2; and Herman L. Shibler, *What's Wrong with Our Schools?* (Indianapolis, 1954), 5–6.

30. Herman L. Shibler, "Evaluation of a Mental-Health Program," in *Mental Health in Modern Education*, ed. Nelson B. Henry (Chicago, 1955), 291–92; "Board OK's 'Four Diplomas,'" *Your Schools and You* 8 (April 1958), 1, 4; Herman L. Shibler, "Organization of Personnel Services," in *Personnel Services in Education*, ed. Nelson B. Henry (Chicago, 1959), 163–64; and Ted Stahly, "High Schools," in *Encyclopedia of Indianapolis*, 676.

31. Shibler, "Evaluation of a Mental-Health Program," 279.

32. "Indianapolis Stacks Up Well by Conant Checklist," 1, 3.

33. Postcard, Elkhart, Picture File Collection, Indiana State Library, "Elkhart County—Elkhart, City of, Folder II," postmarked 1945 or 1946. School superintendents in the 1950s routinely delivered Christmas messages to teachers and pupils. See the regular publication of information on church and Sunday school attendance in Evansville in the *Public Schools Bulletin*.

34. Shibler, *What's Wrong with Our Schools?*, 7–8; George Walker Buckner, Jr., "Schools' Religion Plan Threatened," *The Christian Century* 72 (February 16, 1955): 214–15; H. L. Shibler, "Education ABOUT Religion," *Religious Education* 51 (July-August 1956): 270–71; and H. L. Shibler, "You Can Teach *about* Religion," *The Nation's Schools* 60 (December 1957): 35–37.

35. "Flight for Freedom Scheduled for Showing," *Your Schools and You* 1 (November 9, 1951): 1; H. L. Shibler, "A Letter from the Superintendent," *Your Schools and You* 2 (December 1, 1952): 2; H. L. Shibler, "A Letter from the Superintendent," *Your Schools and You* 3 (January 20, 1954): 2; and "Exhibit Features American Way of Life," *Your Schools and You* 5 (October 6, 1955): 3. Urban school leaders elsewhere also praised the superiority of American capitalism and our way of life and condemned communism. In Evansville, the *Public Schools Bulletin* 32 (December 5, 1955): 2, announced the availability of anticommunist films at the public library, including titles such as "Escape Route," "Conelrad," and "A New Look at the H Bomb." Upon his retirement in 1966, Superintendent Alexander Jardine of South

Bend was remembered for his strong anticommunism, in "The Many Faces of Dr. Jardine," *Trend* 6 (April 1966): 2–3.

36. "Indianapolis Public Schools Granted Principal Award by Freedoms Foundation," *Your Schools and You* 5 (March 1956): 1; "Indianapolis Public Schools Get 11 Freedoms Foundation Awards," *Your Schools and You* 8 (March 1958): 1, 4; "City Schools Win 13 Freedoms Foundation Awards," 12 (March 1962): 3; and "14 Schools Win Freedom Awards," *Your Schools and You* 16 (April 1965): 1.

37. "Shortridge Named as One of the Best Schools in U.S.," *Your Schools and You* 6 (November 1957): 1, 4.

38. *The 1959 High School Class: A Brief Study* (Indianapolis, n.d.), n.p.; and *A Follow-Up Study—Class of 1965* (Indianapolis, 1965), 23. Both documents are in the archival holdings of the Indianapolis Public Schools, at the downtown Education Center.

39. "Counseling and Guidance Services," *Public Schools Bulletin* 43 (February 6, 1967): 2–3; "Local System Has Forty-Two Counselors on Full or Part-Time Basis," *The Trend* 3 (October 1962): 4; and Shibler, "Evaluation of a Mental-Health Program," 287.

40. *The Public School System of Gary, Indiana*, 53, table 5; and Ralph Becker, "Healthy Students Are Most Likely to Succeed," *The School Executive* 70 (November 1950): 77. On the importance of counseling for vocational placement and on mental health work in different Indiana cities, also see "Testing Program, 1954–1955," *Public Schools Bulletin* 31 (September 27, 1954): 3–4; "Guidance Conferences," *Public Schools Bulletin* 34 (March 10, 1958): 2; "Psychological Services Located in New Centers," *Your Schools and You* 1 (August 27, 1951): 3; Herman L. Shibler, "A Letter from the Superintendent," *Your Schools and You* 8 (May 1958): 2; and "Service to Children Is Major Aim of Pupil Personnel Department," *Trend* 3 (October 1962): 1, 4.

41. Daniel W. Snepp, "Can We Salvage the Dropouts?" *The Clearing House* 31 (September 1956): 53.

42. *The Public School System of Gary, Indiana*, a survey completed by the Public Administration Service, is largely a critique of the Gary schools, emphasizing the unwillingness of local leaders to invest heavily in vocational education. An earlier survey of the schools in the 1940s also criticized the schools in a similar way. See William Lynn McKinney, "The Gary, Indiana Public School Curriculum, 1940–1970: A Local History," (Washington, D.C., Final Report, U.S. Department of Health, Education, and Welfare, Grant No. OEg–5–72–0039, 1973), 187–202. I am indebted to Professor Ronald D. Cohen of Indiana University-Northwest for these references.

43. Tyack and Hansot, *Managers of Virtue*, part II, for an understanding of the leading urban patterns in school governance and organization.

44. Harold H. Church, *A Cooperative Study of the Madison Consolidated Schools, Madison, Indiana* (Bloomington, School Survey Series, no. 46, 1956), 13; and Harold H. Church, *A Cooperative Study of the Public Schools of Peru, Indiana* (Bloomington: School Survey Series no. 44, 1956), 12.

45. Church, *A Cooperative Study of the Madison Consolidated Schools*, 29; Harold H. Church, *A Cooperative Study of the Public School Enrollment and the Building and Financial Needs of the School City of Decatur, Indiana* (Bloomington: School Survey Series, no. 31, 1954), 19; Church, *A Cooperative Study of the Public Schools of Peru*, 27;

and Harold H. Church, *A Cooperative Study of the Logansport Public Schools, Logansport, Indiana* (Bloomington, School Survey Series, no. 39, 1955), 30–32.

46. Harold H. Church, *A Cooperative Study of the Public Schools of Columbus, Indiana* (Bloomington: School Survey Series, no. 51, 1957), 28; Church, *A Cooperative Study of the Madison Consolidated Schools,* 33; Church, *A Cooperative Survey of the Logansport Public Schools,* 35; and Harold H. Church, *A Cooperative Study of the Princeton Public Schools, Princeton, Indiana* (Bloomington: School Survey Series, no. 41, 1954), 27.

47. Harold H. Church, *A Cooperative Study of the Public Schools of Wabash, Indiana* (Bloomington: School Survey Series, no. 59, 1961), 23–25.

48. Harvey Kantor and Robert Lowe, "Class, Race, and the Emergence of Federal Education Policy: From the New Deal to the Great Society," *Educational Researcher* 24 (April 1995): 4–5; and Robert Lowe and Harvey Kantor, "Considerations on Writing the History of Educational Reform in the 1960s," *Educational Theory* 39 (Winter 1989): 4.

49. By 1968, in less than a decade, the number of school districts in Indiana declined from 939 to 382. See Madison, *The Indiana Way,* 250. On the new categories, see Harvey Kantor and Barbara Brenzel, "Urban Education and the 'Truly Disadvantaged': The Historical Roots of the Contemporary Crisis," *Teachers College Record* 94 (Winter 1992): 278–314.

50. Madison, *The Indiana Way,* 235.

51. See Maureen A. Reynolds, "The Challenge of Racial Equality," in this volume.

52. That vocational education could defuse the "social dynamite" was claimed by a spokesperson of the Vocational and Practical Arts Association, Robert L. Allen, "The Way Things Are," *The Hoosier Schoolmaster of the Sixties* 1 (April 1962): 11. Similar claims were made when "career education" became popular in the early 1970s.

53. The number of federal education programs soared in the 1960s, as did federal expenditures; see Hugh Davis Graham, *The Uncertain Triumph: Federal Education Policy in the Kennedy and Johnson Years* (Chapel Hill, 1984), xix. Whether the monies actually reached those most in need, poor children, is questioned by some writers, who note that financially strapped districts often used such support for general operating expenses. The impact of such programs is too large a subject to be discussed here, though many local materials exist that are helpful in understanding their impact upon local communities. See, for example, *Your Federal Funds at Work in Indianapolis* (Indianapolis, 1967).

For examples of rising concerns with the education of the poor on the local level, see the following articles concerning South Bend: "Conference on Disadvantaged Children and Youth Sets Stage for Further Study," *The School City Trend* 2 (May 1962): 1; "Advisory Committee on Disadvantaged Children Submits Interim Report," *Trend* 3 (March 1963): 4; on Evansville, see "Poll Shows Concern for Education," *Public Schools Bulletin* 41 (May 31, 1965): 3; "Workshop for 'Target-Area' Teachers Will Stress Motivation," *Public Schools Bulletin* 43 (April 17, 1967): 1, 3; "Urban Sociology Workshop Will Focus on the Deprived Child," *Public Schools Bulletin* 44 (November 6, 1967): 1–2; and "Afro-Asian Workshop Planned for May 6," *Public Schools Bulletin* 45 (April 14, 1969). Indianapolis, Gary, and other cities similarly reflected such concerns with the growing problems in their schools.

On the national scene, see also Julie Roy Jeffrey, *Education for the Children of the Poor: A Study of the Origins and Implementation of the Elementary and Secondary Education Act of 1965* (Columbus, Ohio, 1978); and Harold and Pamela Silver, *An Educational War on Poverty: American and British Policy-Making, 1960–1980* (Cambridge, 1991).

54. "Glass Replacement," *Public Schools Bulletin* 31 (September 26, 1955): 2; "Report Gives School Vandalism Figures," *Public Schools Bulletin* 41 (May 10, 1965): 3; "Destruction of School Property a Major Problem," *Trend* 5 (April 1965): 2; Bernice O'Conner, "Drugs Hit Hoosier Schools," *Indiana Teacher* 13 (Spring 1969): 130–32; Charles J. Leslie, "3 C's Not in Curriculum: Cocaine, Cocktails, Cigarettes," *Indiana Teacher* 114 (Winter 1970): 68–69; Robert L. Prettyman, "Drug Abuse and the Schools: It's Time for Action," *Indiana Teacher* 114 (Summer 1970): 174–75; and Eugene Huber, "Drug Problems Force Reevaluation of Education," *Indiana Teacher* 115 (Winter 1971): 104–105. On the rising problems of school violence and drug use, see William J. Reese, *"Reefer Madness* and *A Clockwork Orange,"* in *Learning from the Past*, 355–81.

55. Frank N. Magid Associates, *The Negro in Indianapolis* (Cedar Rapids, 1969), 128. Also see Emma Lou Thornbrough, "African-Americans," in *Encyclopedia of Indianapolis*, 12.

56. J. Fred Swalls, "Teachers under Indiana Law," in *Yearbook of Indiana Education 1970* (Danville, Ill., 1970), ed. Russell L. Hamm and Max E. Bough, 2. This volume was sponsored by the recently formed Indiana Council of Administrative Associations, while the Indiana Association for Supervision and Instruction took responsibility for its production.

57. John W. Vaughn, "Personalizing Education," in *Yearbook of Indiana Education*, 75, 83.

MAUREEN A. REYNOLDS

The Challenge of Racial Equality

I t is most gratifying to report that school systems which had previously practiced segregation of pupils in their communities have been agreeably surprised by the fine acceptance of the program in all parts of the state." So wrote the Indiana Council for Children and Youth in 1951, commenting upon the state's response to legislation two years earlier that ended eighty years of legally sanctioned segregated schooling. In 1956, Hortense Myers proclaimed in the Indiana State Teachers Association's *Indiana Teacher* that the Hoosier state had a six-year head start on the Supreme Court's order to integrate schools in its landmark decision, *Brown v. Board of Education*, that declared legally segregated schools unconstitutional. Myers added, "And from a survey around the state, integration is not and has not been a serious problem." Hoosiers, who praised their state for anticipating *Brown*, soon found their praise prematurely issued.[1]

After Myers's optimistic words, eight Indiana school districts, Evansville-Vanderburgh, Fort Wayne, Gary, Hammond, Indianapolis, Kokomo, Muncie, and South Bend, were sued by Hoosier African Americans in Indiana's federal district courts to enforce the 1949 state law and the *Brown* decision. Four of those districts—Fort Wayne, Hammond, Muncie, and South Bend—never operated segregated schools under the state law. Desegregation consent agreements signed by Vigo County (Terre Haute) and the Marion school districts avoided litigation in these two districts. The Greater Clark County Schools (Jeffersonville) adopted a minority hiring plan after a district court ordered the federal government to begin court proceedings to cut off federal funds to the district.[2] Unfortunately, in Indiana, as elsewhere in the United States, school desegregation in larger cities with significant minority populations required the threat of, if not actual, court intervention.

Indiana learned that the challenge to realize racial equality in public education could not be met merely by the state legislature passing the 1949 law or the Supreme Court issuing its decision in *Brown*. When studying public school desegregation in Indiana, no one pattern emerges. However, most of what ensued was not unique to Indiana. Except for the interdistrict desegregation order for the Indianapolis Public Schools, the progress in desegregating Indiana's public schools too often mirrored what happened in other states, especially those in the South.

Efforts to obtain racial equality in Indiana schools occurred within a historical context of unusually strong legal discrimination for a northern state. Heavily settled by southerners, Indiana quickly developed discriminatory policies and practices toward African Americans in education and other areas. As early as 1824, Indiana whites objected to black children attending common schools. The 1837 school law restricted public schools to white students. Blacks were later exempted from paying taxes for school purposes.

Between 1824 and 1869, blacks could legally attend only private schools maintained by their own efforts or those of private philanthropy groups, notably the Friends and the Baptists. Consequently, the opportunities available for African Americans to obtain a formal education were more proscribed than those for whites during the formative years of public education in Indiana. Just before the 1869 state legislature convened, Indiana's superintendent of public instruction, Barnabas Hobbs, commented on the educational position of the state's African Americans. Hobbs wrote that African Americans "have been under the necessity of levying on themselves an additional tax to build their own schoolhouses, and for the entire cost of their tuition. The historian will find this a dark chapter in our history."[3]

In 1869, the legislature authorized separate schools for black children with the same rights and privileges as schools for whites. If there were insufficient children to form a separate colored school, school trustees were to provide other means of education using black children's proportion of local funds. Thus, integrated common schools were banned. Shortly afterward, with no colored school available in Lawrence, an African American unsuccessfully attempted and then sued to enroll his school-age children and grandchildren in the local white school. In *Cory v. Carter* (1874), the Indiana Supreme Court held that the fourteenth amendment of the United States Constitution did not make Negroes citizens of the states where they resided and did not apply to the domestic institutions of the states such as common schools. Separate education for the races became

African American Teachers in Madison, 1906. Source: *Twenty-Second Biennial Report of the Department of Public Instruction* (Indianapolis, 1906)

mandated with the proviso that all children receive substantially equal school advantages. Indiana firmly embraced the "separate but equal" doctrine.[4]

Following *Cory*, an 1877 law provided that when no separate school was available black children could attend white schools. Additionally, if black

African American Children in New Albany, 1908. Source:
*Twenty-Fourth Biennial Report of the State Superintendent
of Public Instruction* (Indianapolis, 1908)

children tested for a higher grade than taught in the colored school, they could attend appropriate white schools. Financial concerns rather than egalitarian ideals probably motivated many legislators who voted to allow racially integrated public schools. Separate schools were particularly expensive to maintain for small numbers of children. In the 1880s, the Indiana Supreme Court upheld the 1877 school law from attacks by blacks and whites.[5] More than forty years passed before the next important court challenge to Indiana's laws sanctioning segregated schools.

When Indianapolis and Gary extended segregated schooling during the 1920s, African Americans again legally challenged segregation in public education. Both cities traditionally segregated elementary students but integrated high school students. In 1920, Indianapolis blacks attended all three public high schools. The academic high school, Shortridge, located near black slum areas, was over 10 percent black. Efforts to relocate Shortridge in the city's northern white suburbs became associated with plans to open a colored high school offering academic, technical, and manual coursework so that all black high school students could be required to attend. An African American unsuccessfully sued to prevent Crispus Attucks High School from opening. When Attucks opened in 1927, all African American high school students were transferred there.[6]

Before the 1920s, Gary schools were less integrated than those in Indianapolis. In September 1927, eighteen black high school students joined six other blacks already attending Gary's K–12 Emerson School. White students struck. As a result, all but three of the black students were transferred out of Emerson, a new black K–12 school was planned, and no white students were punished. The Indiana Supreme Court later condoned this return of African Americans to a black elementary school because it purportedly offered high school coursework.[7]

Between the Civil War and when the state legislature abolished segregated schools in 1949, African American Hoosiers received no help from the Indiana courts in obtaining educational racial equality. Indiana courts were not alone in sustaining segregated education. A 1935 issue of the *Journal of Negro Education* analyzed 113 reported cases issued since 1865 involving segregated schools from twenty-nine state supreme courts and the District of Columbia. In all forty-four cases challenging the constitutionality of segregated schools in states with statutory segregation, the courts decreed segregated schools constitutional. The author, Gladys Tignor Peterson, evaluated four of the five Indiana decisions as unfavorable to blacks. The lone favorable decision, *Oliver v. Grubb* (1882), held that an integrated school district could not be forced to segregate.[8]

During the eighty years in which Indiana sanctioned segregated schooling, separate colored schools were never adopted statewide. In 1916, thirty-one of Indiana's ninety-two counties operated colored schools. Eight of those counties had one-room colored schools. Most southern counties conducted segregated schools.[9]

Over thirty years later, during the 1948–49 school year, twenty-one counties had at least one colored school. Eight communities offered separate instruction at the high school level. Nine counties averaged five or fewer students per grade in their colored schools. At the other extreme, nearly four thousand students attended Gary Roosevelt (K–12) and more than a thousand attended Indianapolis Attucks (9–12), Indianapolis Hope (1–9), and Evansville Lincoln (1–12). Cities with colored schools, besides Indianapolis, Gary, and Evansville, included Terre Haute, Marion, Jeffersonville, New Albany, Bloomington, Kokomo, and Lafayette.[10] Indiana's colored schools varied significantly in grade levels taught, enrollment numbers, and statewide distribution at any given time.

Shortly after World War II, both the Gary and Indianapolis school boards discussed ending segregated schooling. In both cities the discussion began after poor whites objected to their schools' apparent designation as transition schools. Whenever the black student population in these cities no longer fit inside existing black schools, overflow students went to a white school. The school boards normally selected those white schools with the poorest students for transition to black schools.

When more Gary blacks were transferred to the already integrated Froebel School in the fall of 1945, another student strike occurred. This time the school board refused the strikers' demand to transfer out all black students. When it became clear that the board would not relent, strikers sought to integrate all Gary schools. Plans were eventually drawn and implemented to end segregation throughout the district. However, segregated residential areas and retention of previous attendance zones kept most Gary schools racially identifiable. Nonetheless, in his 1946 study, *Minority Problems in the Public Schools,* Theodore Brameld was cautiously optimistic about intercultural relations policy in Gary: "Traditional policy largely expedience, recently concern over problem indicates more democratic but still uncrystallized intentions."[11]

In 1948, poor white parents in Indianapolis protested when black students transferred into their children's school. Angry parents argued that if any school desegregated, the whole system should desegregate, including schools attended by wealthier middle-class whites. Discussions to integrate Indianapolis Public Schools (IPS) deadlocked when the board found itself trapped between whites advocating segregation and blacks joined by white supporters seeking desegregation. After the 1949 general assembly abolished segregated schools, IPS attendance zones were redrawn so that most children attended the school nearest their home. Children in integrated neighborhoods sometimes could choose to attend either a black or white school. Inevitably, children attended the school with their race in majority. As in Gary, housing patterns guaranteed that most blacks continued to attend predominantly black schools.[12]

Throughout the years of statutorily sanctioned segregated schooling in Indiana, African Americans worked to overturn or repeal the laws authorizing segregated schools. Lawyers sponsored by the National Association for the Advancement of Colored People (NAACP) were instrumental, along with various civic organizations, in successful efforts that culminated in the 1949 law. While NAACP attorneys used the legislative process to reverse legalized segregated schooling in Indiana, other NAACP attorneys used the federal courts to reverse it in the South. Those lawyers' efforts culminated with the 1954 *Brown* decision.[13]

Back in Indiana, the 1949 legislature passed a law declaring that the public policy of Indiana was to provide nonsegregated public schools. House Bill 242 passed the Indiana House by a vote of 58 to 21 and the Senate by 31 to 5. Only five Democrats voted against the bill. The legislators' voting patterns did not suggest that any section of Indiana adamantly opposed the measure. By 1954, according to the new law, desegregation was to be completed in all school districts. The law did not declare segregated schools unlawful or provide penalties for failure to desegregate. Although the law was arguably not binding, Hoosier public school districts interpreted the law as requiring them to desegregate. However, segregated housing patterns, segregative attendance zones, and liberal transfer policies insured that actual segregation survived in many Indiana school districts long after 1954.[14]

Another reason exists for not characterizing Indiana's anticipation of *Brown* as a sign of Indiana's progressiveness in the area of civil rights. Immediately preceding World War II, only three states besides Indiana, not counting the fifteen former slave states, still statutorily allowed separate schools for African Americans.[15] It may be more significant that Indiana still permitted, rather than that Indiana ended, legally sanctioned segregated schooling five years before the *Brown* decision. Viewed from the standpoint that Indiana authorized colored schools as late as 1949, that obstacles would be encountered to desegregating Indiana's public schools seems almost inevitable.

Segregated school systems attempted at least nominally to comply with the 1949 law's provisions. The *Indiana School Directory 1953–54* shows that about half of the designated colored schools outside Gary and Indianapolis closed after 1949. Only the Wheatland school was still designated as colored.[16] Undoubtedly, most open former colored schools were located in predominantly black neighborhoods and retained predominantly, if not entirely, black student bodies.

Transfer policies perpetuated segregated schools, even in districts that never formally operated colored schools. Whites liberally transferred from majority black schools to white ones, while the reverse occurred with blacks. An African American Indianapolis principal revealed his ignorance about white students needing his approval to transfer out of his school. He thought that they needed only the approval of the white school's principal. Blacks who initially transferred to white schools found that their opportunities to participate in extracurricular activities narrowed, that they seemed to be disciplined more frequently and harshly than white students, and that white students and faculty generally made them feel uncomfortable and unwanted. Not surprisingly, transfers from integrated schools to black schools became commonplace for Hoosier African Americans. After *Brown*, southern school districts often used voluntary transfers to nominally comply with the Supreme Court's order to desegregate. This policy produced results in the South similar to those in Indiana.[17]

Teacher hiring practices prompted some blacks to support segregated education. Prior to the civil rights movement, teaching was one of the few professions open to educated African Americans. However, integrated school districts rarely hired them even to teach in predominantly black schools. When separate colored schools closed after 1949, many African

American teachers lost their jobs or transferred to nonteaching positions or elective classes as happened to Jeffersonville's black teachers. Jeffersonville's public schools fired nontenured black teachers. Tenured teachers transferred to nonteaching positions except for two who taught handicapped students. When the Bloomington colored school closed, one black teacher retired and the other became the librarian for all elementary schools. Initially, school desegregation decreased employment opportunities for Hoosier African American teachers, just as it would for African American teachers in the South when that region finally desegregated in the late 1960s.[18]

Preserving community spirit along with teaching positions caused some African Americans, including teachers and community leaders, in New Albany and Evansville to support sending children to colored schools that remained open. The fate of Jeffersonville's black teachers provided a vivid reminder of what black teachers could expect from school integration. As in the southern states, colored schools nurtured black cultural life in these two cities. Many African Americans feared that closing colored schools might significantly injure the social cohesion of their communities. Recent works such as David S. Cecelski's *Along Freedom Road* and Vanessa Siddle Walker's *Their Highest Potential* document the deep affection many blacks held for their segregated schools, especially the high schools. Outside large cities, blacks found themselves with few places to socialize other than their homes, churches, and schools. The reluctance of blacks in New Albany and Evansville to abandon their colored schools was not an aberration nor was it unwarranted. In retrospect, the closing of colored schools nationwide, along with other factors, harmed the social cohesion of many black communities.[19]

When the promise of 1949 still remained unfulfilled for Hoosier African American children, parents turned to the federal courts. During the 1960s, black parents in Gary, South Bend, and Kokomo, on behalf of their children, sued their school districts alleging illegal segregation. The first suit arose against the School City of Gary. In March 1962, in the absence of its president and its only black member, three white members of the five-member school board approved the superintendent's recommendation that a new high school be built in the black community's center. Citizens opposed to the proposed site argued that another available site might boost racial integration. The board unanimously rescinded the vote, but no compromise followed. The Gary branch of the NAACP provided counsel for Odessa Khaton Bell and other parents to sue the Gary schools.[20]

At the September 1962 trial, sociologist Max Wolff testified that the school district was 100 percent segregated in nearly all schools, except for one or two mixed elementary schools that fed into segregated secondary schools and one mixed secondary school that served as a transition school from white to black. The student body's segregation duplicated itself in teaching and administrative staffs. Wolff noted that new schools were erected within already segregated school zones. Black schools were more crowded, received less money per pupil, produced lower achievement test scores, and offered fewer academic and business courses, but more industrial and homemaking courses, than white schools. Wolff presented a proposal that gave all Gary schools a racial balance of 36 to 72 percent black based on the district's overall racial balance of about 54 percent black.[21]

On January 29, 1963, the federal district court ruled against the plaintiffs. Wolff's testimony was discounted because he lacked experience in either public school administration or education and he failed to cite any authority for his definition of "segregated" other than himself. The court considered the problem in Gary as essentially one of segregated housing. Neighborhood schools were deemed the goal of school zoning. According to the court, no evidence proved that the school board based its decisions on the desire to further segregate schools even when those decisions resulted in greater segregation. Consistent with the then state of desegregation law, the court rejected the plaintiffs' contention that the board had an affirmative duty to balance schools racially.[22]

Plaintiff Bell angrily responded to the court's decision. "The only source of hope for real progress," she wrote, "is through the scant few white and Negro people genuinely dissatisfied with the status quo and who appear bold enough to have formed a minuscule coterie to meet the overwhelming challenge. To date their number is few; maybe tomorrow their number will increase. Only then will Gary begin to realize its potential as a growing city and frustrate those currently leading it down the path to psychological and moral suicide."[23]

Even if the court ruled for the plaintiffs or if Bell's hope became true, racial integration in Gary would have probably been fleeting. Despite segregated schools, whites left Gary's schools in droves. By 1970, the Gary schools were over 60 percent black. Ten years later, they were 87 percent black and almost half of the nonblack students were minority, mostly Hispanic. By the end of the 1980s, Gary's schools were more than 98 percent minority.[24]

The Supreme Court's decision in *Milliken v. Bradley* (1974) ruled against the proposed interdistrict busing of Detroit blacks to suburban school districts. *Milliken* held that surrounding districts that had not practiced unlawful segregation could not be included in school desegregation plans, even if a one-race district resulted.[25] Since 1974, Gary schools faced the continuing challenge of trying to provide effective education in an increasingly segregated setting.

In 1967, federal judges heard evidence on whether the South Bend and Kokomo schools were unlawfully segregated. As in the Gary suit, the NAACP provided counsel to the plaintiffs. In April 1966, African Americans filed suit against the South Bend Community School Corporation although South Bend never operated colored schools. The suit sought to stop the construction of a new school at the Linden Street site where the student body was more than 90 percent black. A ceiling in the Linden Street school buckled in December 1966 with children in the classroom. After an injunction hearing, the judge found the school safe and suitable for continued occupancy by its regularly enrolled students.[26] On the third day of its September 1967 trial, the plaintiffs settled when the defendants agreed not to build the new school at the Linden site and to seek to improve the racial balance in all schools.[27] Because of the then state of federal school desegregation law, it seems unlikely that the plaintiffs would have won. However, the abrupt end left the issue of school desegregation in South Bend unresolved and waiting for further litigation.

In July 1967, the federal district court conducted a hearing into allegations that Kokomo schools were still illegally segregated. At that time, most blacks attended the elementary and junior high schools, including the former colored school, in the two areas where most Kokomo blacks lived. The Kokomo schools had only seven black teachers (none at the high school level), no black administrators, and no black school board members. At the trial, witnesses testified to physical and verbal abuse of black children by white teachers and students, to the inferiority of facilities at the schools attended by most blacks, and to the school board's decision to replace a white school even though a 1954 school survey recommended that a black school be replaced first. After absolving the Kokomo schools of practicing illegal segregation, the court nonetheless closed the two most segregated Kokomo schools.[28]

Indiana's last school desegregation case won by the school district defendant concerned Muncie schools. Muncie never maintained separate colored schools prior to 1949. In the late 1960s, just over 11 percent of Muncie's public schoolchildren were black. Most blacks lived in two neighborhoods whose elementary schools were more than 80 percent black by the 1969–70 school year. White children passed these two black elementary schools to attend predominantly white schools despite available classroom space in the black schools.[29]

Although the Muncie elementary system was considerably more segregated than its secondary system, racial problems associated with the high schools provoked the desegregation litigation. In the late 1960s, Muncie high school students attended one of two schools that were both about 13 percent black. A third high school scheduled to open in 1970 was located in an overwhelmingly white area. African Americans feared that the new high school altered the then desegregated status of Muncie high schools. Muncie provided no transportation to high school students so that attending the new school might be difficult for poor blacks. The court considered it premature to presume greater segregation when the third high school opened.[30]

Despite racial proportions that evidenced integrated Muncie high schools, considerable racial tension existed particularly at Southside High School. At that school, there were no black honor society members (although some were qualified), cheerleaders, or choral members of "Southern Aires." In 1968, only two custodians of the school's 103 full-time employees were black. When the school opened in 1962, the Southside student body selected Southern and Confederate titles and symbols for their school. The "Rebels" played before the Confederate flag while students screamed the legendary yell of Confederate soldiers. The "Southern Belle and Her Court" reigned over homecoming. Understandably, African American students deeply resented their school using titles and symbols associated with their ancestors' enslavement.

The Indiana State Advisory Committee's report to the U.S. Commission on Civil Rights recommended that the school administration take immediate action to eliminate the Confederate titles and symbols, to assign black teachers, counselors, and clerical personnel to the school, to restrict local administrators' autonomy particularly in disciplinary matters, and to ensure that all extracurricular activities were biracial. However, the district court found that the admittedly offensive symbols did not deny black students access to school facilities. The court concluded, "the adoption of symbols by the majority of students is merely the exercise of their First Amendment right of free speech and the state has not insinuated itself into private acts of discrimination."[31] Racial tension at Muncie's Southside High School highlighted how physical integration alone failed to advance greater racial harmony.

By the late 1960s and early 1970s, changes in the federal law raised African American plaintiffs' chances of winning desegregation lawsuits brought outside the South. Title VI of the Civil Rights Act of 1964 prohibited discrimination in schools receiving federal funds. By that time, almost all public schools received such funds. During the early 1970s, the Supreme Court charged school boards with affirmative duties to disestablish dual school systems. Courts began examining the effectiveness of desegregation efforts to determine whether a school district was unlawfully segregated. In *Keyes v. School District No. 1, Denver* (1973), the Supreme Court found that the Colorado school district, which never maintained statutorily segregated schools, had nonetheless maintained an unlawfully segregated dual system. *Keyes* was the first Supreme Court case that found unlawful segregation in a district that never operated statutorily segregated schools.[32]

Since 1970, Indiana federal courts have directed desegregation in the Evansville-Vanderburgh, Fort Wayne, Indianapolis, and South Bend public schools. Unlike earlier lawsuits, none of these lawsuits resulted in victories for the school district defendants. However, only in the Evansville and Indianapolis cases did the judge, S. Hugh Dillin, find the schools illegally segregated. Both Evansville and Indianapolis previously maintained segregated systems. The Fort Wayne and South Bend school districts, which never practiced statutory segregation, settled without admitting that they operated illegally segregated public schools.[33]

Late in the 1960s, the U.S. Office of Civil Rights (OCR) began investigating racial discrimination in the public schools of Evansville, Fort Wayne, and South Bend. The Evansville case was resolved first without protracted litigation. As previously noted, Evansville historically maintained a dual school system prior to 1949. Between 1949 and 1970, little progress toward integrating Evansville's elementary schools took place. Lincoln was not discontinued as an all-black high school until 1962. After Lincoln's conversion to an elementary school, white students living within walking distance still attended white schools that were farther away. At no time in its existence was Lincoln ever less than 99 percent black.

Under pressure from OCR in 1971, the school board prepared to implement a school desegregation plan that effectively desegregated its schools, until the board interpreted the Nixon administration's actions as an indication that federal agencies were backing off from enforcing school desegregation. Judge Dillin considered the board's reversal proof of continuing unlawful segregation in Evansville-Vanderburgh schools. The court's ruling and the resulting desegregation plan ended active desegregation litigation in this school district.[34]

In the mid-1960s, about 13 percent of Fort Wayne's and 15 percent of South Bend's students were black. At the same time, only 4 percent of Fort Wayne's and 6 percent of South Bend's licensed school personnel were black. In elementary schools, 83 percent of Fort Wayne's and 51 percent of South Bend's black students attended majority black schools. As in most American cities, segregated housing patterns contributed to segregated schools. OCR investigations of both districts languished from the late 1960s through the mid-1970s.[35] Despite surface similarities between the two communities, they adopted vastly different desegregation plans.

Fort Wayne's desegregation efforts consistently tried to avoid forced busing to integrate elementary schools. In 1971, secondary schools integrated when Fort Wayne's inner-city junior and senior high schools closed and their students transferred to outlying schools. Desegregating the elementary schools stalled. The Fort Wayne Urban League's executive director, Charles B. Redd, in 1973 protested that the district was making white elementary schools whiter and black elementary schools blacker. He asserted, "It is evident that the FWCS [Fort Wayne Community Schools] never has and does not intend to, at present, desegregate the schools entirely." In response to such complaints, the school district proposed an elementary desegregation plan that created magnet programs in seven inner-city elementary schools and closed three other schools while reassigning their students to twelve predominantly white schools. Under the plan, whites who did not choose a magnet program largely remained in their present schools.

Upset because the proposal put a disproportionate burden for desegregation on their children, African American parents sued the school district in 1977. Although black parents considered it only a first step toward achieving school desegregation in Fort Wayne, a settlement prevented any involuntary busing of elementary children. Integration depended on the successful implementation of a magnet system.[36]

For six years, no proposed magnet schools materialized. Although residents strongly opposed forced busing, they nonetheless rejected a tax increase to finance magnet schools. In February 1984, OCR found twenty-two of thirty-six Fort Wayne elementary schools severely racially unbalanced. A biracial group of parents formed the Parents for Quality Education with Integration and sued the district in September 1986. This suit settled in 1990 with a plan that again bypassed forced busing in favor of voluntary magnet schools. As of the fall of 1992, all fifty-two of Fort Wayne's public schools were racially balanced with 6,000 children voluntarily participating in magnet programs. Implementation required extensive federal funds. The plan expired after the 1996–97 school year.[37]

After the federal government filed a lawsuit against the South Bend schools, a settlement reached in 1981 relied heavily on busing white and black students. The school district was divided into pieces of a pie. Each piece contained a high school into which its lower schools fed. Nobody seemed pleased with the plan. The NAACP objected because it failed to protect already integrated neighborhoods. Whites objected to their children being bused for integration. Nevertheless, the desegregation plan remained in place. Despite the two districts having similar proportions of black students in the mid-1960s, by 1990 the Fort Wayne schools were 27 percent minority, while the South Bend schools were 35 percent minority. In her national study of school desegregation plans, *The Carrot or the Stick for School Desegregation Policy: Magnet Schools or Forced Busing* (1990), Christine H. Rossell determined that white flight from urban public schools was slower when voluntary magnet programs were implemented as opposed to mandatory assignment magnet programs. Rossell's study suggests that South Bend's experience of greater white flight with a mandatory desegregation plan than Fort Wayne's with a voluntary plan is consistent with national trends.[38]

Indiana's longest continuous school desegregation lawsuit involves Indianapolis and Marion County schools. By the mid-1960s, all of IPS's high schools were desegregated except for Attucks, which remained all black. However, of IPS's 106 elementary schools, two-thirds taught virtually one race. At that time about 30 percent of IPS's enrollment was black. Only 24 elementary schools had mixed teaching staffs, although all the high schools had such staffs. In the middle of opposing interest groups, the school board failed to take any significant action to further integration. Despite minimal integration of IPS schools, white flight thrived. On May 31, 1968, the U.S. Justice Department filed suit against the IPS Board of Commissioners to force school desegregation.[39]

Subsequent to being sued, the board unsuccessfully attempted to desegregate on its own. The fate of its proposal to close the two most identifiably black high schools, Attucks and Shortridge, typified the board's ineffectualness in directing IPS's desegregation. Attucks symbolized African American community tradition. Shortridge had until recently been nationally recognized for academic excellence. The schools' respective champions undermined any efforts to close them.[40] Under these circumstances, any significant desegregation of IPS schools probably required court intervention.

Following a month-long trial in July 1971, Judge Dillin announced that IPS operated an unlawfully segregated school system from the date of *Brown* in 1954 through the time of the trial. He ordered the immediate desegregation of IPS schools and faculties, but feared that IPS would soon be a one-race district unless an interdistrict plan could be implemented. In order to fashion such a remedy, Dillin joined all Marion County school districts and those bordering Marion County in surrounding counties to the lawsuit. The appellate court later dismissed the actions against those districts outside Marion County.[41]

Ten years passed between the court's finding IPS unlawfully segregated and the implementation of an interdistrict desegregation plan in 1981. After 1974, the Supreme Court's decision in *Milliken v. Bradley* prevented the implementation of an interdistrict plan unless outlying districts committed acts causing segregation within the segregated district or civic boundary lines deliberately supported racial segregation in public schools. In 1968, the Indiana legislature made the boundaries of Indianapolis coextensive with that of Marion County, exempting only the cities of Beech Grove and Speedway. Under the Uni-Gov legislation, most government services within Marion County were combined, except for the public schools.

In his opinion, Judge Dillin pointed out that Richard Lugar, then Indianapolis mayor, testified that the Uni-Gov bill would have failed if it consolidated Marion County's school districts. According to Dillin, "The inference is that the representatives elected by the vote of suburban residents—many of whom had recently moved to the suburbs from the central city to escape the threat of desegregation posed by the filing of this very suit in 1968—would have voted against Uni-Gov but for exclusion of the schools." Additionally, evidence suggested that county residents' resistance also prompted decisions to build Marion County low-income housing within IPS's boundaries. Consequently, legal grounds existed for one of the few post-*Milliken* interdistrict plans in the United States.[42]

The court's plan provided that African American students from selected neighborhoods inside IPS be bused to designated township school districts. Township children were not ordered into IPS; Judge Dillin claimed that he could not transfer them as long as the township school districts remained separate entities. Two townships with already sufficiently integrated schools were exempted. After the plan's implementation, the township schools' enrollments were 10–20 percent black. A proposed IPS plan with two-way busing might well have increased white flight from the county. Statistics showed that white students in IPS dropped by half after initiation of the desegregation lawsuit.

Equally important, since disclosure of a possible countywide plan a decrease of about 11 percent occurred in the white student population of township schools. A similar increase occurred in the surrounding counties' public schools. Contrary to federal law, the plan clearly placed an unequal burden for desegregation on blacks. Many Indianapolis blacks resented being discriminatorily burdened with correcting a wrong they did not cause.[43] However, massive resistance by suburban whites was probably avoided by not ordering their children into IPS schools. Indianapolis did not become another Boston.

Since 1981, the court approved two major changes to the intradistrict plan that controlled school integration within IPS. Overcrowding in elementary schools coupled with excess capacity in high schools prompted the conversion of two high schools, Attucks and Marshall, into junior high schools and four junior high schools into elementary schools for the 1986–87 school year. The closing of Attucks as a high school outraged blacks. Graham E. Marsh, an Attucks graduate and head football coach, most astutely lamented, "Most black high schools across the nation have become junior highs, then faded into obscurity." Supporters of Marshall, the newest IPS high school and one perceived as white, felt that their school was chosen for conversion to appease blacks. Earlier the superintendent recommended that Attucks and Arlington, both perceived as black schools, be converted. Both Attucks and Marshall supporters failed to prevent their high schools from becoming junior high schools. When the school year began in September 1986, IPS enrollment was 51,000, down 1,050 from the year before. Although IPS enrollment was steadily declining, this unusually sharp drop provoked speculation that the high school controversy prompted it.[44]

In 1993, the IPS intradistrict plan was modified to permit execution of a school choice plan. Under the plan, each school must maintain a racial balance within 15 percent of the system's overall 50–50 racial balance. Judge Dillin, who still presided over the case, approved the plan because about one-third of the IPS schools were not within the desegregation guidelines of the 1981 and 1986 plans.[45] No major changes have occurred in the interdistrict plan that affects the township school districts.

Determining the effect of school desegregation in furthering better race relations in Marion County is more difficult than chronicling the case's legal aspects. A survey of IPS high schools immediately before the implementation of the intradistrict desegregation plan found whites more likely to be in the academic track and less likely to be in the fine and practical arts tracks than blacks. This pattern of tracking, now sometimes referred to as resegregation, continues nationally. The overall attitudes of most students toward their other-race schoolmates was fairly positive despite interracial friction. Students tended to share parental racial attitudes and to base attitudes on earlier experiences with the other race.[46]

After the first and second years of the interdistrict plan's operation, studies surveyed the interracial attitudes at the six township school districts participating in the desegregation plan. The findings supported those of the earlier IPS survey. The vast majority of students from both races reported friendly contact with students of the other race, although if given the opportunity, both races interacted more often with their own race in the halls and at lunch. Blacks were less certain than whites about whether the teachers wanted blacks in the township schools. African American students felt more positive about being in township schools during their second year. They unequivocally wanted more black teachers.[47]

Interracial conflict in the Marion County township schools continues to receive occasional publicity in the local press. Perhaps the most significant conflict occurred in January 1991 when a riot prompted Warren Central High School to close for two and a half days. At a Friday night talent show, African American students tore up a handmade American flag. Early the next week, these students were suspended for changing their act between the rehearsal and performance. The Gulf War's start aggravated the situation. On the Wednesday morning following the performance, African American students participated in a peaceful protest of the suspensions. During lunch, a riot began between white and black students. Reportedly whites taunted blacks to "Go back to Africa" and blacks berated a white wearing patriotic attire.[48]

In the aftermath, African American parents voiced dissatisfaction with Warren Township school officials for allegedly disciplining blacks more severely than whites and being pro-white in their curriculum and hiring practices. Black parents made similar complaints about Decatur and Washington township schools. The failure to hire more black teachers may not reflect discriminatory hiring practices but instead the relatively flat pool of black teachers during the last twenty years. Unlike most of their ancestors, educated African Americans now find greater opportunities in higher paying and more prestigious fields such as law, accounting, and medicine.

More college-educated blacks has not meant increased numbers of black teachers.[49] Considerable racial strain may still exist in Marion County public schools even though daily contact between the races appears to be generally peaceful. African American complaints in Marion County about discriminatory discipline, hiring, curriculum, and other practices are common in many American school districts.

Throughout the state, desegregation after the 1949 change in the Indiana law and the 1954 *Brown* decision has been hindered by segregated neighborhoods and by white efforts to keep their children in racially segregated schools through liberal transfer policies and gerrymandering of school boundaries. Desegregation was accomplished most easily in smaller communities and in those cities with relatively small black populations. According to the 1990 national census, African Americans constitute about 8 percent of Indiana's population. Almost 90 percent of all Hoosiers remained non-Hispanic white. The census revealed that less than 10 percent of the population is black in 89 of Indiana's 92 counties. More than 90 percent of Indiana's blacks reside in Allen, Lake, LaPorte, Madison, Marion, St. Joseph, and Vanderburgh Counties. African Americans heavily congregate in a few large cities such as Fort Wayne, Gary, and Indianapolis whose school districts do not fully include their surrounding white suburbs. These demographics ease school integration in most areas of the state, but seriously impede it in the school districts where most blacks actually live.[50]

As of 1990, 11 percent of the enrollment in Indiana elementary and secondary schools was black. However, in IPS minority enrollment was 52 percent, in Gary 98.5 percent, in Fort Wayne 27 percent, and in South Bend 35 percent. The physical desegregation of Evansville-Vanderburgh schools became relatively simple after the desegregation order, because as late as 1990, the district was only 14.5 percent minority. Between 1970 and 1980, Evansville experienced the lowest percentage of white flight among northern cities with court-ordered school desegregation plans. Nationally, it has been easier to desegregate schools in those districts with a relatively small black population. Unlike the situation in many other states, in Indiana racial issues pertaining to schools largely involve only blacks and whites. In 1990, more than 97 percent of Indiana's elementary and secondary students were either black or white. Fewer than 2 percent of the students were Hispanic and fewer than 1 percent Asian/Pacific.[51]

At this time, it appears that in most Indiana school districts, the student bodies are racially balanced under federal guidelines. Desegregation law requires that the proportions of racial groups within a school fall between 10 or 15 percentage points of each group's proportion within the entire district.[52] Consequently, the fact that Gary schools are more than 98 percent minority does not mean that they are illegally segregated although people might understandably consider them segregated.

What is less clear than whether Indiana's schools are now legally desegregated is whether racial integration caused better attitudes toward other races or better education for African American Hoosiers. It is difficult to know if incidents such as that at Warren Central are ephemeral or indicate significant racial tension that normally remains below the surface. There is no reason to believe that the Indiana courts will soon be able to permanently withdraw from intervening in public school desegregation. The Indianapolis case remains open, the Fort Wayne magnet program expires in 1997, and as shown most black Hoosiers, like many blacks nationwide, reside in comparatively poor urban school districts. Until those issues are favorably resolved, the challenge for racial equality in education persists in Indiana and the nation.

NOTES

1. Indiana Council for Children and Youth, *Indiana's Children: A Report for the Midcentury White House Conference on Children and Youth* (1951), 33; *Brown v. Board of Education*, 347 U.S. 483 (1954); Hortense Myers, "Integration: A Two-Way Process," *Indiana Teacher* 101 (October 1956): 88.

2. Indiana Department of Public Instruction, *Indiana School Desegregation: A Brief Historical Overview* (July 1979); *Brown v. Weinberger*, 417 F. Supp. 1215 (Washington, D.C. 1976).

3. Indiana. *Laws* (1837), 15; Indiana. *Laws* (1953), 124; Richard G. Boone, *A History of Education in Indiana* (Indianapolis, 1941), 237–39; J. C. Carroll, "The Beginnings of Public Education for Negroes in Indiana," *Journal of Negro Education* 8 (October 1939): 650–54; Indiana Superintendent of Public Instruction, *Sixteenth Report* (1869), 23. For a comprehensive review about the education of African American Hoosiers before 1900, see Emma Lou Thornbrough, *The Negro in Indiana before 1900* (Bloomington, 1985), chaps. 6 and 12.

4. Indiana. *Laws* (1869), 41; *Cory v. Carter*, 48 Ind. 327 (1874).

5. Indiana. *Laws* (1877), 124; *Oliver v. Grubb*, 85 Ind. 213 (1882); *Mitchell v. Gray*, 93 Ind. 303 (1883).

6. *Greathouse v. Board of School of Com'rs*, 151 N.E. 411 (Ind. 1926); Emma Lou Thornbrough, "Segregation in Indiana during the Klan Era of the 1920's," *Mississippi Valley Historical Review* 27 (March 1961): 604–606, 616–18.

7. *Cheeks v. Wirt*, 203 Ind. 121 (1931); Thornbrough, "Segregation in Indiana during the Klan Era," 606–609; Ronald D. Cohen, *Children of the Mill: Schooling and Society in Gary, Indiana, 1906–1960* (Bloomington, 1990), 95–97; Indiana. *Laws* (1949), 604.

8. Gladys Tignor Peterson, "The Present Status of the Negro Separate School as Defined by Court Decisions," *Journal of Negro Education* 4 (July 1935), 354–65.

9. Emma Lou Thornbrough, *Since Emancipation: A Short History of Indiana Negroes, 1863–1963* (Indianapolis, 1963), 53–54.

10. *Indiana School Directory 1948–1949*.

11. Cohen, *Children of the Mill*, 177–84; Thornbrough, *Since Emancipation*, 57–58;

Theodore Brameld, *Minority Problems in the Public Schools: A Study of Administrative Policies and Practices in Seven School Systems* (New York, 1946), 228.

12. Robin M. Williams and Margaret W. Ryan, eds., *Schools in Transition: Community Experience in Desegregation* (Chapel Hill, 1954), 53–54; Board of School Commissioners, *Report on Racial Integration in the Indianapolis Public Schools* (1965), 34; *United States v. Board of School Commissioners,* 332 F. Supp. 655 (S.D. Ind. 1971).

13. Emma Lou Thornbrough, "African Americans," in *Peopling Indiana: The Ethnic Experience,* ed. Robert M. Taylor, Jr., and Connie A. McBirney (Indianapolis, 1996), 27; Richard Kluger, *Simple Justice: The History of Brown v. Board of Education and Black America's Struggle for Equality* (New York, 1975); Mark V. Tushnet, *The NAACP's Legal Strategy against Segregated Education, 1925–1950* (Chapel Hill, 1987).

14. Indiana. *Laws* (1949), 604; Indiana, *House Journal* (Indianapolis, 1949), 628–29; Indiana, *Senate Journal* (Indianapolis, 1949), 814; Thornbrough, *Since Emancipation,* 60.

15. Kluger, *Simple Justice,* 169.

16. *Indiana School Directory 1953–1954.*

17. Williams and Ryan, *Schools in Transition,* 56–63; Kenneth J. Meier, Joseph Stewart, Jr., and Robert E. England, *Race, Class, and Education: The Politics of Second-Generation Discrimination* (Madison, Wis., 1989), 46–48.

18. David B. Tyack, *The One Best System: A History of American Urban Education* (Cambridge, 1974), 225–28; Thornbrough, *Since Emancipation,* 63–64; Myers, "Integration," 90; Williams and Ryan, *Schools in Transition,* 75–76; David S. Cecelski, *Along Freedom Road: Hyde County, North Carolina, and the Fate of Black Schools in the South* (Chapel Hill, 1994), 8–9.

19. Cecelski, *Along Freedom Road,* 9; Vanessa Siddle Walker, *Their Highest Potential: An African American School Community in the Segregated South* (Chapel Hill, 1996); Williams and Ryan, *Schools in Transition,* 74–79.

20. Odessa Khaton Bell, "School Segregation in Gary," *Integrated Education* 1 (October-November 1963): 33.

21. Max Wolff, "Segregation in the Schools of Gary, Indiana," *Journal of Educational Sociology* 36 (February 1963): 251–61.

22. *Bell v. School City of Gary,* 213 F. Supp. 819 (N.D. Ind. 1963), *aff'd,* 324 F.2d 209 (7th Cir. 1963).

23. Bell, "School Segregation in Gary," 35–36.

24. Cohen, *Children of the Mill,* 241.

25. *Milliken v. Bradley,* 418 U.S. 717 (1974).

26. *Copeland v. South Bend Community School Corporation,* 376 F.2d 585 (7th Cir. 1967); David Robinson, "Ceiling Falls at Linden School," *South Bend Tribune,* 9 December 1966, 1, 19.

27. Roger Birdsell, "Linden School Trial Settlement Hinted," *South Bend Tribune,* 12 September 1967, 19, 23; Roger Birdsell, "Settle Linden School Suit," *South Bend Tribune,* 13 September 1967, 1, 17.

28. Ken Atwell, "Question Lack of Negro Administrators," *Kokomo Tribune,* 19 July 1967, 1–2; Ken Atwell, "NAACP Secretary Tells of Pupil Abuse," *Kokomo Tribune,* 22 July 1967, 1; Ken Atwell, "Witness Says Students Not Properly Educated," *Kokomo Tribune,* 2 August 1967, 1–2; Ken Atwell, "Judge Denies School Injunction," *Kokomo Tribune,* 10 October 1967, 1–2; Ken Atwell, "Dalton Moves on Court Order," *Kokomo Tribune,* 25 July 1968, 1, 9.

29. *Banks v. Muncie Community Schools*, 433 F.2d 292 (7th Cir. 1970).

30. Ibid., 293–94.

31. *Banks*, 297–99; Indiana State Advisory Committee to the U.S. Commission on Civil Rights, *Student Friction and Racial Unrest at Southside High School, Muncie, Indiana* (April 1968), 3, 10–12.

32. Civil Rights Act of 1964, Pub. L. No. 88–352, Title VI, 78 Stat. 253; Center for National Policy Review, *Justice Delayed & Denied: HEW and Northern School Desegregation* (Washington, D.C., 1974), 1, 11–15; *McDaniel v. Barresi*, 402 U.S. 39, 41 (1971); *Swann v. Charlotte-Mecklenburg Board of Education*, 402 U.S. 1 (1971); *Keyes v. School District No. 1, Denver*, 413 U.S. 189 (1973).

33. *Martin v. Evansville-Vanderburgh School Corporation*, 347 F. Supp. 816 (S.D. Ind. 1972); *Board of School Commissioners*, 332 F. Supp. at 677–78; Indiana Advisory Committee to the U.S. Commission on Civil Rights, *Equal Opportunity in the Fort Wayne Community Schools: A Reassessment* (Washington, D.C., 1979), 5; *Parents for Quality Education v. Fort Wayne Community Schools*, 728 F. Supp. 1373 (N.D. Ind. 1990); *United States v. South Bend Community School Corporation*, 511 F. Supp. 1352 (N.D. Ind. 1981).

34. *Martin*, 817–20; *Justice Delayed & Denied*, 99–101, 109.

35. Indiana Civil Rights Commission *1967 Progress Report* (1967), 10–11; *Racial Isolation in the Public Schools: A Report of the U.S. Commission of Civil Rights* (Washington, D.C., 1967), 14–15; James W. Whitlock, *Fort Wayne Community Schools* (Nashville, 1975), 225–27; Williams and Ryan, *Schools in Transition*, 117–19; Weinberger, 1221–22, 1224.

36. Charles B. Redd quoted in Indiana Civil Rights Commission, *Public Inquiry on Discrimination in Education—Fort Wayne* (21 September 1973), 3–4; Whitlock, *Fort Wayne Community Schools*, 232–33; Brad A. Altevogt and Michael F. Nusbaumer, "Black Parents and Desegregation in Fort Wayne," *Integrated Education* 16 (July-August 1978): 31–34; *Equal Opportunity in the Fort Wayne Community Schools*, 5.

37. *Parents for Quality Education v. Fort Wayne Community Schools*, 728 F. Supp. 1373 (N.D. Ind. 1990); Larry Hayes, "Race relations at stake in FWCS vote," *Fort Wayne Journal-Gazette*, 25 October 1992, 5C.

38. *United States v. South Bend Community School Corporation*, 511 F. Supp. 1352 (N.D. Ind. 1981); Gale Hinchion, "Racial plan a delicate weave," *South Bend Tribune*, 17 December 1980, 1, 17; Gale Hinchion, "More integration hurdles pop up," *South Bend Tribune*, 26 February 1981, 28; *United States v. South Bend Community School Corporation*, 710 F.2d 394 (7th Cir. 1983); *Digest of Education Statistics 1992* (Washington, D.C., 1992), 98; Christine H. Rossell, *The Carrot or the Stick*.

39. *Report on Racial Integration in the Indianapolis Public Schools*, 34, 38, 41; William E. Marsh, "The Indianapolis Experience: The Anatomy of a Desegregation Case," *Indiana Law Review* 9 (June 1976): 900, 903–904; Thornbrough, *Since Emancipation*, 62.

40. Marsh, "The Indianapolis Experience," 907–10, 912–15; *Burns v. Board of School Commissioners*, 302 F. Supp. 309 (S.D. Ind. 1969).

41. *Board of School Commissioners*, 332 F. Supp. 655–81; *United States v. Board of School Commissioners*, 368 F. Supp. 1191 (S.D. Ind. 1973); *United States v. Board of School Commissioners*, 503 F.2d 68 (7th Cir. 1974).

42. *Milliken*, 721–22; *United States v. Board of School Commissioners*, 456 F. Supp.

183, 187 (S.D. Ind. 1978); *United States v. Board of School Commissioners*, 573 F.2d 400 (7th Cir. 1978).

43. *Untied States v. Board of School Commissioners*, 506 F. Supp. 657 (S.D. Ind. 1979), *aff'd*, 677 F.2d 1185 (7th Cir. 1982); Emma Lou Thornbrough, "The Indianapolis School Busing Case," in *We the People: Indiana and the United States Constitution* (Indianapolis, 1987), 87–89.

44. Deborah Pines, "Attucks, Marshall slated to become junior highs," *Indianapolis Star*, 11 April 1986, 1, 10; Bruce C. Smith, "Marshall faithful stunned at IPS decision," *Indianapolis Star*, 11 April 1986, 10; Lynn Ford, "Attucks switch ends era for blacks," *Indianapolis Star*, 12 April 1986, 8; Barb Albert, "D-Day for reorganization," *Indianapolis Star*, 2 September 1986, 31; Cecelski, *Along Freedom Road*, 9.

45. *United States v. Board of School Commissioners*, No. IP 68-C–225 (S.D. Ind. February 9, 1993).

46. Martin Patchen, *Black-White Contact in Schools: Its Social and Academic Effects* (West Lafayette, 1982), 23, 54–55, 112–14, 162–63; Cecelski, *Along Freedom Road*, 170.

47. J. John Harris III, Richard C. Pugh, and Camilla A. Heid, *Beyond School Desegregation: A Study of Student Perceptions and Needs in Six Suburban Township School Districts in Marion County, Indiana—Year Two* (Indianapolis/Bloomington, 1983), 134–36.

48. Kevin Morgan, "Scuffle Closes Warren Central," *Indianapolis Star*, 17 January 1991, B1, B3; Jim Nelson, "Disturbance at Warren Central," *Indianapolis Recorder*, 19 January 1991, A1, A8; Lynn Ford, "Warren Central reopens amid tight security," *Indianapolis Star*, 23 January 1991, E1.

49. "Racism Alleged at North Central," *Indianapolis Recorder*, 16 September 1989, B1, B3; Morgan, "Scuffle Closes Warren Central," B1, B3; John R. O'Neill, "Decatur Township Candidates Hear Concerns about Racial Issues," *Indianapolis Star*, 24 April 1990, D3; Meier, Stewart, and England, *Race, Class, and Education*, 76–77.

50. Bureau of the Census, *1990 Summary Population and Housing Characteristics Indiana*, 64–65.

51. Karl Trauber, "Desegregation of Public School Districts: Persistence and Change," *Phi Delta Kappan* 71 (September 1990): 20; *Digest of Education Statistics 1992*, 60, 98; Rossell, *The Carrot or the Stick*, 52–54.

52. Trauber, "Desegregation of Public School Districts," 19.

BARRY BULL

School Reform in Indiana since 1980

Across the United States, the 1980s marked a major change in state involvement in schools. Issued in 1983, *A Nation at Risk*, the Reagan administration's first and most influential report on education, emphasized three assertions that both defined and stimulated this change.[1] First, the quality of education had diminished considerably in the United States since the early 1960s. Second, this educational decline had the effect of weakening the U.S. economy. And, third, the responsibility for reversing the decline rested with individual states rather than the federal government. In accord with these themes, state after state, usually led by their governors, enacted significant legislative reforms of their public schools.

Indiana was an active participant in this state-initiated school reform movement. Between 1980 and 1994, more than 200 education reform provisions were put in place, almost all by Indiana's General Assembly. And these reforms have covered the full range of educational issues, from preschool to postsecondary education, from the schools' planning and instructional procedures to their expected results, from the discipline of students to the working conditions of teachers and other school professionals.

This chapter reports on three aspects of this recent spate of reform. First, it considers the overall pattern of reform. Second, it traces the evolution of two major categories of reform. And finally, it analyzes and reflects upon the form and consequences of education reform in the state.

Indiana Schooling
for the
Twenty-first Century

The Indiana Department of Education
and
The Indiana Curriculum Advisory Council
of the
State Board of Education

In Search of the Educational Millennium (1987). Courtesy Indiana
Department of Education

In Indiana, education reform gathered strength in the early 1980s and
has been fairly constant ever since.[2] Figure 1 reports simple counts of
reform provisions enacted in each of the fifteen years between 1980 and
1994. Although 1987 was a peak, the enactment of new reforms and the
modification of earlier reforms have been consistent activities of state

Figure 1.

NUMBER OF MAJOR REFORM PROVISIONS, 1980-1994

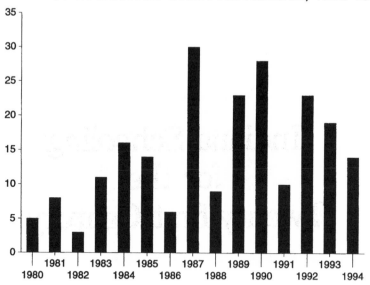

government since 1984. Whereas 1994 was widely seen as an "off" year for education, with no major reform initiatives passed by the General Assembly, its fourteen reform provisions exceed the number enacted in any year prior to 1987 except for 1984. Clearly, popular and political expectations about the level of involvement of state authorities in the schools have undergone a dramatic shift.

The most visible reforms have been included in a series of five omnibus education initiatives sponsored by Indiana's governors and state superintendents of public instruction. These five initiatives are summarized briefly in Table 1.

The movement toward omnibus reform began in 1982 when the General Assembly established the Governor's Select Advisory Commission for Primary and Secondary Education. Appointed by Governor Robert Orr, the sixteen members of the commission included three state senators and three state representatives of both political parties. Meeting over a two-year period, the commission recommended over thirty specific changes in state law, twelve of which were eventually enacted, most in the 1983 and 1984 legislative sessions. Among the important changes made on the recommendation of the commission were the reorganization of the State Board of Education into a single body appointed by the governor, the mandated offering of kindergarten by all school corporations, state financial assistance to school corporations with limited local resources,

Table 1.

INDIANA'S OMNIBUS EDUCATION REFORM INITIATIVES

YEAR	INITIATIVE	SELECTED REFORMS ENACTED
1982	Governor's Select Advisory Commission for Primary and Secondary Education	Teacher shortage programs Computer learning Gifted and talented program support State Board reorganization Expanded Prime Time Teacher incentive program Mandated kindergarten State minimum competency testing Awards for school improvement State financial assistance to low- spending corporations
1987	A+ Program for Educational Excellence	ISTEP testing program Student remediation/retention program Performance-based accreditation Performance-based awards Japanese/Chinese learning initiatives Beginning teacher internship Professional evaluation mandate Fund for education technology Minimum school day definition School year increase to 180 days At-risk student program
1989	Governor's Excel Program	School report card Funding for adult literacy education Education Employment Program K–12 drug education mandate Summer enrichment programs At-risk preschool grants Early teacher retirement Challenge Incentive-Innovation grants
1990	Bayh-Evans Joint Education Program	Pilot higher-order skills test Board of Workforce Literacy Funding for adult high school students Drug-free schools committees Technology Preparation mandate Pilot parent education programs Education technology program 21st-century Schools pilot Latchkey program mandate and pilots
1992	Workforce Development Act	Gateway test for high school graduation Application and interdisciplinary focus for state test Remediation plan for students who fail Gateway test Vocational and academic achievement certificates Regional workforce development plans Adult Gateway and achievement testing Grades 1-12 career education mandate Student high school career plan State college preparation curriculum Exit interview requirement for dropouts

Reaching for an A+. Courtesy Indiana
Department of Education

and the expansion of Prime Time, a program to reduce class sizes in the
early elementary school grades.[3]

A+, adopted in 1987, is widely regarded as the state's most comprehensive reform legislation. As originally proposed by Governor Orr and
Superintendent of Public Instruction H. Dean Evans, A+ included more

than thirty reform proposals, over half of which were eventually adopted in some form by the General Assembly. The most significant of these provisions were the increase in the minimum length of the school year from 175 to 180 instructional days; the statewide uniform ISTEP test, originally administered at seven grade levels; mandatory remediation and retention in grade for students who do not pass ISTEP; a state school accreditation program based on expected levels of student attendance, graduation, and ISTEP scores; a mandatory, year-long internship program for beginning teachers; and categorical funding to support specified programs for at-risk students.[4]

Evan Bayh, elected governor in 1988, sponsored or cosponsored three omnibus education initiatives. The first, passed by the General Assembly in 1989, was the Excel Program. It included a requirement that all school corporations publish annual fiscal and performance reports; a mandate for drug, alcohol, and tobacco education in all grades; a program to help potential dropouts finish school; and a grants program to schools to support innovative instructional programs.[5]

Governor Bayh and Superintendent Evans joined in 1990 to support a reform initiative that included experimentation with forms of state testing of higher-order skills, a requirement that all high schools offer a technology preparation curriculum based on guidelines and models developed subsequent to 1987 legislation, an education technology program to fund innovative computer-based instruction, and a requirement that all elementary schools provide after-school childcare, or latchkey programs.[6]

Finally, in 1992, Governor Bayh proposed and the General Assembly passed workforce development legislation that had implications for public schools, area vocational schools, postsecondary vocational/technical institutions, universities, and the state Department of Workforce Development. The major public school provisions included a requirement that students pass the Gateway examination to graduate from high school, a change in content for the state tests to focus on the application of learning to realistic problems, a requirement of remediation plans for high school students who fail the Gateway test, a requirement of career education for all students in grades 1–12, a state model for the college preparation curriculum, and a requirement that all high school students adopt a career plan that meets college preparation or technology preparation requirements. In addition, the Workforce Development Act authorized but did not fund state tests that would enable high school students to earn certificates of achievement in various academic subjects and vocational fields.[7]

As Figure 1 suggests, A+ represented a major turning point in state involvement in education policy. In the seven years prior to A+, state policymakers enacted on average nine reform provisions each year. Starting in 1987, however, there have been an average of nearly twenty reform provisions enacted annually.

Table 2.

Accountability and Testing. These reforms make schools, school corporations, and students responsible for particular educational outcomes, usually based on statewide definitions and measures of the desired results.

Adult and Workforce Education. These reforms provide education to out-of-school adults, particularly those with limited educational backgrounds, and prepare elementary and secondary students for roles in the workforce.

Curriculum and Instruction. These reforms define the curriculum that schools must offer, regulate the use of instructional materials, and establish course requirements for students.

Early Childhood Education. These reforms enhance the availability and quality of educational services provided to preschool children, children in grades K–3, and their parents.

Education Governance. These reforms redefine the structure, composition, and responsibilities of decision-making authorities at the state and school corporation levels.

Education Professionals. These reforms redefine the licensing requirements, conditions of service, and educational opportunities for current and prospective professional educators in the public schools.

Educational Technology. These reforms provide for acquiring educational technology equipment (especially computers), planning for and testing the use of technology, and training teachers in techniques of instruction using technology.

Instructional Time. These reforms regulate the length of the school day and school year and define how school time is to be used.

School Finance. These reforms change the amount, use, and distribution of state and local funding for public schools.

School Restructuring. These reforms enhance the authority of schools to plan and conduct their own educational programs and foster the use of innovative educational techniques.

Special Populations. These reforms provide special learning and other opportunities for particular groups of students, including disadvantaged, disabled, and gifted students.

Students. These reforms regulate the attendance, conduct, and discipline of public school students and the student records schools must maintain.

Other. These are miscellaneous reforms that do not fit into the other categories.

As important as these omnibus initiatives have been, they include fewer than 40 percent of the reform provisions that have been enacted during the past decade and a half. To be sure, about a third of the reforms enacted outside the five major initiatives have been refinements of those initiatives. However, the number of new reforms enacted outside these initiatives is greater than those included within them.

The list of specific reform provisions included in the omnibus education initiatives provides a general sense of the subject matter of those reforms. However, because many of the reforms took place outside the

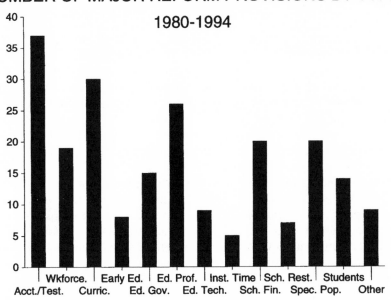

Figure 2.

NUMBER OF MAJOR REFORM PROVISIONS BY TYPE
1980-1994

omnibus initiatives, the full picture of reform requires an analysis of all of the reforms that have been enacted. Table 2, which defines thirteen different categories into which the reforms can be classified, illustrates the scope of the reforms.

Figure 2, which reports simple counts of the enacted reforms in these various categories, provides a sense of the major emphases of state education policy change over the past fifteen years.

Two categories have dominated state education reform according to this analysis—accountability/testing and curriculum/instruction—together representing about a third of all reform provisions. While accountability was a topic of concern prior to A+, most of these reforms were enacted beginning in 1987. By contrast, curriculum was a consistent topic of reform across the entire fifteen-year period. These two arenas of reform will be treated in more detail later in this chapter.

Although accountability and curriculum are of special importance, one should note that two-thirds of the policy changes have taken place in other categories. And some of these other reforms can be regarded as especially significant. At least six initiatives are worthy of special mention and explanation:

- Prime Time. Started as a pilot in 1981, Prime Time was phased in state-wide starting in 1984. The program provides state incentives to hire additional teachers and teacher aides to bring down average class sizes in grades K–1 to 18:1 (24:1 with an aide) and in grades 2–3 to 20:1 (27:1 with an aide). Prime Time has been the reform that has earned Indiana the most national attention.[8]

- Minimum school year and school day. These provisions of A+ are Indiana's response to the national concern that American students' poor academic performance was partially the result of a lack of instructional time for academic subjects. These reforms lengthened the school year from 175 to 180 days (the length of the school year in 35 other states), mandated that elementary students receive five hours of daily instruction and secondary students receive six, and required schools to make up days canceled because of emergencies.[9]

- Educational Opportunity for At-Risk Students. Also a part of A+, this program assists students who are deemed to be at risk of failure or dropping out. Funds are distributed to school corporations according to local percentages of children in poverty, single-parent families, and adults without a high school diploma. These funds must be used for one or more of ten different types of projects beyond the schools' regular instructional programs. Projects most widely used include expanded school counseling, tutoring, and alternative educational programs.[10]

- Twenty-First Century Scholars Program. Enacted in 1990, this program promises college financial aid to students from low-income families who enroll in eighth grade and fulfill a pledge to maintain a C average, to graduate from high school, to abstain from using alcohol and illegal drugs, and not to commit other specified crimes.[11] By 1994, more than 21,000 students had enrolled in the program. In 1995, the General Assembly provided funding for the first class of the program's students to enroll in college in the 1995–96 academic year.[12]

- Indiana 2000. Enacted in 1991, this program was Indiana's response to President George Bush's America 2000. Under this program, individual schools choose, through a process of school and community involvement, to develop their own plans for restructuring the schools to achieve the national educational goals. If those plans are approved by the State Board of Education, Indiana 2000 schools receive a small implementation grant, and their school corporations are authorized to invoke waivers of certain state statutes and regulations on the schools' behalf. By 1993–94, 138 schools had been approved, and another 68 had received planning grants to assist in the application process.[13]

- Professional Standards Board. In the early 1980s professional certification was the focus of several specific statutory reforms, such as the requirement that all new applicants pass a state test, the repeal of the requirement that teachers have a master's degree for permanent certification, and the enactment of continuing education requirements for certificate renewal throughout the careers of education professionals.

School Reform in Indiana since 1980

This legislative activism in professional licensing was supplanted by the idea of a separate governing body for the licensing and education of education professionals, something that was placed on the state reform agenda in 1987 with the proposals for A+ but not adopted until 1992. At that time, the General Assembly moved the State Board of Education's authority over these matters to a governor-appointed board consisting of the superintendent of public instruction, one school superintendent, one principal, one local school board member, three employees of teacher education institutions, and nine public schoolteachers.[14]

While Indiana's state authorities were frequently and significantly modifying the rules and expectations under which the public schools operated, they simultaneously enhanced their financial support of schools. In current dollars, total state spending on schools more than doubled between 1980 and 1990. After correcting for inflation, this represents a 48 percent increase in spending per student, above the national increase of 33 percent for the same period. Despite these increases, spending per student in Indiana still lags behind the national average slightly, although the gap has narrowed considerably. At the same time, Indiana continued to increase the proportion of school funds that derive from state rather than local taxes. In 1980–81, about 54 percent of general fund school revenues came from state sources; by 1991–92, this figure was about 65 percent.[15]

Although much of this additional funding went to increases in basic state support for schools, some was allocated to specific new programs, notably Prime Time, the At-Risk program, and ISTEP summer remediation. In part, such earmarked funding of reform was a result of a conviction that reform without funding was doomed to fail, based partly on a perception that a 1978 State Board of Education effort to promote local accountability had been ineffective because "the General Assembly did not see fit to allocate resources" to support it.[16] Yet less than 5 percent of the state's education budget is devoted to earmarked funding of reforms, and few of the reform provisions enacted have specific funding for local schools attached to them. Many school corporations have a mixed response to the lack of earmarked funding for reform, complaining, on the one hand, that the state has failed to fund its mandates but wanting, on the other hand, the sort of flexibility in the use of funds that earmarked funding would restrict.

In the case of A+, additional funds were raised by an increase of the state uniform income tax rate from 3.0 to 3.4 percent. Since that time, educators, including former Superintendent of Public Instruction Evans, have protested that much of the funding raised for A+ was "used for other government programs." A document prepared by the Indiana Department of Education on the fifth anniversary of A+ claimed that of the $320 million raised in 1992 by the earlier tax increase only $125 million had gone to support A+. However, because there were other increases in state school support that were not earmarked to particular elements of reform, it is difficult to ascertain precisely whether or not money intended for the schools was actually diverted to other purposes. Nevertheless, this is still a common complaint among some school officials.[17]

While state funding of education has been used to support and stimulate other types of reform, two significant reforms to the state basic funding formula were also enacted during the past fifteen years. In response to concerns that state property tax controls imposed in 1973 had frozen in place historical inequalities in school corporation funding, the General Assembly added in 1986 a per-pupil revenue equalization element to the formula. The basic strategy has been to provide additional state funds for school corporations that spend less than a target amount per student. As the target amount is raised each year, the spending levels of more and more low-revenue school corporations are increased. In 1989–90, the highest spending school corporation spent 2.3 times as much as the lowest-spending corporation on each student. Just two years later, the highest spending corporation spent at only 1.8 times the rate of the lowest-spending corporation.[18]

Although parity across corporations has not been achieved, recent progress toward spending equity was one factor that encouraged a group of fifty school corporations that filed suit in 1987 against the state for unfair inequalities to suspend the suit in 1992. Another factor was an agreement between the school corporations and Governor Bayh that led to a major change in the state's funding formula adopted by the General Assembly in 1993. To date, the group of school corporations has not reactivated the suit, pending experience with the results of the new formula.[19]

The 1993 school formula revision marks an important expansion of the goals of the state's school funding system. Previously, the funding formula was intended to control local property taxes, to provide for funding stability by ensuring incremental annual increases in revenue, and, as noted, to equalize revenues per pupil from the bottom up. While the new formula continues to pursue these goals by somewhat different means from in the past, it also seeks to attain taxpayer equity by ensuring that property tax rates will be the same in school corporations that spend the same amount on the education of each student. To this end, property tax rates are to be adjusted upward or downward in stages over six years until a target tax rate indexed to each school corporation's per-pupil revenue is achieved. For those corporations that lower property tax rates, state funds will make up the difference. Although this new formula has some of the features of what school finance specialists call reward-for-effort formulas, in which school corporations are rewarded equally for equal tax effort, it lacks one key element: Local schools do not have the option to raise or lower their local tax effort and, thereby, their school spending because per-pupil revenues and tax rates are tied strictly to what a school corporation spent in the previous year.[20]

Thus, recent school reform in Indiana has been wide ranging, continuous, and supported by enhanced funding. Despite its breadth, reform has also focused on particular aspects of schooling. As noted, accountability/testing and curriculum/instruction are the two categories with the largest number of reforms. This section analyzes the form these two types of reform have taken and the way they have evolved over the past fifteen years to ascertain the primary principles on which state reform has been based and major trends in education policy change.

Conceptually, accountability and testing need not go together. Schools could, for example, be held accountable for providing certain services to students, employing teachers with certain types of qualifications, or offering certain courses of study. In fact, this process-oriented accountability is the traditional means by which state control over schools has been exercised in Indiana and elsewhere in the United States, at least until the mid-1970s. But since then, accountability has increasingly been related to the outcomes of schooling.

Outcome-oriented accountability became an issue in Indiana in 1977 when the General Assembly's Senate Education Committee conducted a study of minimum competency testing. The committee held five meetings and issued an unofficial staff report but did not make any formal recommendations. In the 1978 legislative session, Representative James Jontz introduced a bill that would have required school corporations to identify minimum basic skills, especially in reading comprehension, writing, and computation; to test students once in grades K–4, once in grades 5–9, and in grade 10; to provide remediation for students who do not meet local basic skills standards; and to administer a graduation test in grade 11.[21]

Almost simultaneously, the State Board of Education adopted the Comprehensive Assessment and Program Planning System (CAPPS). CAPPS required each school corporation to identify local standards of student performance starting with reading, composition, and spelling and adding other subjects later; to develop an annual plan for evaluating its curriculum in light of the local standards; and to establish a testing program at four grade levels to assess student satisfaction of the standards.[22]

In light of the State Board action, the General Assembly did not pass the Jontz bill but established a joint House and Senate select committee to study the issue once more. The committee recommended legislative monitoring of the implementation of the State Board policy and continued legislative attention to the issue of student competency, but it did not endorse any specific legislation on the subject. A year later, a legislative study committee recommended that CAPPS be allowed to run through a full ten-year cycle, with legislative monitoring in the interim. No legislation was passed on this topic until 1984.[23]

This initial action on minimum competency testing illustrates one premise of school reform in Indiana, namely that testing and accountability are intimately related. The State Board of Education clearly viewed testing as part of a larger process of school evaluation and improvement. At the same time, the Board's policy and the General Assembly's deferral of action reveal another premise of reform in the early 1980s: that accountability is a local responsibility for which the state has, at most, a role in establishing a general framework. However, this second premise was to be severely challenged and eventually denied during the next decade of reform.

Despite teacher and administrator acceptance of CAPPS and their belief that the program had improved both the school curriculum and student basic skill performance, citizens and legislators came to doubt its effectiveness. Questions about the authority of the State Board of Education to require annual reporting and to disapprove local plans led to the suspension of local reporting and more generalized concerns over the ability of CAPPS to enhance the level of student achievement.[24]

Such concerns led the General Assembly in 1984 to pass legislation establishing the Indiana Basic Competency Skills Testing and Remediation program (IBCST). This legislation required uniform state tests in reading, mathematics, and writing in three grades chosen by the State Board of Education (grades 3, 6, and 8) and a program of state-funded and State Board approved summer remediation for students who failed to achieve State Board minimum scores. The IBCST program took away much of the flexibility that local school corporations enjoyed under CAPPS to determine the test to be used for evaluation, the subjects in which testing was to be conducted, the grade levels to be tested, the minimum competency requirements, and the form and timing of remediation.[25]

With this legislation, the earlier premise that accountability is a local responsibility came clearly under attack. It began to be replaced by a belief that accountability is a joint responsibility of the state, students, and schools, with the state responsible for setting the standards for student achievement, students for meeting those standards, and schools for providing the assistance that students need to meet the standards. Equally important, the state also assumed responsibility to pay for the costs of testing and remediation. Indiana's commitment to this new belief about accountability was strengthened under A+.

Accountability under the 1987 A+ legislation had three critical elements—a transition from IBCST to the Indiana Statewide Testing for Educational Progress (ISTEP), the replacement of the CAPPS planning process with the Performance-Based Accreditation (PBA) system, and the establishment of a Performance-Based Award system. ISTEP, like IBCST, mandated state testing and remediation, but it also included tests for grades 1, 2, 9, and 11 in addition to grades 3, 6, and 8. Students who did not meet the ISTEP standards through grade 8 were required not only to attend summer remediation but also to be retained in grade unless they passed a retest.[26]

Measuring School Achievement. Courtesy Indiana
Department of Education

PBA requires that schools assess their performance against standards
established by the state for expected attendance rate, ISTEP scores, and
graduation rate. At least once every five years, each school must commission a committee of administrators, teachers, parents, and community
members to complete a self-study, select goals, and prepare a school im-

provement plan to achieve those goals. The school's improvement plan and student performance must be approved by the State Board of Education for the school to be fully accredited. Schools not approved are put on probation and given up to three years to improve their performance and their plan.

The Performance-Based Awards program provides cash payments to schools based upon their students' attendance rates, ISTEP English/language arts scores, ISTEP mathematics scores, and ISTEP total battery scores. Forty percent of the award funds are allocated equally per student to every school that improves its performance on two or more of the four criteria. Sixty percent of the funds are distributed to these same schools based upon their overall level of improvement on the four criteria together, with more funds per student going to the schools showing greater overall improvement. The state initially distributed about $10 million per year through this program, but that amount was later reduced to $5 million per year.[27]

Under A+, schools lost the flexibility and control over planning for improvement that they were permitted under CAPPS. They also lost some control over the decision about whether to retain students who do not meet state standards after remediation. In sum, with A+ almost all traces of the premise that accountability is an exclusively local responsibility were erased. The state is in clear control of outcome standards; students' academic lives are significantly determined by those standards; and schools' internal planning processes and their public reputations are dictated by state rules and decisions.

The 1992 Workforce Development Act put the finishing touches on this outcome-oriented and state-directed conception of educational accountability. That legislation established but did not fund a new state testing system called the Indiana Performance Assessment for Student Success that was to go fully into effect in the fall of 1995. Originally, the law required students to pass the Gateway test in tenth grade to graduate from high school and to take particular high school courses if they failed the test. The Gateway test and IPASS tests required in grades 3, 4, 8, and 12 were to assess not only students' basic skills but also their capabilities to apply academic knowledge to real-life problems.

Action in the 1995 session of the General Assembly made important changes in this law but left many of the provisions in place. Objections to the costs of IPASS and the potential invasiveness of the new types of test items led the General Assembly to enact a modified version of ISTEP that still tests students' applied skills as well as their basic skills and includes a graduation test. However, only those students who do not complete the state's college preparation requirements will be required to pass this test in order to graduate. In 1996, the General Assembly repealed the requirement for mandatory summer remediation and retention of students who do not pass ISTEP. The new legislation requires school corporations to pay one-third of the cost of remediating students who do not perform satisfactorily on ISTEP, but it allows localities to determine which students are to be served, what form remediation is to take, and at what time the remediation will occur.[28]

Although accountability and testing have been perhaps the most visible and highly publicized reforms, the curriculum and instructional process of schools have received nearly equal attention. Prior to 1980, regulation of the curriculum was a primary way in which state authorities in Indiana exerted control over public schools. Through statutes and State Board of Education rules, the state defined the educational process of schools by specifying the subjects that must be offered and the courses that students must complete. For example, the State Board required that all public high schools offer a minimum number of semester-long courses in specified subjects, depending upon the size of the school. Similarly, the state required that high school students complete a specified number of courses in particular subjects in order to graduate.[29]

It is important to note two things about these earlier types of curriculum controls. First, they permitted local schools to determine the outcomes of schooling within the broadly specified curricular categories. And, second, they gave schools and students considerable flexibility in selecting specific content within the required subjects, determining content of the curriculum beyond the minimum requirements, and scheduling of instruction. As noted, changes in state testing policy during the past fifteen years have shifted to the state the determination of many instructional outcomes. And other changes in the state's curriculum controls during the 1980s reduced schools' flexibility in content selection and scheduling.

Recent reforms of the curriculum can be roughly classified into two categories—those that deal with the curriculum as a whole and those that deal with more specific aspects of the curriculum. Four reforms dealing with the entire curriculum are especially worthy of note:

• The State Board of Education required that a particular number of minutes of instruction be provided to students in grades 1–8 each week in each of seven subjects. For students in grades 1–3, for example, 22.5 of the state's minimum 25 hours of weekly instruction were accounted for under these rules. As of the 1994–95 school year, however, these requirements become recommendations within the framework of a detailed set of learning opportunities that schools must provide to students.[30]

• The State Board of Education approved specific proficiencies that students are to achieve at various grade levels as guidelines for the content of the legislatively mandated IBCST and ISTEP tests. At the same time, the Board required that the curriculum offered in the schools must prepare students to demonstrate these proficiencies.[31]

- The State Board of Education adopted a number of different programs for high school students, including increased basic graduation requirements (from 16 required semester courses plus 16 electives to 22 required courses plus 16 electives), an honors diploma (36 required courses plus 11 electives), and a college preparation curriculum (36 required courses plus 4 electives). Depending upon the program, state specification of required courses for high school students has thus increased from 33 percent of a full four-year course load (16 of 48 courses) to 75 percent of the full course load (36 of 48 courses).[32]
- The Workforce Development Act originally required high school students to select a college preparation or a technical preparation course of study. Subsequently, this mandate has been modified so that students must choose a course of study that meets State Board unified requirements for both college and technical preparation.[33] The intent of this mandate is to eliminate the general studies program or track from Indiana's high schools.

Requiring a curriculum that matches the state proficiencies has clearly connected the state's control of the instructional process to its determination of school outcomes. Moreover, these proficiencies coupled with the minutes-of-instruction requirements strictly reduced schools' flexibility to define specific content within required broad subject areas. Both the minutes-of-instruction requirement at the elementary and middle school levels and the new programs at the high school level reduced the proportion of the curriculum outside the state's control. And all four of these sets of reforms greatly reduced schools' options in scheduling instruction both within and across grades. During the past fifteen years, then, the extent of explicit state direction of the schools' curriculum and instructional processes has generally increased through the modification of state policies governing the curriculum as a whole.

This was also the result of the various more specific curricular reforms that were enacted:

- Computer literacy was added to the subjects included in the State Board's CAPPS program.
- Grants were authorized to enhance arts instruction.
- Incentives were provided to encourage teaching Japanese and Chinese in secondary schools.
- Sex education was required to emphasize abstinence as a means to prevent teenage pregnancy and disease.
- Schools were required to allow students to attend college courses and to grant them appropriate credit toward high school graduation for passing those courses.
- Foreign language textbooks were added to those that must be adopted by the State Board of Education.

- A technical preparation curriculum was piloted and subsequently required for all school corporations.
- AIDS instruction was required.
- Drug, alcohol, and tobacco education was required in all grades K–12.
- State grants, adopted textbooks, curriculum guides, and inservice education were provided for teaching geography.
- Summer enrichment programs were authorized.
- Advanced placement courses in mathematics and science were required in all high schools.
- Career education was required in all grades 1–12.[34]

A few of these reforms include state financial assistance for their implementation, but most do not. These new specific curriculum requirements have further reduced local flexibility within required subjects, such as health, and decreased the time, money, and energy available for the development and offering of subjects not required by the state. Moreover, the connection between these specific reforms and the more general curricular requirements is often tenuous at best. For example, the need to add career and drug education to the early elementary school curriculum may conflict with the heightened focus on reading and mathematics instruction required by the state proficiencies and the ISTEP tests.

Some proponents of outcome-oriented accountability claim that this approach should make it possible for the state to provide more leeway to schools in determining their own programs of instruction. Whatever the truth of this claim, it does not describe the course that reform has taken in Indiana, where state definition of outcomes has stimulated and been accompanied by additional regulation of the instructional process.

Without question, then, the state role in defining and regulating the processes and outcomes of schooling has increased dramatically. It is important to consider just what this heightened state involvement was intended to accomplish and whether that intention has been fulfilled.

Even in the early 1980s when criticism of public education was at its most strident, no one doubted that there were some genuinely effective local school systems. The problem was that there were too few of them. For, it was said, the political, social, and fiscal conditions under which local decisions were made often militated against the sort of comprehensive, universal, and consistent policies that were needed to make schools as good as they could be. State involvement in education was undertaken in the belief that state authorities could do better in part because they held ultimate fiscal authority and in part because they could detach themselves from the narrow and parochial interests that made local improvement so difficult to achieve. This section considers briefly the extent to which that belief has been borne out in the past fifteen years of experience with state education reform in Indiana.

State education reform can be understood as attempting to overcome two problems with the traditional locally oriented system for controlling public schools. The first problem is the lack of uniformity in school programs and opportunities. The variation in policy across Indiana's nearly 300 locally controlled school corporations and their roughly 2,000 public schools is likely to be considerable. Clearly, in many aspects of schooling, Indiana has solved this problem. Today all students take the same standardized test in specified grades; all high school graduates have accumulated the requisite 38 semester courses in specified subjects; all schools have undergone the same accreditation process and been judged according to the same standards. Of course, above these minimums, school corporations are free to impose higher standards, requiring, for example, fifth-graders to take a locally chosen standardized test or high school graduates to take a home economics course.

The recent reforms have established a uniform and reasonably detailed floor of expectations for the schools' educational outcomes and processes. The worry of some critics of reform in the early 1980s that schools would simply refuse to comply with or would tacitly subvert the intentions of state reform now seems to be controverted by the evidence. Schools across the nation have complied, sometimes enthusiastically, with their states' reform mandates. Indiana schools have been no less willing to conform to the new state requirements, even though some school board members, administrators, and teachers have complained about them.[35]

The second problem that state reform attempts to overcome is that local school policies often are not based upon a comprehensive and coherent vision of education. Two strategies in Indiana have attempted to address this problem. The first has been the development of omnibus education initiatives in which many different aspects of education policy are changed at the same time. The second has been an effort to link various elements within each omnibus initiative together. Neither of these strategies has been entirely successful.

The simple fact that there have been five separate omnibus initiatives, two under Governor Orr and three under Governor Bayh, is an indication of the difficulty in making state reform coherent. While certain themes have tied these initiatives together, particularly accountability, there have also been important differences between them. The explicitly partisan nature of the politics of public office at the state level has fostered a need to enact new programs that are different from those of one's predecessors. For example, Governor Bayh's new school restructuring and workforce development initiatives have helped him establish a political identity distinct from that of Governor Orr.[36]

Furthermore, over half of the new reforms enacted have not been part of any omnibus initiative. For example, the impetus for Prime Time and the technology preparation program developed prior to and outside the omnibus reforms. To be sure, both of these reforms were eventually embraced within omnibus initiatives, Prime Time by the Governor's Advisory Council and A+ and "tech prep" by the Workforce Development Act, but this is not true of many of the other nonomnibus reforms. For example, eight of the thirteen specific curriculum reforms listed earlier in this chapter have been entirely independent of the five omnibus education initiatives. Thus, the use of an omnibus approach to reform has not prevented many other particular issues and interests from claiming the attention of the state's education policymakers.

In the case of the curriculum, this has led to a clear tension within the policies themselves, with one set attempting to tie the curriculum to the state's definition of student outcomes and another set operating independently from those outcomes. This expression of particular political interests within state education policy has occurred even within the arena of accountability and testing, where most of the policies have been enacted within omnibus initiatives. For instance, in the 1992 Workforce Development Act, the State Board of Education was required to develop new standards and tests in English/language arts and mathematics, but additional standards and tests were permitted in science, history, and geography. In 1993, the arts were added to this list, as was business in 1994. Even though the new assessment program may never embrace any of these optional subjects, the potential influence of such special interests makes coherence of state education policy more difficult to achieve.

As a result of independent action, some aspects of state education policy have been almost entirely unaffected by the omnibus reforms. This is significantly the case in the reform categories of the curriculum and the education profession, and it is particularly true in school finance, where none of the significant changes in the state's basic tuition funding formula have been part of the omnibus initiatives.

This has not been the result of inattention on the part of the omnibus reformers. For example, tuition formula reform was an important part of the A+ proposals, in which a shift to a cost-based system of funding was recommended but never enacted. Nor is it the result of a lack of significant reform in school finance; as already noted, bottom-up equalization and taxpayer equity have been enacted. Rather, school finance seems to run on a separate track from other types of reform, in part as a result of the committee organization of the General Assembly. For example, one effort at more comprehensive education reform in 1993 by B. Patrick Bauer, chair of the House Ways and Means Committee, was eventually stripped of its nonfinance elements prior to passage.[37]

Thus, a number of realities of state politics have weakened the comprehensiveness and coherence of recent state education reform—partisan political competition, the influence of special interests, and the division of power within state government. Whether, in light of these realities, state reform turns out to be less fragmented than local reform is still an open question.

In sum, while the enhanced state control over education that has resulted from the past fifteen years of reform has produced a certain uniformity across schools and school corporations in the state, it is less clear that it has generated a coherent vision of schooling. Of course, whether it is in the best interest of the citizens of the state for education policy to be either uniform or coherent is a question that a simple history of events may not be able to answer. But an understanding of those events can help to demonstrate the importance of the kind of public debate and philosophical reflection that may be needed to answer such a question.

Among the considerations that scholars and citizens may bring to bear on the emerging state control of education are questions that arise from the very nature of state government itself. First, state government, informed by the federal constitutional doctrine of checks and balances, is deliberately fragmented. In addition to the traditional division into legislative, judicial, and executive branches, state governance of education is characterized by a complex division of the executive power itself into the fiscal authority of the governor's office, the administrative authority of an elected superintendent of public instruction, and separate rule-making authority of a State Board of Education and now a Professional Standards Board, both of which are appointed by the governor. Second, state government is explicitly partisan, with the governor, members of the General Assembly, and the superintendent of public instruction chosen in partisan elections. Both characteristics of state government contrast with the doctrine that informs local governance of schools. School boards, unlike other units of local government, have responsibility for a single public institution. Originally, those boards held all the executive powers and even many legislative powers necessary for the governance of schools, including even the power to tax local property. Even though almost all local boards are elected, those elections are at least nominally nonpartisan. Thus, the shift from local to state control of education in Indiana, as in other states, represents a change not just in the locus but also in the structure of the authority to govern schools.

The possible effect of fragmentation and partisanship on the coherence of state education policy has already been noted. The creation of well-coordinated and consistent policy within a system that is so divided and politically competitive is at the very least challenging if not utterly futile. But several other potential consequences of this relocation of school authority need to be examined and monitored as well.

One obvious consequence may be on the perceived responsiveness of schools to the concerns of local community members and parents. Until recently, public schools were the one major governmental institution over which local communities exercised decisive authority. But the increased volume and intensity of state regulation of both the outcomes and the processes of schooling have left local boards in the frustrating position of being expected to respond to local priorities but often without the authority to do so. Even when they have the requisite authority, local boards and administrators may use the generally enhanced power of the state as an excuse for failing to respond. For example, in 1993 the General Assembly included the funding for the at-risk program in the basic state grant for school corporations with the lowest ratios of at-risk students rather than giving them a separate earmarked grant as in previous years. Those with the highest ratios of at-risk students still received a designated grant. In low at-risk corporations all across the state, local boards and administrators told constituents that at-risk programs had to be discontinued for lack of state funding, even though they had been given undesignated money sufficient to fund those programs at previous levels.

A second, less obvious consequence of the shift to state control may lie in the extent to which the public is willing to support public schools financially in the future. At least two possibilities suggest that school funding may become less generous when it is regulated entirely at the state level. On the one hand, there is intensified competition for state funds that may reduce the proportion of the state budget devoted to schools. Despite the genuine increase in funding per student reported above, the proportion of the state General Fund allocated to schools actually dropped from a high of 50.1 percent in 1982 to 46.0 percent in 1993. On the other hand, state decision makers may be less willing than local communities to fund public education; after all, state funding goes to schools statewide, schools that the public consistently finds to be less adequate than their own local schools. For example, the Phi Kappa Delta poll shows that 41 percent of the public give an A or B to their local schools but only 20 percent do so for the nation's schools in general.[38]

A third possible consequence of state control may lie with the ability or willingness of public schools to explore innovations that solve local educational problems. In part, this reduced ability to innovate may stem from efforts to comply with new state regulations; as state laws keep changing, much of the local energy that might be devoted to solving local problems is inevitably needed to implement state programs. In part, reduced innovation may derive from the well-documented tendency for legislated minimums to be treated as maximums; a lack of local decision-making authority may breed among local boards and even teachers themselves a tendency to limit their aspirations to what the state has mandated.

In any case, these possible effects of increased state control over education—effects on coherence, responsiveness, funding, and innovation—provide an important agenda for future research on Indiana's schools. No matter how well intended these reforms may be, their consequences need to be monitored and debated.

NOTES

1. National Commission on Excellence in Education, *A Nation at Risk: The Imperative for Educational Reform* (Washington, D.C., 1983).

2. The analysis throughout this section relies heavily upon Indiana Education Policy Center, *Education in Indiana: An Overview* (Bloomington, Ind., 1994) and Indiana Education Policy Center, *Calendar of Education Reforms in Indiana, 1980–1994* (Bloomington, Ind., 1994).

3. Governor's Select Advisory Commission for Primary and Secondary Education, *Preliminary Report* (Indianapolis, Ind., 1982); Governor's Select Advisory Commission for Primary and Secondary Education, *Second Report* (Indianapolis, Ind., 1983); and Governor's Select Advisory Commission for Primary and Secondary Education, *Final Report* (Indianapolis, Ind., 1984).

4. Indiana Department of Education, *The Future Is Now* (Indianapolis, Ind., 1987); P.L. 390, *Indiana Acts,* 1987.

5. P.L. 342, *Indiana Acts,* 1989.

6. P.L. 51, *Indiana Acts,* 1990.

7. P.L. 19, *Indiana Acts,* 1992.

8. P.L. 111, *Indiana Acts,* 1984.

9. P.L. 390, *Indiana Acts,* 1987.

10. P.L. 390, *Indiana Acts,* 1987; Indiana Education Policy Center, *Education in Indiana,* 77.

11. P.L. 56, *Indiana Acts,* 1990.

12. Indiana Youth Institute, *High Hopes, Long Odds! Materials for Pocket 8* (Indianapolis, Ind., 1994), 4.

13. P.L. 240, *Indiana Acts,* 1991; Indiana Education Policy Center, *Education in Indiana,* 12.

14. P.L. 46, *Indiana Acts,* 1992.

15. Indiana Education Policy Center, *Education in Indiana,* 116 and 107.

16. Indiana Department of Education and Indiana Curriculum Advisory Council of the State Board of Education, *Indiana Schooling for the Twenty-first Century* (n.p., 1987), 33.

17. Indiana Department of Education, *A+ Program Reaches Five-Year Anniversary* (n.p., 1992), 4.

18. P.L. 65, *Indiana Acts,* 1986; Indiana Education Policy Center, *Education in Indiana,* 109.

19. Ibid.

20. P.L. 278, *Indiana Acts,* 1993.

21. Select Joint Committee to Study Minimum Competency Testing in Elementary and Secondary Schools, *Final Report* (Indianapolis, Ind., 1978), 1 and Attachment C.

22. Ibid., 1 and Attachment B.

23. Ibid., 16; Interim Study Committee on the Implementation of the DPI Comprehensive Assessment and Program Planning System (CAPPS), *Report* (Indianapolis, Ind., 1979).

24. Donald Ferris, James Higgins, Edward Wolpert, and Clint Chase, *Indiana Comprehensive Assessment and Program Planning System (CAPPS): An External Evaluation* (Indianapolis, Ind., 1982); Indiana Department of Education and Indi-

ana Curriculum Advisory Council, *Indiana Schooling for the Twenty-first Century,* 59.

25. P.L. 126, *Indiana Acts,* 1984.

26. P.L. 390, *Indiana Acts,* 1987.

27. Mark Buechler, Gayle Hall, and David Ebeling, "Indiana School Improvement Award Program," in Indiana Center for Evaluation, *Evaluation of the Progress and Impact of the PL 390 Educational Initiatives* (Bloomington, Ind., 1990), 51; Indiana Legislative Services Agency, *Various Public Education Programs Enacted and Funded by the Indiana General Assembly and Administered by the Indiana Department of Education (1983–1992)* (n.p., 1992), 7.

28. P.L. 34, *Indiana Acts,* 1996; P.L. 340, *Indiana Acts,* 1995; P.L. 19, *Indiana Acts,* 1992.

29. Indiana Department of Education and Indiana Curriculum Advisory Council, *Indiana Schooling for the Twenty-first Century,* 19.

30. Indiana Education Policy Center, *Education in Indiana,* 70.

31. Indiana Department of Education and Indiana Curriculum Advisory Council, *Indiana Schooling for the Twenty-first Century,* 20.

32. Indiana Education Policy Center, *Education in Indiana,* 71; Indiana Youth Institute, *High Hopes, Long Odds!,* 5.

33. P.L. 19, *Indiana Acts,* 1992; P.L. 24, *Indiana Acts,* 1994.

34. Indiana Education Policy Center, *Calendar of Reform.*

35. Susan Fuhrman, William Clune, and Richard Elmore, "Research on Education Reform: Lessons on the Implementation of Policy", in Allen R. Odden, ed., *Education Policy Implementation* (Albany, N.Y., 1991), 207–11; Indiana Center for Evaluation, *Evaluation of the Progress and Impact of the PL 390 Educational Initiatives* (Bloomington, Ind., 1990).

36. Susan Fuhrman, "The Politics of Coherence," in S. Fuhrman, ed., *Designing Coherent Education Policy* (San Francisco, 1993), 9–11.

37. See the initial version of House Bill 1003, which eventually was passed as P.L. 278, *Indiana Acts,* 1993, in which the new taxpayer equity formula was enacted.

38. Indiana Education Policy Center, *Education in Indiana,* 105; Stanley M. Elam and Lowell C. Rose, "The 27th Annual Phi Delta Kappa/Gallup Poll of the Public's Attitudes toward the Public Schools," *Phi Delta Kappan* 77: 1, 42.

Contributors

BARRY BULL is professor of philosophy of education and educational policy studies at Indiana University at Bloomington. He is also former director of the Indiana Education Policy Center. His research focuses on ethical issues in education policy.

LAURIE MOSES HINES is a doctoral candidate in history of education and American studies at Indiana University at Bloomington. Her areas of research include the history of teachers and American cultural experience in the Cold War era.

DAVID G. MARTIN, a product of Indiana public schools, received a B.A. in political science from Indiana University and an M.A. in curriculum and instruction from the University of Colorado. He is currently completing his Ph.D. in the history of education and American studies at Indiana University at Bloomington.

WILLIAM J. REESE is professor of educational policy studies and of history at the University of Wisconsin–Madison. Former editor of the *History of Education Quarterly,* his most recent book is *The Origins of the American High School* (Yale University Press, 1995).

MAUREEN A. REYNOLDS received her B.A. in history from the University of Notre Dame and a law degree from Northwestern University. Now a doctoral student in history of education at Indiana University at Bloomington, she is writing her dissertation on the relationship between party politics and Indiana public schools during the Civil War.

TED STAHLY is a doctoral candidate in the history of education at Indiana University at Bloomington. Formerly an elementary schoolteacher and cabinetmaker, he was a lecturer in educational foundations at Indiana University–Purdue University at Indianapolis from 1992 to 1995.

ALEXANDER URBIEL is an assistant professor of history in the School of Social Sciences and Human Services at Ramapo College of New Jersey.

SCOTT WALTER is a doctoral candidate in history of education and American studies at Indiana University at Bloomington. He holds M.A. degrees from Georgetown University and The American University. He is currently at work on his dissertation, "The Children Are the Revolution: Radical Education in Twentieth-Century America."

Index